W9-ARF-347

REVOLUTION, REFORM, AND
THE POLITICS OF AMERICAN TAXATION,
1763–1783

Revolution, Reform, and the Politics of American Taxation, 1763-1783

Robert A. Becker

LOUISIANA STATE UNIVERSITY PRESS
Baton Rouge and London

Designer: Joanna Hill
Typeface: Linotype Aster
Typesetter: Modern Typographers, Inc.
Printer: Thomson-Shore, Inc.
Binder: John H. Dekker & Sons

Library of Congress Cataloging in Publication Data

Becker, Robert A. 1943–
    Revolution, reform, and the politics of American
taxation, 1763–1783.

    Bibliography: p.
    Includes index.
    1. Taxation—United States—History. 2. Taxa-
tion, State—History. 3. Revenue—United States—
History. I. Title.
HJ2368.B4   336.2′00973   79-19729
ISBN 0-8071-0654-2

For my father,

ARTHUR J. BECKER,

because there were always histories close at hand

Contents

Preface

Reform is a bit like improvement or progress: nearly everyone favors it (at least in the abstract), but then agreement evaporates in debate over whether a particular "reform" really represents a change for the better. Advocates of every proposed alteration in colonial and state tax laws between 1763 and 1783 hailed each one as a necessary reform; proponents of other changes, and those who doubted any change at all was needed, damned the same measures as blatantly unjust or fiscally insane or both. Different interest groups, with conflicting ideas about the direction in which equity and progress and therefore reform lay, sometimes put forth mutually exclusive "reform" programs simultaneously. Reform obviously always involved change of some sort, but as obviously all changes were not necessarily reforms.

Anyone who intends to examine tax reform movements should establish some standard for judging the difference between reform and mere change. In the following chapters, that standard is the idea, often publicly embraced by colonial legislators and just as often discreetly forgotten when it came time to write the laws, that taxes ought to be levied in proportion to each man's ability to pay. Only changes that moved a colony's tax laws closer to this ability-to-pay ideal are here called reforms. It is important to remember, however, that although eighteenth-century colonists often used the term *ability to pay*, they did not usually mean by it that taxation ought to be either progressive or graduated. Rather they meant that all should pay an *equal* proportion of their wealth or income in taxes. Even after the Revolution began, few argued that the rich should pay a greater proportion of their wealth than the middling sort or the poor.

Two subjects one might expect to find in a book on the politics of American taxation are not much discussed in this one. The first is national finance—the various currency emissions, funding plans, and money-raising schemes hammered out by the perennially broke Continental Congress during the Revolution. Since Congress had no independent taxing power until 1789, its various plans were ultimately supported (or not supported) by state taxes, and since there is an excellent study of congressional finance—E. James Ferguson, *The Power of the Purse: A History of American Public Finance, 1776–1790* (Chapel Hill: University of North Carolina Press, 1961)—I have concentrated on the colonial and state legislatures. The second subject not covered is religious taxation. My primary interests were how the various colonies raised their *general* public revenues, and the politics involved in the process, and how these things changed in the Revolution. Religious taxes and the furor they caused as Baptists in New England and minority sects elsewhere objected to paying taxes to established churches seemed to involve a highly emotional issue—freedom of religion—distinct from the matters with which I was most concerned.

Finally, I should add that this study is not (nor did I intend it to be) an exercise in either statistical compilation or quantitative analysis. Some interesting studies, which apply quantitative methods to questions involving colonial and state taxes, are beginning to appear. My interests, however, lay in a different direction.

Throughout the notes, journals of the various colony and state legislatures are cited by date only. Many of the legislative journals are available in several forms (manuscript, contemporary broadside, pamphlet and newspaper printings, and modern edited versions). With few exceptions, I used the journals available in William S. Jenkins (ed.), *Records of the States of the United States: A Microfilm Compilation Prepared by the Library of Congress in Association with the University of North Carolina.* And unless otherwise noted, all citations to the *William and Mary Quarterly* are to the third series.

I doubt that anyone can write history today without owing thanks to a great many people who help along the way, and I am no exception. I am indebted to several colleagues and friends who read the manuscript, or parts of it, at various stages and who saved me from more errors than I like to think about. I owe special thanks to Merrill Jensen of the University of Wisconsin, who directed the early stages of this study and who criticized the early drafts closely, and special thanks, too, to M.R.W., who was always ready with encouragement when I wanted it, and criticism when I needed it.

The staffs of the State Historical Society of Wisconsin, the New-York Historical Society, and the Louisiana State University Library helped make working in those places both profitable and pleasurable. The Research Council of Louisiana State University provided a timely grant that allowed me to put the manuscript through yet another revision.

Portions of Chapters Three and Six were published earlier in the *William and Mary Quarterly,* and they appear here with the *Quarterly*'s permission.

PART ONE

The Colonies
Before the War

In this world nothing can be said to
be certain, except death and taxes.
—BENJAMIN FRANKLIN, 1789

Introduction

In 1815 John Adams observed that there was a difference between the war for American independence and the American
Revolution, and historians have been trying ever since to define
that difference and to measure the changes in American society
that accompanied independence. Much of their work has centered on broad questions such as the ideological origins of American union, the basis of sovereignty in the new nation, or the
structure of government under the old colonial charters, the
Articles of Confederation, and the Constitution of 1787. Half a
century ago, however, J. Franklin Jameson pointed out that the
Revolution need not be defined only by vast changes wrought by
prominent men acting on a continental stage, that seemingly
lesser changes in law and custom that affected the day-to-day
lives of millions of quite ordinary colonists were also significant
clues to the meaning of the Revolution.[1]

The world of most colonists was, after all, not continental but
local. Most of them were farmers first and foremost, and they
lived in some ways as far from the halls of Congress after 1775 as
they had from the Court of St. James before. Their world was
small, their attention focused on the people and things that were
closest to them and therefore mattered most: their families,
their land, their crops. They were more likely to be concerned,
day in and day out, with the weather than with continental politics, with crop yields and commodity prices than with the prerogatives of the king. What lawyer James Madison might say at
Congress about the powers of Parliament and the rights of man

was doubtless important to those who could understand it. But would the Shenandoah flood this spring? For many colonists that kind of question was equally important. After the war, essayist John Dickinson of Philadelphia viewed his state's unicameral legislature with alarm. What many other Pennsylvanians viewed with even greater alarm was the Hessian fly moving west toward their wheat. John Adams' scholarly pronouncements from Boston about the nature of the British constitution were important, all might agree. But so were the questions of how large the poll and land taxes would be this year and whether the collectors would take grain in payment. If the Revolution made a significant difference in the ordinary lives of ordinary people (and historians are by no means agreed that it did), then that difference grew in large part from the policies adopted by the new state assemblies after 1775, policies that affected people's land and crops and therefore their prosperity, and sometimes their survival. Much of the impact of the Revolution on the common lives of common men can be traced by comparing the legislative policies of the new state governments with those of the old colonial assemblies. What changed? And in what ways?

Recent histories of the Revolution have concentrated heavily on institutional changes that accompanied independence and on the ideological origins and implications of the struggle.[2] Yet there is at least as much to be learned about the nature of the Revolution—what it meant to those who lived through it—by examining the actions of the new governments as by studying their structures; at least as much to be understood by examining what rebel legislators did as by examining what they said. The chapters that follow describe the changes that accompanied independence in one area of colonial life: internal taxation—the annual levying and collecting by each colony of its own taxes to pay the ordinary expenses of government and the extraordinary costs of fighting natural disasters, Indians, and Frenchmen.

Internal taxation is not one of the more dramatic topics of the period. Most historians who deal at all with the politics of taxation focus on the dispute between England and the colonies. Colonial historians have shown a casual interest at best in the tax rate on farmland in the Carolina piedmont and a less than enthusiastic commitment to tracking the wanderings of Virginia poll taxes through a wilderness of legal prose that often said very little at very great length. In fact, there is no history of taxes in the colonies overall, and there are very few of taxes in the individual colonies. Those few are, with rare exceptions, dry institutional studies that examine laws in a vacuum, separated from the political context in which they were drafted, adopted, and applied.[3] Few American colonists and no colonial legislators would have made that mistake.

Internal taxation was anything but a marginal topic for most colonists. Colony taxes were frequently of far more immediate concern to many than the constitutional questions being debated with England. Unlike such temporary aberrations as the stamp tax or the Townshend revenue duties, the colonies' own taxes had to be paid year after year, on the coasts and in the backlands, in good times and in bad, no matter what the state of English-colonial relations. Internal taxes were often at the brawling center of colonial politics and at the center of politics in the emerging state governments after 1775. Occasionally a colonial assembly that overwhelmingly objected to a parliamentary tax would, at the same session, divide bitterly over an internal tax.

The politics of colonial taxation were extremely complex. The particular tax system that existed in each colony by 1763 was the result of well over a century of shaping and fitting competing interests against each other, of dealing and trading between farmers and merchants, new towns and old, seaports and inland villages, and each reflected the unique political and economic history of the colony involved. Change came but slowly, for it had to make its way against the massed weight of habit and tradition. "Because it's always been done this way" ("always" meaning within living memory) was a powerful argument against innovation, and it is important not to read into the eighteenth-century colonies either the brash enthusiasm for change that marked the new nation as it drove west in the nineteenth or the liberal faith in the power of legislation to reform that characterized it in the twentieth. By the end of the colonial period many traditions were eroding under the impact of an expanding frontier, the imperial wars, the Great Awakening, and other influences, but the colonies were still a long way from the day when "new" would come to mean improved and "change" would come to mean progress. In 1763 England's American colonists still lived in a world that valued its traditions highly.

The colonists developed no radically new form of taxation when they came to the New World, for they took their taxes as they took most of their political and social institutions, from the mother country but with a difference. The establishment of separately governed colonies in the New World permitted dominant factions in each to choose which institutions and patterns of life from the Old World they wanted to keep and which they preferred to leave behind. New Englanders, for example, adopted the English farming village as the basis for initial settlement and local government, while Virginians preferred the county and country estate pattern. Thus by the eighteenth century the colonies were, despite their common English origin, marked by a wide diversity of ideas, institutions, and ways of life.

It was the same with taxes. Free from the unifying influence of a central government and having established early the right to control their own internal revenues, colonial legislators selected from among the many kinds of taxes collected in England only those that suited their particular needs and interests. In the final decades before independence each colony relied on a different mixture of poll, property, and commerce taxes. By 1763 no two colonies had exactly the same revenue laws. They differed so much one from another in the ways they raised money that it makes little sense to speak of "American" taxation before 1776 at the earliest.

Yet this diversity of law and practice concealed an underlying uniformity of purpose: throughout the American colonies, tax laws overburdened the politically impotent in general and the poor in particular and favored the politically powerful and the wealthy, particularly the landed wealthy. Some colonies relied heavily on poll taxes, which were regressive because they required all adult white men to pay the same amount regardless of their wealth or income. Other colonies taxed land equally by the acre regardless of its location, quality, productivity, or market value, which worked to the advantage of large landowners, particularly in the East and along the coastal plain in the South. Such men generally owned the best land with good access to local and international markets, yet they paid the same tax for each acre of their land as did those who held small lots of marginal land in the piedmont or mountain counties, far from the sea. Some colonial legislatures adopted both types of discriminatory taxation and employed other methods designed to make tax laws work to the advantage of those who wrote them. Tax discrimination took different forms in different colonies and was much more pronounced in the South than elsewhere, but the pattern was evident almost everywhere.

No one could have argued with Benjamin Franklin's famous dictum about the certainty of death, but few colonial treasurers thought there was anything certain about the taxes they had to collect. The revenue laws they administered were tightly enmeshed in the colonies' internal politics, so the laws changed as the membership of colonial legislatures shifted with the fortunes of one faction or another.

Even where the basic tax laws did not vary much from year to year, the size of the taxes, the vigor with which they were collected (or not collected), the "coin" acceptable in payment, and the distribution of the taxes among towns and counties all varied with political shifts in the legislatures, for control over taxes was one of the important rewards for political success in eighteenth-century America. Those who were not well represented by the legislative majorities that wrote the tax laws complained and frequently did more than complain. They hampered collections by concealing taxable property or by supporting local officials who obligingly applied wildly improbable interpretations, rendering the tax laws all but ineffective. Sometimes they went as far as violence. But on the whole they complained and protested and demanded reforms without much success before 1776.

CHAPTER ONE

New England

Men should be taxed in proportion to their ability to pay: by 1763 this had become so self-evident a truth in New England that few public men dared deny it, but as with most self-evident truths, they had some difficulty determining what it meant in a practical way. How should a man's ability to pay be determined? New England legislators taxed to raise the money needed for government salaries, provision of necessary services, and occasional extraordinary expenses. It was not, in their view, the proper function of government to redistribute riches from the upper classes to the lower, and so they accepted income rather than wealth as the proper measure of people's ability to pay. The New Hampshire assembly, for example, wanted each man "compelled to pay in proportion to his income," and Massachusetts claimed to tax "incomes and profits." But income was often hard to determine in eighteenth-century America, and profits could be concealed fairly easily. Hiding property was more difficult, though not impossible. Colonial farmers were notorious for driving livestock into the forest at assessment time, and gold or silver plate was as easy to hide as it was difficult to acquire. Nevertheless, income-producing property tended on the whole to be highly visible, and as a matter of convenience New England legislators preferred to tax it rather than income per se when they had a choice. The primary source of internal revenues in New England in the decade before independence was the general property tax, which included taxes on more than just real property. Lawmakers assumed that the amount of cleared land a man owned, his livestock and buildings, or a merchant's stock-in-trade, were more or less accurate measures of probable income and therefore of ability to pay.[1]

Periodically in each colony, taxpayers submitted inventories of their taxable property to assessors or to town selectmen, who accepted the lists they were satisfied with or altered those in which they found evidence of fraud or concealment. From these inventories, each town computed its total taxable worth and reported it to the general assembly of the colony, which then compiled a valuation list (or general estimate, as it was often called) showing the total taxable worth of the colony as a whole and of each town in it. The assemblies used the lists to apportion internal taxes among the towns or to determine how high the property taxes had to be to raise the necessary money. Local assessors used the lists to collect from each individual his share of the province's taxes plus whatever local town or county taxes might be added on. In theory the system provided for taxes levied in direct proportion to each man's property, hence to his presumed income and therefore to his ability to pay. In fact, it did nothing of the kind. The laws were riddled with loopholes, special-interest provisions, and inequities and were subject to endless political manipulation.

First of all, only Connecticut and New Hampshire reassessed property annually. Elsewhere the general estimates might be as much as five years apart, and each year the taxes were increasingly out of line with the changing distribution of taxable property among the people. Furthermore, the assemblies normally relied on the taxpayers themselves to make assessments (risky, to say the least) and on locally chosen assessors, whose methods were primitive and whose accuracy was often as debatable as their impartiality. Rhode Island assessors, for example, estimated the taxable value of land by trying to determine what it might have rented for over the previous fifteen or twenty years. Connecticut and Massachusetts relied less on their assessors' discretion and fixed by law the taxable value of real property, varying it according to the quality of the land involved, its location, use, and productivity.[2]

The Massachusetts law directing assessors to take a new general estimate in 1771 was typical. They were told to rate agricultural property according to its average yearly rent, but the values were to be determined by use and productivity. For each farm, assessors had to report the number of acres of pasture "and the number of cows the same will keep"; orchards were to be rated according to "the number of barrels of cyder that can be made upon the farm, one year with another." Plowland was reported along with its annual yield of corn or other grain. They rated salt marsh according to "the tons of hay produced therefrom by the year." New Hampshire, on the other hand, had no law guiding assessors in establishing uniform values for property until 1770.[3]

New England's commercial development was more rapid than that of the grain-exporting colonies in the middle region or of the staple-growing colonies of the South. Yet even as late as 1775 most New Englanders were farmers, not tradesmen, merchants, or artisans, and most of them lived in rural areas rather than in anything remotely resembling a city. Merchants were often influential enough to exact major tax concessions, especially in Rhode Island, but for the most part New England's colonial assemblies were dominated by country men from country towns and villages.[4] The tax laws they wrote consistently undervalued agricultural property and agricultural income. The values set for some livestock in the Massachusetts statutes remained unchanged from 1694 until shortly before the Revolution, while real livestock values were generally higher. Land values for tax purposes in Connecticut were fixed by law, and for years at a time they trailed far behind market values. Strong farm blocs in Connecticut and New Hampshire forced through laws permitting payment of taxes in commodities at fixed rates rather than in money. New Hampshire, for example, accepted corn, rye, peas, wheat, beef, flax, pine and oak boards, and eleven other items (including codfish) for provincial taxes.[5]

Those same legislators made certain that laws reached out to tax merchants, moneylenders, artisans, lawyers, and others who did not live off the land. Massachusetts taxed ships "of every kind, upwards of ten tons burthen . . . whether at home or abroad," which prevented shipowners from dodging taxes simply by having their vessels at sea at assessment time. The colony also taxed merchants' "whole stock-in-trade, including all goods, wares, merchandise, at home or abroad, of their own property, paid for or not; also including by factorage," and "money at interest which any person has more than he or she pays interest for." Rhode Island, with its restricted farming hinterland and powerful merchant community, granted ships at sea and their cargoes discounts as high as 66 percent. On occasion, merchants were permitted a 50 percent deduction on their stock-in-trade. New Hampshire, Rhode Island, and Massachusetts taxed money at interest; Connecticut taxed the income of moneylenders instead. Connecticut assessed retail merchants at 10 percent of the wholesale cost of the goods they ordered from outside the colony.[6]

By the 1770s all of the New England colonies had adopted faculty taxes of one sort or another ("faculty" meaning a man's skill or ability) as a way of taxing nonfarmers. Connecticut assessors, for example, estimated the annual "gains and returns" of craftsmen and tavern keepers as best they could. Massachusetts' faculty tax was the most extensive. It taxed "the incomes or profits which any person or persons . . . do or shall receive from any trade, faculty, business or employment what so ever, and all profits which shall or may arise by money or commissions of profit, in their improvement."[7]

The predominance of country members in the assemblies made things difficult for New England cities, which were in fact little more than medium-sized towns in the late colonial period. Boston's fifteen thousand people made it the colonies' third-largest city in 1774. Nevertheless, urban-rural tensions were beginning to appear, and they were especially evident in Massachusetts. Boston's complaint about provincial taxes was simple: its representatives thought that their constituents paid too much in general property taxes and that other special taxes (such as excises on wines and liquors) were laid on Boston residents merely to lower the rates on country property. The excise law

first passed in the 1750s over the loud objections of city representatives that Boston would pay the bulk of the taxes and that
its real purpose was to avoid angering country voters through
increased property taxes. There was a great deal of money at
stake, and most of it was finally paid in the eastern ports, particularly Boston. The tax raised £14,000 in 1763 alone and was
continued over the steady opposition of Boston's representatives
into the middle of the 1760s, when they finally succeeded in
having it removed.[8]

Boston did have a special tax problem that it shared with
most other colonial cities: the heavy burden of poor relief. From
1763 to 1774, city taxes for local purposes, in addition to what
residents paid in provincial taxes, varied between £4,000 and
£8,000 annually, and much of the money went for poor relief
(Appendix, table 1). Between May, 1766, and May, 1767, for
example, Boston spent £3,057 (more than 60 percent of the city's
taxes in 1767) on welfare services of one sort or another.[9] The
resulting high city taxes produced a flight to the suburbs to
avoid them, and the laws regularly contained provisions to
check it:

> Whereas it has been the practice of some of the inhabitants
> of the town of Boston to remove to some other town in this
> province, and there to reside some months, to avoid paying
> their part of the taxes in the town of Boston, to which they
> really belong, to the great injury of said town,
>   Be it therefore enacted,
>   That when any inhabitant of the town of Boston shall
> remove to any other town in this province, and shall, on one
> year after, remove back to said Boston, and shall have been
> taxed in said town, he shall be subject to pay said taxes, in
> like manner as he would have been had he not have re-
> moved from said Boston.[10]

Collecting city taxes was extremely difficult. Boston in 1763
owed the colony more than £4,000 in back taxes plus £8,570 in
current taxes. Two years later it still owed £4,397, and by 1767
six city collectors were behind almost £8,000 in their collections.
Collector Samuel Adams was responsible for half the deficit.
Always short of money, the city regularly petitioned the General

Court for outright grants for poor relief, for delays on loan payments, and for money for special purposes like combating small-
pox epidemics.[11]

Boston may have been a hotbed of rebellion after 1763, when
it played a major role in the developing crisis with England,
but as far as more mundane matters of legislative interest were
concerned, the city was an urban island in a rural sea. The General Court remained under the control of men from country
towns, whose opinion of the city was summed up by Braintree's
John Adams. He considered Boston a "dirty town," a moral
swamp packed with taverns, a place of "parade, pomp . . . frip-
pery, folly, flopping, luxury and politics." Adams complained
about Bostonians who drank, ate off silver plate, rode in carriages, played cards, and in general corrupted the colony, all the
while complaining about their taxes, when "people in the country were obliged to wear homespun threadbare, eat salt pork
and beef, drink cyder and small beer and turn every stone and
save every penny to pay their taxes, and did it cheerfully too."
Legislative committees charged with reducing the cost of poor
relief in the city produced such helpful suggestions as shipping
all the poor "who belong to Europe," and who were willing to
go, back across the Atlantic at the colony's expense. Nevertheless, the city's tax problems diminished between 1761 and 1772.
Not only did the province taxes as a whole fall during this period, but Boston's share of them fell too, from 11 percent in
1761 to 9 percent in 1772, although rising city poor taxes ab-
sorbed some of the gains.[12]

Legislators sometimes discriminated in favor of particular
trades or occupations when they used tax incentives to promote
development. Connecticut encouraged manufactures by exempting locally produced goods when taxing merchants' stock-in-
trade. It encouraged opening new land by exempting newly
cleared acreage from all taxes for four years. The colony had a
small direct trade with England, and it imported most of its
overseas products through New York, Boston, or Providence.
To encourage local merchants, the assembly placed special import taxes on goods brought into the colony by nonresident

traders. To develop a fishing fleet, it exempted fishing vessels from the property tax and fishermen from poll taxes. New Hampshire's estimate of the income from "all stock, whether money at interest or improved in trade," at a ludicrously low 1 percent a year was similarly designed to attract new business.[13]

Some kinds of property were not taxed at all. Owners of wilderness land often paid no colony rates, depending on the terms of the original grants, on whether it was held in common by a group of proprietors or had been divided, and on whether it was within an organized town. The laws varied from colony to colony. Speculators could often buy land or receive it as a grant, sell portions of it to settlers, and hold the remainder virtually untaxed while it grew in value. In Connecticut, no town paid province taxes until it had the right to send representatives to the assembly, and some untaxed towns there and in New Hampshire were no more eager to be represented in (and taxed by) their assemblies than were the colonies as a whole to be represented in (and taxed by) Parliament. Such towns had to be dragged protesting and complaining into the assembly and onto the tax rolls. Massachusetts, however, did tax unrepresented towns. Why taxation without representation should be tyranny with respect to England but not tyranny in Massachusetts was, as one newspaper writer said at the height of the Stamp Act crisis, "a mighty shrewd question."[14]

Except in Rhode Island, which commonly taxed unimproved land, the special provisions of the laws favoring land speculators caused endless trouble. Frontier settlers commonly complained to their legislators that they took all the risks of converting wilderness into productive farmland and paid taxes that were "very heavy considering our poverty," but nonresident proprietors reaped the benefits. They demanded, and sometimes got, permission to tax all land within their towns in order to construct roads, bridges, and public buildings. In effect, that meant adding the unimproved land of nonresident proprietors to the local tax rolls. Proprietors, on the other hand, complained that settlers were wasteful and improvident, that in full knowledge of all the terms they had agreed to settle on the land, and that it would be unfair to tax the proprietors' "wild land that lays on rocky mountains and spruce swamps," or in other unpleasant and presumably unprofitable locations, equally with the improved land of resident settlers.[15]

Questionable assessments, undervalued farm property, special-interest exemptions—all of these undercut the New England colonies' claim that they taxed strictly according to each man's ability to pay. Such maneuverings were all but inevitable in any tax system prepared by elected officials with interests to protect and constituents to serve. But another aspect of the New England tax laws reduced to a polite fiction the assemblies' professed commitment to the ability-to-pay standard. This was the colonies' heavy reliance on poll taxes for a significant portion of their public revenues. The poll taxes were equal taxes paid by adult men regardless of their wealth or income. In Rhode Island the rate was commonly sixpence per poll for each £1,000 of tax money the colony needed to raise. Connecticut merely added a fixed sum—commonly eighteen pounds—to the taxable estate of each man between the ages of sixteen and seventy. Thus if the property tax in Connecticut was one penny for each pound of assessed value, the poll tax was eighteen pence. When the property tax doubled, of course, the poll tax automatically doubled along with it. New Hampshire had a similar system. Massachusetts levied a flat rate of so many pence per poll each year. In every case but the last, when property taxes went up, poll taxes automatically went up in the same proportion, and in Massachusetts the result was the same, since the General Court raised and lowered the poll tax whenever it raised or lowered the property tax.[16]

Poll taxes accounted for a large part of New England's internal revenues. In a general property tax of £6,000 levied by Rhode Island in 1769, poll taxes raised about £1,200, or 20 percent. Massachusetts expected poll taxes to yield approximately £18,500 in 1765, about 37 percent of the total general property tax. Connecticut poll taxes probably accounted for at least one third of the colony's regular internal revenues, and perhaps more.[17]

Fraud or politics or both (it was not always clear where one left off and the other began) diluted even more the connection between New England taxes and the ability-to-pay principle.

People, after all, had much to gain by making a thriving community appear to be, at assessment time, a poverty-stricken pocket of barren fields and ramshackle homes inhabited by poor but honest folk. When Colonel William Williams of Pittsfield, Massachusetts, wrote to his brother-in-law, urging him to settle nearby, he had nothing but praise for the area. The place was unbelievably healthy, he reported. It made "barren women . . . that have left off for 5, 6, 7, and 9 years begin anew, and now and then bring one, but as many as two [children] at birth after residing a suitable time among us." So few people died out of their season that the probate judge had to struggle by on a mere two pounds a year in fees. More important, there were fortunes to be made quickly at Pittsfield, and Williams listed people who had made them. But when the same Colonel Williams petitioned the General Court for a remission of the town's taxes, he had a different story to tell. Then he glumly reported that it took years and cost a fortune merely to clear land and begin farming, and that when at last a struggling Pittsfield farmer brought in a crop, he had no convenient market in which to sell it and precious little profit to show for all his work. Williams was far from being the only New Englander with optimism to spare for everyone but the tax assessor.[18]

The problems caused by political manipulation of the laws were more serious. Taxation was a complex matter, and the interest groups involved in the politics of New England taxation are difficult to define precisely. It is deceptively easy to speak of landholders versus merchants and to forget that many professional men and many merchants speculated in wilderness land. Furthermore, all landowners did not share common interests all the time. Small farmers generally wanted tax exemptions for some undeveloped land (their woodlots, for example, or a "reasonable" amount of land held against future cultivation), but they had little to gain if all wilderness land was exempt. Often, the divisions between interest groups had less to do with occupation than with wealth. The wealthy, whatever their professions, generally preferred high poll taxes as a means of reducing property taxes. The relatively poor, on the other hand, much preferred that poll taxes be kept as low as possible and that property taxes be raised instead. Sometimes, however, the divisions depended simply on party politics, on whether a particular tax or remission could be expected to produce votes on election day. Mere location could be the most important factor, since legislators rarely missed a chance to shift taxes from their own constituents, of whatever profession or degree, to someone else's. The tax laws that passed colonial assemblies generally reflected the balance of influence among various interest groups and political factions, for throughout New England and in the colonies as a whole, control over the tax laws was both a prize bestowed for victory at the polls and a weapon designed to ensure reelection. Thus the men who wrote the colonies' tax laws did not, as traveler Andrew Burnaby noted in 1759, always act with that "strict regard to probity and honour which ought invariably to influence and direct mankind." That strict regard was especially scarce, Burnaby thought, in Rhode Island.[19]

"The character of Rhode Islanders is by no means engaging or amiable," complained Burnaby, "a circumstance owing principally to their form of government," which "is entirely democratical."[20] In that last observation at least, he was by eighteenth-century standards not far wrong. Women of course could not vote, nor could slaves, but most adult white men could. In the twenty years before independence, more than three out of four were eligible to vote, though in any given election not many more than half bothered to. But in Rhode Island, those who did vote had a greater impact on government than did voters who lived in royal or proprietary colonies, where the governors and councils were appointed. Rhode Island governors were popularly elected every spring, and so were their councils. Delegates to the assembly were elected every six months. A faction that won the spring elections, therefore, normally controlled all branches of government including the judiciary, since judges were elected by the assemblymen each year. Thus the winning faction might pass new laws or repeal old ones, establish new policies or revise existing ones, almost as it pleased. When one faction came to power, it generally purged the bench of its political opponents and installed loyal supporters. Whatever faction dominated the spring elections, then, won virtually complete control over the colony's revenue system for at least six months but more often for a full year. It could retain, alter, or abolish old taxes, institute new ones, redistribute taxes among the towns, and either rigidly collect them or prudently not collect them.[21]

In the two decades before independence, two political parties battled for control of Rhode Island's government, one led by Samuel Ward and the other by Stephen Hopkins. Ward was politically associated with Newport, the colony's leading seaport. He drew his political support from there and from the surrounding towns in the southern part of the colony. Stephen Hopkins drew his support primarily from Providence and the surrounding counties in northern Rhode Island. By 1755, when Hopkins was first elected governor, the town was growing rapidly and becoming a port prosperous enough to rival Newport. From 1755 on, politics in the colony reflected the personal rivalry of the two men, the economic rivalry of the two ports whose interests they represented, and the sectional rivalry of the two regions from which they drew their support. Both men and the factions they led understood the political use of taxation, and Rhode Island offers the best example of the way taxes in New England were manipulated for political ends.[22]

The French and Indian War brought to Rhode Island, as it did to all the colonies, higher taxes and an increased public sensitivity to paying them. After 1755, there were always votes to be lured by pledging to end "unjust" taxes or to reduce "burthensome" ones, though Rhode Islanders often seemed to think all taxes burdensome and any tax passed by the opposition faction unjust. Hopkins lamented publicly that anyone, even Ward, would risk impeding the war merely to dupe a few misguided voters by promising lower taxes, and Ward regularly accused Hopkins of raising taxes to unconscionable levels merely to line the pockets of his innumerable friends.[23]

War also brought prosperity to New England, which made the higher taxes easier to bear. The troops the colonies raised and the soldiers England sent to America had to be fed and supplied, and New England farmers reaped windfall profits. The war made commerce both more dangerous and more profitable, and Rhode Island merchants did well providing goods and services to the king's forces, which paid in specie, and to the French in the West Indies, who also paid in specie. Trade with the French, who were, properly speaking, the enemy, angered the Admiralty, outraged the army, and embarrassed New England's friends in old England, but New England traders rarely let any of that interfere with their profits. Parliament primed the colonies' economies still more when it purchased their hesitant cooperation in the war with substantial cash subsidies. By 1762, however, the good times were ending. Drought, severe winters, and heavy shipping losses plunged Rhode Island into depression. Reports that Parliament intended to revive the moribund Molasses Act of 1733 and to impose new restrictions on colonial trade in general, and on the molasses trade with the French West Indies in particular, made the future look darker still. Like all the New England colonies, Rhode Island imported from the mother country goods worth far more than the agricultural products it exported. The result was a perennial balance-of-payments problem, which the colony solved in part by trading with the French West Indies, legally if it was convenient, illegally if it was not. Among other things, New Englanders imported molasses from the French West Indies and converted it into rum for export to other colonies, Europe, and Africa, where it could be traded for slaves, money, or both. The proposed new Sugar Act of 1764 threatened to disrupt this commerce by imposing a threepenny tax on each gallon of foreign molasses imported into the colonies. Rhode Islanders from both political factions and merchants and traders from both leading ports joined to protest the Sugar Act and later the threat of direct taxation by Parliament posed by the Stamp Act.[24] Although the postwar depression helped unite the colony's factious people against the external threat of parliamentary trade restrictions and taxes, it had a quite opposite effect locally. Internally, the depression encouraged division rather than union, and intensified party struggles. As important as it was for each faction and interest group to influence legislation and to control as much as possible the distribution of the colony's taxes during the war, it was doubly so during the depression that followed.

The influence of politics on Rhode Island's taxes was evident long before the war ended. In 1761, at a time when Hopkins was governor but Ward controlled the assembly, the legislature ordered a general estimate of all taxable property in the colony so that future taxes might be more accurately distributed among the towns. The estimate did not please many of Ward's supporters when it was completed in February, 1762. Of the twenty delegates who entered a protest against it on the house journals, fifteen came from either Newport County or Kings County, both Ward strongholds. Only one came from Providence County. But in the spring, Ward captured the governor's chair and the assembly. Since the general estimate displeased them, Ward's legislators prepared a tax law that ignored it and redistributed some of the tax load from southern towns to northern ones. Representatives from the latter complained, but to no avail. Ward had the votes, and there was little they could do but wait for the colony's mercurial voters to return Hopkins to power. During the wait, Smithfield (in Providence County) refused to pay the new taxes at all.[25]

In 1763 Hopkins became governor again. His administration promptly resurrected the estimate and redistributed the taxes. Smithfield's taxes dropped £104. The pattern was thus set. Whenever Ward's faction won office, it scrapped the estimate and shifted taxes onto northern towns. When Hopkins triumphed, he reinvoked the estimate and shifted taxes south again. In 1765, when Ward returned to office, taxes went up in three Providence County towns and down in six southern towns. The tax law of 1765 increased taxes £468 over the previous year, and Ward's assembly arranged things so that 70 percent of the increase would have come from Providence County taxpayers alone, provided the money could have been collected. The Providence delegates in the assembly, supported by others from the rest of the county, insisted that the estimate of 1762 was the only legal basis on which taxes could be distributed and that therefore the present tax was "arbitrary, unequal . . . oppressive" and illegal. Three towns in Providence County—Providence, Scituate, and Cumberland—flatly refused to pay it. Ward's assembly threatened to sue them the next year for double what they owed, conveniently overlooking the facts that Newport had not yet paid the 1765 tax either and owed substantial amounts on its 1763 and 1764 taxes.[26]

There was little good news for the northern towns in 1766. Ward retained the governorship and control of the assembly. In December the house offered to repeal the troublesome estimate of 1762, but the council refused, insisting that it was already void because the legislature had ignored it in several subsequent tax laws. To repeal formally a law that had already been repealed de facto, the council thought, would be redundant. It would also have been unwise, since formal repeal might have raised awkward questions about the legality of the taxes passed by Ward's followers since 1762. The council's political prudence if not legal logic prevailed. The old estimate was neither repealed nor applied; the new tax law passed in 1766 simply ignored it.[27]

Once again Hopkins' loyal supporters objected. The three delinquent towns complained that the assessors in 1766 had worked by "mere guess and conjecture," since they spent only one day at their task and could not possibly have determined fair property assessments for the whole colony in so short a time "without supernatural assistance." The towns likened their refusal to pay an unjust Rhode Island tax to the colonies' refusal to pay the stamp tax. "If ever the time should happen," they warned, "when the passions of any prevailing administration should be the rule of their government, a matter of taxation without any other rule or guide than mere arbitrariness would be the object of their particular attention." They denounced the new tax as a "high act of arbitrary power and despotism and an exercise of such authority as is utterly inconsistent with a British constitution, and most evidently tending to slavery."[28]

An arbitrary tax "tending to slavery": with the Stamp Act fresh in mind, few could have missed the implications. If colonists had the right to decide for themselves whether the Stamp Act was arbitrary, despotic, and in violation of the British constitution and to refuse obedience to it, then might not other colonists within a particular colony claim with equal justice the same right with regard to their own taxes? There were of course differences between the two cases. That no one denied. The colonies sent no representatives to the Parliament that passed the Stamp Act, but the three protesting towns were all represented in the Rhode Island assembly. In fact it was their representatives in the assembly who challenged the constitutionality of the tax. Understandably, then, they based their objections on other grounds and used arguments that anticipated some of those later developed by John Dickinson in his *Letters from a Farmer in Pennsylvania*. Even though the towns were directly represented in the legislature, the tax was still unconstitutional, they claimed, because of the nature of the law (it was arbitrary) and the intention of its framers (despotic).[29] The origins of their protest were partisan and local, and the protesting delegates were hardly motivated by a disinterested concern for high constitutional principle alone. Nevertheless, the question they raised was fundamental and would be asked with greater frequency and growing urgency as independence approached: to what extent might the principles raised against England by the colonies be applied internally?

Ward's council replied to the attack the following February, when it insisted that the three delinquent towns be forced to pay. The councillors saw no similarity at all between the right of Rhode Islanders in general to nullify an arbitrary parliamentary tax and the refusal of the northern Rhode Islanders to pay a tax levied by their own assembly. The "supreme authority of the General Assembly of this colony in matters of taxation," they explained, was established "by every idea of government, the English Constitution in general and . . . the constitution of this

colony in particular." In effect they claimed for the colonial government the same supreme authority within the colony that
Parliament claimed for itself within the empire.[30]

The last general estimate was for all practical purposes dead
by the spring of 1767, when Stephen Hopkins again became governor, but it was far from forgotten. There were scores to be
settled, and the Hopkins administration quickly began settling
them. The legislature absolved the three towns from punishment
for refusing to pay their 1765 and 1766 rates and gave them an
additional four months to pay only what they would have paid
if the estimate had been in force during those years. Furthermore, the "sums taken off the towns of Providence, Scituate and
Cumberland" would be "proportioned among the towns which
shall be found to have been too light in the taxes assessed in the
years 1765 to 1766." Few doubted that the towns "found to have
been too light" would be towns that supported Ward. Representatives from southern towns now moaned about the injustice
of burdening them with other people's delinquent taxes and predicted the "total ruin of all public credit" if the assembly gave
such "encouragement to every town in the colony to refuse paying their taxes." The list of protesting towns read for the most
part like a map of Ward's areas of strength: Hopkinton, Wester-
ly, Newport, Charlestown, South Kingstown, North Kingstown,
Richmond, and Exeter.[31]

Normally, the whole amount of the colony's taxes was apportioned among the towns according to assessed property values.
Each town therefore had "the advantage of its polls," which
meant that poll taxes collected in the town were subtracted from
the town's total tax quota and only the remainder was raised by
a property tax. Thus while the poll tax was uniform across the
colony, property rates might vary considerably from town to
town, being higher in thinly settled areas with high assessed
valuations and lower in heavily populated towns with low valuations. In the spring of 1767 eight delegates, all but one from
either Kings County or Newport County, proposed a major revision in the system. They suggested that in the future the income from the poll taxes colony-wide be deducted from the total

amount to be raised *before* taxes were apportioned among the towns. Each town would, in short, lose the advantage of its polls, and only what remained after poll taxes had been subtracted would be apportioned among the towns according to their assessed property values. Say, for example, the assembly approved a £12,000 tax. Under the existing system, all of it would be apportioned among the towns according to their property assessments. But under the proposed new system, the yield from the poll tax (£2,400 at the usual sixpence rate) would be subtracted first, and only the remaining £9,600 would be apportioned among the towns according to their taxable property. In short, the delegates who suggested the change wanted property taxes made more nearly uniform across the colony, and the poll taxes of the populous towns used to lower property taxes in the less populous towns. That kind of reshuffling appealed especially to the landed wealthy, particularly if they lived in towns with high assessed values relative to their number of taxable polls (Appendix, table 2). Such towns were heavily concentrated in the south, the area usually aligned with Samuel Ward. Newport County, for instance, had the highest assessed value per taxable poll of any county in the colony (£321); Providence County had the lowest (£187). The three poorest towns in the colony by this measure were Scituate (£135), Gloucester (£133), and Cumberland (£132), all in Providence County. The four richest were Jamestown (£421), Middletown (£430), Portsmouth (£419), and South Kingstown (£459), all in Newport and Kings counties.[32]

A Hopkins legislature killed the plan in June, 1767, but in February, 1769, the southern towns tried again and for a time they succeeded. Josias Lyndon was governor. He had been elected in May, 1768, with the backing of both factions in hopes of creating a coalition government and of ending the factional brawling that continually disrupted the colony. By 1769, however, the spirit of compromise, never very evident in Rhode Island in the best of times, had evaporated, and the experiment in coalition government collapsed when the assembly developed a distinct pro-Ward bias. In February the assembly passed a new general estimate into law, agreed to lower property taxes by raising poll taxes to six shillings (which would have placed fully 40 percent of the total tax burden on polls), and agreed to subtract the money raised on polls from the total tax quota before apportioning the remainder among the towns.[33]

The changes—they were hardly reforms—did not survive long. Within two months Stephen Hopkins' ally Joseph Wanton became governor, and Hopkins' supporters regained control of the government. The new legislature that met in May declared the taxes assessed in February "erroneous" and it reapportioned them in such a way that taxes went up in every town in Newport County and down in every town in Providence County except Providence itself. At the same time, lawmakers lowered the poll tax to the usual rate of sixpence for each £1,000 of tax, making the 1769 poll tax three shillings rather than six, and restricted it to men over twenty-one rather than men over eighteen. Finally, they reinstituted the old system of distributing taxes among the towns. Twenty-four delegates protested the changes, all but four from either Newport County or Kings County. Although skirmishing over taxes had enlivened virtually every legislative session after 1761, following Wanton's victory in 1769 the Hopkins group retained the governorship and control of the legislature. As independence approached and the Ward faction grew increasingly feeble, tax laws in Rhode Island passed with relative ease and unprecedented quiet.[34]

Factional politics explains a great deal about the pattern of Rhode Island taxation before the Revolution but it does not explain everything. One other major division within the colony affected taxes, and in the long run it was a more significant division than that between the political factions, since it survived the Revolution and became a major focus of state politics after 1776. This was the division between the merchant community and the agrarian community, and it was not always reflected in the party struggles because the conflicting interests of the two communities sometimes crossed party lines.

When legislators debated rules for determining the taxable value of different kinds of property, the division between those who were primarily merchants and those who were primarily farmers became clear. Farmers from all over the colony, regardless of their political leanings, tried to fix the value of agricultural property as low as possible and that of commercial property as high as possible. Merchants, tradesmen, and manufacturers from Newport or Providence or anywhere else tried to do the reverse. It was *after* the taxable value of different kinds of property had been established (or, put another way, after the apportionment of taxes among individuals within the towns was settled) and the assembly turned to the apportionment of taxes among towns that merchants and farmers in the north joined against merchants and farmers in the south and the factional alignments firmed up. As far as taxes were concerned, the council was generally more sympathetic to the merchant community, while the house more often reflected the farmers' interests. In 1767, for example, rural representatives complained that they would be "greatly oppressed by paying a much larger share of the public taxes than in justice they ought, in proportion to the merchants and traders," unless the laws were changed. Appraising land for tax purposes at twenty times the annual rent was a gross overvaluation, they argued (in 1762 they had thought twelve times the yearly rent too high), and rating distilleries and mills at only fifteen years' rent set them "certainly not higher, if so high, as the true value." And why, they asked, should some personal property be assessed at full value when merchants enjoyed a one-third discount on ships and cargoes at sea?[35]

When assessors reported a plan for a new general estimate to the legislature in 1768, the house and council agreed only that it was unacceptable. They could not agree on the proper definition of trading stock or on what discount, if any, should be permitted for unimproved land or for merchants' ships. The house insisted, furthermore, that money or merchandise anywhere in the world belonging to Rhode Islanders be taxed and demanded a one-third discount on unimproved land. The council argued that money invested by Rhode Islanders in English public securities should be tax exempt, as should trade goods belonging to Rhode Islanders stored in and taxed by other colonies. The two chambers battled until October and then compromised. The house agreed to keep the discount on ships at sea and to exempt money invested in English public securities; the council agreed that all merchants' "book debts or other accounts, as well without the colony as within," should be taxed.[36]

Debates like these continued with hardly a pause throughout the crises with England that preceded independence. Certainly Rhode Islanders were as deeply involved in the struggle against parliamentary taxes as their neighbors were. They watched Parliament's maneuverings as apprehensively, memorialized against English taxes as earnestly, thundered against tyranny as loudly, and rioted with perhaps more enthusiasm than other New Englanders. But through it all, Rhode Islanders rarely lost sight of local issues, those matters of commonplace legislative concern that affected their daily lives and businesses directly and constantly. Common opposition to the Sugar Act scarcely diminished their quarreling over local taxes, and the same assemblymen who, in the name of justice and equity, stood united against the Stamp Act argued violently about their own levies and used the laws, whenever they got the chance, to punish their political opponents and reward the faithful.

Rhode Island was unique. No other New England colony was so open to tax manipulation for political ends. Even in Connecticut —like Rhode Island, a charter colony with a popularly elected governor, council, and house of representatives and a two-party political system—the relationship between taxes and factional politics was less clear-cut. Rhode Island's taxes were easy to manipulate because the legislature assigned a tax quota to each town every year, and the dominant faction could therefore punish or reward towns as the need arose. But Connecticut levied its taxes a different way. Each year the general assembly established the colony pound rate, that is, a uniform amount each taxpayer had to pay for every pound of his assessed value. The legislature did not assign tax quotas to the towns, and therefore if the tax collections were to be manipulated for political ends, as they unquestionably were, it could be done most easily at the town or county level by local selectmen and assessors, rather than by the general assembly. This reduced but by no means eliminated the chances for playing politics with the taxes. In an independent charter colony where land values fell nearly 50 percent after the Seven Years' War and where farm prices and profits fell along with them, where the people owed their own colonial government some £80,000 in back taxes by 1765, where the running dispute with England over the Stamp and Townshend acts pushed the question of taxes to the fore in the popular mind, and where two well-established factions battled each year for control of a completely elected government, it could hardly have been otherwise.[37]

The roots of Connecticut factional politics lay in the Great Awakening, when the colony split into two warring religious camps. Those who accepted the Awakening, the New Lights, established their power primarily in eastern Connecticut. Those who rejected it in favor of a more conservative style of congregational worship, the Old Lights, retained power in western Connecticut. Religion was never very far removed from politics in old New England, and the Old Light–New Light controversy soon broadened into political divisions.

By 1765 the religious differences, although still potent, had been to some degree overtaken by events and submerged in other issues. Connecticut's governor in the early 1760s was Thomas Fitch. He spoke not only for the Old Lights in religion but also for those who favored fiscal orthodoxy and opposed currency inflation and tax reductions, for those who disliked the land speculation schemes of the Susquehanna Company, and for those who wanted opposition to English taxation kept orderly and well within the bounds of law. If New Light zealots wanted Fitch and his supporters removed from office so that the work of the Lord might go forward, others wanted him removed in order that currency might be made more plentiful, taxes be reduced, the Susquehanna Company be blessed by the government, and the danger of English taxation in America be stamped out by whatever means were necessary, the law notwithstanding. Fitch was no more pleased with the stamp tax than were his New

Light opponents. He had written to England often, saying that the colony could not afford to pay a stamp tax, but he was appalled by the mobs that rioted and forced the Connecticut stamp distributor Jared Ingersoll to resign, and he worried about where such mobbish proceedings might lead. In the name of order and the public peace, rather than out of any particular agreement with the principle or practice of parliamentary taxation, Fitch called for the arrest and trial of Stamp Act rioters. Furthermore, he was under orders from England to swear to uphold the Stamp Act on pain of a £1,000 fine and removal from office. He delayed as long as he thought he could, but in October, 1765, Fitch took the necessary oath. From that day forward, he and the Old Lights were branded by their opponents as supporters of parliamentary taxation and English despotism, enemies to American liberty, and purveyors of the cowardly doctrine of nonresistance to tyranny. In 1766 the New Lights, campaigning as Sons of Liberty, defeated Fitch and elected their man, William Pitkin, governor.[38]

Pitkin's victory had a dramatic effect on Connecticut taxes. Fitch and his council had fought recommendations by the house of representatives for substantial tax reductions, but the new governor and his supporters were more amenable to tax relief. The legislature had previously authorized a tax of eight pence per pound of assessed value, to be collected in 1766; the new Pitkin administration canceled it. Nor were any general taxes collected under Pitkin in 1767, 1768, or 1769. From the end of the Stamp Act crisis through the Townshend Acts troubles, while the colonists complained mightily about the crushing burden of parliamentary taxes and memorialized endlessly about the injustice, Connecticut citizens paid no province rates at all.[39]

Fitch's followers and the Old Lights cried foul and insisted that the colony treasury was not nearly healthy enough to justify a suspension of taxes and that the policy had but one transparent purpose: to buy popularity for the Pitkin administration and ensure its reelection. They had insisted upon tax suspensions, the Old Lights wailed, only "in order to establish the reputation of those gentlemen who were elected when those changes in government first took place."[40] The reasons for the Old Lights' anger are evident: already charged, somewhat unfairly, with being soft on tyranny, they found it doubly difficult to campaign against a party and a governor whose policy with respect to England was no taxation for revenue and whose policy at home seemed to be no taxation, period.

After 1766 the Old Lights never regained control of the colony, although they continued to campaign year after year, and the rhetoric of all involved touched on taxes whenever there were votes to be lured. Eliphalet Dyer, for instance, promised the legislature that a new grant of land for the Susquehanna Company, which was closely associated with the New Light faction, would raise so much revenue that the colony would never again need to levy peacetime general taxes. Benjamin Gale, however, warned that such a grant would sink Connecticut so deeply into debt that recovery would take a century. When the colony began collecting taxes again in 1770, during the administration of New Light governor Jonathan Trumbull, his opponents charged, somewhat inconsistently, that no taxes would have been needed but for New Light mismanagement, incompetence, nepotism, and fraud. In May, 1768, a New Light–dominated general assembly quietly revised collection rules so that towns were no longer required to pay the taxes of their paupers. It soon became evident that towns politically close to the Pitkin administration benefited out of all proportion to their tax assessments. New London, a Pitkin stronghold, with an assessed value of £37,000, received £1,100 in abatements for paupers. Fairfield, an Old Light town, valued at more than £61,000, got only £307. Lyme (in New London County), valued at £27,000, enjoyed an abatement of £588, but Milford (Fairfield County), with a similar assessment, was allowed only £85 for its paupers. The matter became a public scandal that embarrassed the New Light faction into repealing the abatement plan within a year, but Old Light essayists regularly retold the story at election time.[41]

An Old Light essayist raised a more important issue in January, 1767. Writing in the *Connecticut Courant*, "Plaind Facts" pointed out that if one counted the governor and lieutenant governor, the council contained nine men from towns east of the Connecticut River, where the New Lights were strongest, and only five men from towns west of it, where the Old Lights prevailed. And yet, Plaind Facts went on, the west-bank towns were assessed at £1,013,799 and the east-bank towns at £564,736. In other words, west-bank towns paid twice the taxes east-bank towns paid. Plaind Facts did not challenge the accuracy of the assessments, for he was after much more than a reduction of taxes. Indeed, the more taxes paid west of the river, the stronger his case. He argued that the west-bank towns ought to be represented on the council in direct proportion to the taxes they paid. Or as "Candor" subsequently put it, also in the *Courant*, "We should have our rulers where we pay our money for them."[42]

The argument made little sense in any but partisan political terms. As New Light writers countered, one might with equal justice draw a line east and west across the colony and demand representation from each side according to tax assessments. And they ridiculed the idea that councillors should be chosen on the basis of "acres of land or according to the amount of pounds, shillings and pence in the public list." God, they explained, had for his own good reasons placed the balance of talent and ability in eastern Connecticut, and until he changed his mind and rearranged things, "everyone should be easy with their present rulers." Newspaper debate on the matter lasted for months, and it raised the notion of an upper house that directly represented property and income rather than population, a notion that would receive more serious consideration after 1775.[43]

The connection between factional politics and taxation was more tenuous in Massachusetts and New Hampshire. Both were royal colonies, and the governors owed their appointments to the crown. Francis Bernard and Thomas Hutchinson of Massachusetts and John Wentworth of New Hampshire had no choice but to support crown policy publicly, however unpopular, and no matter what their own private opinions might be. As the conflict with England worsened, there emerged in both colonies a government or court party, beholden to the governor and therefore to the crown and committed to upholding parliamentary authority in America, and a popular party, centered in the houses of representatives and committed to opposing parliamentary taxes. As time went on, the opposing factions were separated more by their stands on imperial affairs than on purely internal issues. By contrast, the factions in Rhode Island and Connecticut, where neither side was recognizably "royal," divided more often over internal policy than imperial affairs. In Massachusetts and New Hampshire, therefore, internal tax policy sometimes opposed merchants to farmers or arrayed town against country, but such conflicts were rarely reflected in the party divisions after 1763. In fact, internal taxes were central elements of party struggle before the Revolution only in the proprietary and charter colonies that had no royal establishment. Internal taxation intruded on the struggle between the Massachusetts popular party and the Bernard and Hutchinson factions, or on the contest between the New Hampshire popular party and Governor Wentworth's administration, only incidentally during the decade before independence.

A peculiar quirk of the Massachusetts tax laws, for example, permitted Thomas Hutchinson to force the Massachusetts General Court in 1770 to meet in Cambridge rather than in Boston. Hutchinson called the legislators to Cambridge in hopes of reducing the influence of the Boston popular party and the Boston town meeting on their deliberations. Members of the house protested the move, charged Hutchinson with harassment, and refused to do any business until they were returned to Boston. Hutchinson stood fast: time and the tax laws were on his side. Massachusetts law as a rule provided for taxing in the *entire* colony public debt (at this time about £80,000) each year, though no one actually expected such a massive tax to be collected. Before the warrants went out, the General Court invariably approved a supplementary tax law reducing the levy to a fraction of the public debt and extending the rest of the collection to some future date. But if the supplementary law was not passed, the treasurer had no choice but to issue warrants for the collection of the full amount.[44] In June, Hutchinson warned the house that unless it agreed to sit at Cambridge, the full tax would be collected. The house replied that the people of Massachusetts "had much rather be subject even to the immediate payment of that whole sum, distressing as it would be, than to concede to so pernicious a precedent." All through the summer, neither side moved. On September 27 Hutchinson told the house that warrants for the collection of an £80,000 tax had gone out but that he would accept an act recalling them, provided it came from Cambridge. The house quickly determined that the people of Massachusetts had undergone a wondrous change of heart. Overriding the objections of Samuel Adams and John Hancock, the members agreed to work at Cambridge and then hastily set about recalling the tax warrants. But they had learned their lesson and they took steps to prevent their being coerced that way again. A new law provided for taxing in the debt in three installments rather than in one indigestible lump. Their prudence paid off in 1771, when Hutchinson vetoed a tax law because it did not exempt the salaries of royal officials. The collectors then levied a tax in accord with the previous installment law, which included taxes on royal officials.[45]

The Seven Years' War had been good to New England; all the colonies prospered from it, so much so that Governor Bernard of Massachusetts was almost sorry to see it end. "By the ceasing of the war," he warned his General Court, "several sources of the current wealth of this province will be shut up." The "spirit of industry, frugality and economy, all of which have been of late too much relaxed by an unusual flow of money, much exceeding what could naturally arise from the common produce of this country," would have to be revived.[46]

The war created private prosperity but it also created public debt. Massachusetts alone spent £800,000 on the war, and all the New England colonies faced the coming peace with debts to pay. A postwar depression and new imperial restrictions on trade, as well as a growing scarcity of specie and—as wartime paper money was retired—of currency of any sort, made paying those debts more difficult.[47] And yet, the New England colonies were spectacularly successful in paying them while keeping their taxes low, at least in comparison with those paid in England. The war added £60,000,000 to England's national debt, which nearly doubled it. From 1756 to 1766, £14,500,000 had to be raised annually; the amount had been £6,000,000 a year before the war. Old taxes went up and new ones were added. Land taxes in England doubled during the war to four shillings per pound of annual rent and stayed there after the peace. In addition, Englishmen paid a bewildering array of other taxes, including window taxes, assorted excise taxes, and a stamp tax. In 1761 a new brewery tax drove the price of their product up a sobering penny a pot. Two years later, rioting broke out over new cider taxes. By the 1770s, English taxes reached a level of at least one pound sterling per capita.[48]

No New England provincial tax during the postwar years ever reached that level. In fact, the period 1763–1774 was one of declining taxes. The highest tax Rhode Island passed during those years was £12,468, which came to only about five shillings per capita. In 1773 and 1774 the tax fell to £4,000, the poll tax to twopence, and the per capita rate to two shillings. No new taxes at all were levied in 1767 or 1768 (Appendix, table 3). In Connecticut the twopence per pound tax of 1774 amounted to less than one shilling eight pence per capita, and no new colony taxes at all were levied from 1766 to 1769 (Appendix, table 4). Property and poll taxes in New Hampshire never rose above seven pence per capita and in 1774 they dropped to less than half that. As the 1770s began, Governor Wentworth reported "with the greatest pleasure that . . . no man can justly say the taxes are heavy, for the whole does not exceed three shillings eight pence proclamation money to each rateable in the province. Perhaps if exactly known, and taken, not three shillings six pence; an instance I believe heretofore unexampled in any province or country whatever"[49] (Appendix, table 5). In 1764 and 1765 Massachusetts levied its highest postwar taxes (£50,000), which came to only four shillings seven pence per capita. No tax at all passed in 1768, when

Governor Bernard prorogued the legislature for refusing to repeal its circular letter condemning the Townshend duties. From 1766 on, taxes in the Bay Colony dropped until they hit a low of £10,312 in the tax law of 1774 (Appendix, table 6). Applying 1776 population figures to the 1774 tax (the last before the Revolution) yields a per capita rate of less than one penny sterling.[50]

Understandably, colonial leaders were not eager to make Parliament aware of how low their taxes were. Connecticut's governors, for example, went to great lengths to keep as murky as possible London's view of the colony's financial condition. Secretary of State Hillsborough found it nearly impossible to get a straight answer about the colony's finances out of its governors or its agents in England. He requested copies of Connecticut's legislative journals, and when he did not get them, he asked agent William S. Johnson to explain. Johnson told him that the Connecticut legislature kept no journal, only "short notes . . . which would be perfectly unintelligible" without the colony secretary on the spot to interpret them properly. Hillsborough thought this a very peculiar method of doing business and said so. After some pointed references to the dangers of becoming "too much a separate independent state," he sarcastically asked if Connecticut might condescend to send him at least its laws.[51]

In 1769 Johnson cautioned Joseph Trumbull to let Parliament know "as little as possible of our internal circumstances and police, especially in point of taxation, which they will never clearly understand, and which may be liable to much misconstruction." What Johnson feared was that Parliament might understand only too well. He advised the son of the soon-to-be governor Jonathan Trumbull to "meet ministerial art with American prudence." Just how successful "American prudence" was in obscuring matters became apparent in 1774, when Silas Deane, newly chosen representative to the Continental Congress, tried to gather information about the "immense sums" Connecticut "must have" contributed during the Seven Years' War. He complained to Governor Trumbull that he could find "no authentick record kept of it. . . . Our enemies boldly assert that we have expended nothing but what we have been largely repaid for, and we have no record to contradict them." "What excuse," he demanded of Trumbull, "can be made for neglecting to preserve the exact account of the charge of the last war?"[52] One wonders what Trumbull replied.

Rhode Island also apparently tried to keep England in the dark about the size of the colony's taxes to redeem its paper money. In 1766 a committee preparing a new compilation of the laws asked whether laws "relating to the emitting and sinking of paper bills shall be inserted in the new law book." The assembly ordered that "all those laws respecting the public monies, such as emitting, sinking or any way regulating thereof, being matters only concerning the public treasury or revenue, or debts due thereon, or arising therefrom . . . be omitted in the new law book." In January, 1768, Hillsborough asked Rhode Island for a "complete collection, either in manuscript or print," of its laws. In June the assembly told the governor to send him "an authenticated printed copy of the public laws of the colony." If the "authenticated printed copy" sent to Hillsborough in 1768 was the "new law book" prepared in 1766, it contained precious little information about Rhode Island's public revenues.[53]

New Englanders from every colony complained that it was unfair to judge the magnitude of their taxes by the province rates alone. The New Hampshire assembly conceded that its province tax was not very high in 1773, yet "the tax upon the whole county, town and parish which must be paid by the people cannot be deemed inconsiderable." And it is true that town and local taxes often exceeded the province rates. Concord, New Hampshire, for example, raised £100 for town expenses in 1770, when the colony rate for the town totaled only £31. Hanover taxed itself £135 for town projects in 1774 but paid only £7 to the colony. With the exception of Boston, the same was generally true in Massachusetts. Brookline, for instance, paid a province tax of £102 in 1770 and a town tax of £140. In Connecticut, the towns generally raised three times as much by taxes as did the colony.[54]

Several factors account for the low colonial taxes. First of all, England compensated the colonies for their efforts in the French and Indian War. In 1760 alone, Parliament voted the northern colonies £200,000 sterling in subsidies. Massachusetts' share came to £60,000, and in 1759 it had received subsidies totaling more than £70,000 sterling. Parliament eventually granted Connecticut nearly £240,000 sterling, which permitted substantial tax reductions. Connecticut slashed a planned fourteen-pence tax to tenpence in 1761 and a seven-pence tax to fivepence the following year. In 1763 it collected only sixpence out of a planned fifteen-pence tax. During the next two years, the compensation payments permitted the reduction of another fifteen-pence tax to eight pence and still another to seven pence. It canceled completely an eight-pence tax planned for 1766. Compensation grants to New Hampshire permitted taxes planned for 1763 to be cut by more than 44 percent and the elimination of £9,000 in taxes planned for 1764 and 1765. The colony complained endlessly that it had not been granted enough, but the governor reported in 1770 that £6,000 more had been received from Parliament, which provided "an immediate and very easy remedy" for the colony's debts "without augmenting the province tax."[55]

The relatively low cost of running colonial governments also helped keep taxes low. Schools, poor relief, and road construction and maintenance were largely the responsibility of the counties or towns, though there were exceptions. Connecticut shared taxes with the towns for school expenses, and most colonies occasionally used province funds for roads or bridges. On the whole, however, such services were local concerns.[56]

The cost of running Rhode Island for one year in the 1760s was not much more than £2,000. Connecticut got by on about £4,000 for regular expenses, plus another £2,000 for education. Massachusetts needed considerably more, about £18,000. These differences were caused in part by the pay of officials in the various colonies. Government salaries in Rhode Island, for example, ranged from low to nonexistent, and most public officers were expected to derive the major portion of their income from fees established by law, and kickbacks established by custom, in return for services they performed or, occasionally, did not perform. Deputies and assistants received no fixed pay at all, and as late as 1768 the governor of Rhode Island drew the princely sum of £30 in pay. In Connecticut, the governor got ten times as much. When he was on speaking terms with his General Court, Francis Bernard of Massachusetts earned £1,300 a year, and pay for the house and council members added between £3,000 and £7,000 to the annual taxes.[57] New Hampshire's expenses were probably not above £2,500 a year. The governor was convinced that they were kept low by scrimping on his pay and housing, and he took what small comfort he could in sarcasm: "the small paring you have voted [me]," he told the house in 1769, "is the object of my pity . . . however, if one honest taxable in the province is comforted in the one penny thus saved to him out of the money from my pocket, I do rejoice at the vote."[58]

Tax collections even of such small amounts were often lax, to say the least. "Collecting taxes has laid the foundation for the ruin of many great families," wrote John Adams, and the reason is not far to seek. Uncollected taxes in Massachusetts amounted to £95,375 in June, 1763, and a decade later they still totaled more than £61,000 (Appendix, table 7). In 1767 the town of Winchendon asked to be excused for the past six years' taxes, none of which had it paid, and the collector of Dunstable asked to be excused from paying money due since the 1730s.[59] Arrearages in New Hampshire were considerably lower, but so were its taxes. An audit in the summer of 1765 revealed £469 in sterling emissions and £4,253 in new tenor paper bills overdue. Arrearages for 1768, 1770, and 1774 respectively were £331, £222, and £300.[60] Connecticut taxpayers were in arrears nearly £80,000 by the end of 1765. The delinquencies could be traced, the Connecticut colonial agent insisted, to the people's inability to pay, but it seems more likely that they came from the treasurer's unwillingness to collect. By 1767 the vast sums uncollected became a public scandal. The assembly forced treasurer Joseph Talcott to resign and began charging interest on uncollected taxes. By 1769, however, £45,000 still remained in arrears, and some of it was not collected until 1780.[61]

Rhode Island's tax difficulties were not all politically inspired. Far from it. The colony had a history of tax delinquency, stretching back at least a century. Its people, north and south, no more eager to pay taxes than were other New Englanders, were equally negligent in doing so. Politics entered the picture not through nonpayment of taxes, which was common, but through the selective enforcement of the laws, as when the Ward-dominated assembly ordered the treasurer to sue Providence, Scituate, and Cumberland for back taxes and ignored the fact that Newport had not paid those same taxes. Despite various plans adopted to speed collections, payment in Rhode Island remained spotty. An investigation in the summer of 1767 revealed that some Rhode Island towns still owed money for their 1762 and 1763 taxes and that the colony as a whole was behind more than £7,000.[62]

Despite all this—the partial and complete cancellations, the spotty collections, and the relatively light rates—by 1775 the New England colonies had retired most, and in some cases all, of the debts they contracted in the Seven Years' War. The year before, Governor Wentworth congratulated the New Hampshire assembly on "the prosperous and growing state of the Province, which is of late years increased in culture, commerce, and population, while the same time the province taxes are greatly diminished to individuals." The house replied that "the colony's being so free from debt, for which reason the provincial tax will be light to individuals," afforded them "an additional pleasure." Thomas Hutchinson, in his *History of the Colony and Province of Massachusetts Bay*, gave a glowing account of Massachusetts in the early 1770s:

> It is certain that there had been no period when the province . . . felt less of the ordinary burdens which must at all times be felt, more or less, by the people of every government. . . . From the surpluses of former funds and from debts due to the government for lands which had been sold, there appeared a fund sufficient to raise money not only for the service of the present year [1770], but of some years to come, so as to render any tax unnecessary. The whole debt of the province at the expiration of the last war had been since paid by taxes of less than £20,000 sterling a year, except about £40,000 which was charged part upon the present and part upon the next, and if raised by a poll or capitation tax would not exceed six shillings a head in each year, equally

divided among the male inhabitants subject to taxes. No excise of any sort was then paid, and only an inconsiderable impost remained.

Three years later, Hutchinson was able to tell the legislators of Massachusetts that the province was "entirely free from debt." And in 1769 Connecticut's London agent learned, probably from Joseph Trumbull, that the colony he represented was "nearly out of debt."[63]

The remarkable thing about the politics of taxation in New England before the Revolution is not that there was so much debate over internal taxes but that so little of it extended to the basic principles that underlay the laws. Critics normally complained not that the laws were inherently unjust but that fair laws were being unfairly applied. It is always risky to assume that silence implies consent, but it is undeniable that most New Englanders apparently accepted quietly and with little visible protest the combination of poll, property, and faculty taxes by which they funded their governments in the final decades before independence. Few complained publicly about the regressive nature of the poll taxes or asked how such taxes could be squared with the ability-to-pay principle that in theory underlay New England's tax laws. In this, New Englanders were unlike residents of the southern colonies, where the principles that lay behind the tax laws were challenged loudly, frequently, and sometimes violently.

The New England colonies, however, were like those farther south in that the men who wrote the revenue laws guarded their autonomy jealously. Legislators well understood that without it they would not have been able to respond as they had to postwar economic problems, by adopting a variety of relief policies. Some colonies accepted commodities in payment of taxes, thus easing the currency scarcity. Some cut taxes sharply after the war, eliminated them altogether, or delayed collections for months or years at a time. Occasionally, as in Connecticut, overdue taxes were permitted to run on and on, and though they might accumulate interest, they amounted to a loan by the colony to the taxpayers in troubled times. The independence of the colonies where taxes were concerned permitted each to apply its own form of tax relief to its own special needs and to raise revenues through its own particular mixture of poll, property, and trade taxes, a mixture that in each case reflected the needs and interests of the dominant legislative factions. Each New England colony guarded its tax autonomy against encroachment by England or by other colonies. Connecticut made the point emphatically when it instructed its delegates to the Albany Congress of 1754 that in arranging for the common defense, they were to commit the colony to no expenses "save for the present occasion and let that be so guarded that nothing be urged hereafter so as to bring it in precedent."[64]

In the post-Revolution years, the New England states would face problems similar in kind, though much more severe in degree, to those they faced as colonies after 1763. Most of their actions, roundly condemned after the war as dangerous innovations of an unleashed democracy, were those taken by legislatures long before independence. Although none of this was apparent before 1776, one thing did seem certain: New Englanders would not look kindly on any challenge to their local autonomy over taxes, from whichever side of the Atlantic—and from whatever external government, English or American—it might come.

CHAPTER TWO

The Middle Colonies

In spite of the brawling over taxation that went on in New England after 1763, an overall unity of form and theory marked the region's taxes. All the New England colonies relied on property taxes as a regular source of income. All were nominally committed to the idea that taxation ought to be related to ability to pay and that property, variously defined, was an acceptable measure of that ability. In the middle colonies, even this minimal uniformity of theory dissolved into a patchwork of different policies and expedients imposed in accord with the relative strength of the contending political factions in each colony. Nevertheless, an important unifying principle, implicit rather than publicly avowed, did underlie many middle colony tax policies: the interests of the landed wealthy should be protected whenever politically possible. In New York that principle lay behind the legislature's stubborn reluctance to pass new land taxes or to continue such taxes any longer than was absolutely necessary. In New Jersey it permitted landowners to exempt much of their property by applying some creative definitions to key terms in the tax laws. In Pennsylvania it explained, at least in part, the assembly's continuing efforts to tax the Penn family estates and thereby to reduce taxes on native Pennsylvania landowners.

In no two of the middle colonies were property taxes administered in precisely the same way, and in no two did they fall on exactly the same items. During the 1760s the New York assembly assigned a quota of the total property taxes to each county, to be raised on "estates real and personal." Several subsequent acts governing collections in the counties directed assessors to list taxable wealth at 4 percent of the "real" value of the property involved. But "estates real and personal" did not necessarily mean all such estates. The laws offered the landed wealthy numerous loopholes, and all the counties of New York did not apply the laws in the same way. The definition of taxable property, for instance, sometimes changed from county to county. Richmond and Suffolk counties taxed unimproved land, but most of the upriver counties did not, which practice worked to the advantage of the great landed families of the Hudson River valley, like the Livingstons, who owned thousands of acres of wilderness land. And the manor lords shifted the taxes on their improved land to their tenants, who had to pay those taxes in addition to their rents or lose their leases. With their wild lands held tax free, their tenants paying the taxes on most of their developed property, and the rents they collected not taxed at all, the manor lords reaped all the benefits from their tremendous holdings nearly tax free.[1]

Furthermore, not until 1775 did New York begin supplying county tax assessors with a standard list of rates for land and other property to guide them in their work. Many assessments therefore were little more than guesses made by "comparing one man's appearance or known substance with another." Accuracy in such circumstances was not always possible, and when possible, it was not always prudent. Assessors in New York City, councillor and merchant John Watts explained, could not "be over-nice" in making such estimates, for "the circumstances of people in commerce, where the greater part live by credit, won't bear it."[2]

Finally, New York legislators' attitudes toward land taxes of any sort reflected the attitudes of the landed families who dominated New York politics in the late colonial period: they tolerated the general property tax only as a short-term war emergency measure, and the shorter the term the better. When, by the end of 1767, a substantial part of the colony's war debt had been retired, the New York general property tax lapsed into welcome oblivion.[3]

New Jersey's general property tax was more permanent. The colony redeemed its wartime paper money by an annual tax of no more than £15,000 on estates real and personal, and legislators expected the whole debt to be retired by 1783. As in New York, each county had a quota to raise, but the New Jersey legislature supplied assessors with detailed lists of taxable property: homes, all kinds of commercial mills, stills, breweries, and boats, male slaves or servants over sixteen, livestock, and all "profitable tracts of land held by patent, deed or survey, where on any improvement is made and no other tracts."[4] There was some doubt, however, at least in the minds of landowners, about what "tract" meant. The New Jersey assembly complained that assessors, interpreting the word too loosely, called all the land in a tract improved land if any part of it was improved. A man who owned one hundred acres of land, only ten of which produced anything profitable, was, the assembly complained, taxed for one hundred acres of profitable land. Governor William Franklin, however, replied that New Jersey landowners had found in the law a wide and profitable loophole that all but eliminated taxes on much unimproved land. "Many persons who have larger tracts than what they think proper to occupy," he explained, "sever by lease only a part of them for farms, and let the rest lie waste." Once the unproductive lands were separated by lease, they became separate tracts and therefore nontaxable, by which means owners "only pay taxes for what they actually receive a profit from."[5] Tenant farmers in New Jersey, furthermore, could not subtract land taxes from their rents if their leases required them to pay those taxes. Thus a New Jersey landlord with favorable leases, and his wilderness property separated into untaxed tracts, could escape most of the property taxes, just as his New York counterpart could.

New Jersey taxed a few occupations such as merchant and shopkeeper in a drastically cut-down version of the New England faculty tax. Merchants, for example, were rated after 1769 at no less than five shillings nor more than five pounds, at the discretion of assessors. New Jersey assessors received detailed instructions, embodied in the laws, setting forth values for some kinds of property, such as livestock, and giving minimum and maximum values for other kinds, including land. These varied according to the location of the land and its quality. After 1769, for instance, improved tracts in Cumberland County could be assessed at no less than five nor more than thirty-five pounds per hundred acres. Similar land in Somerset County had to be rated between nine and fifty pounds. Within such limits, the laws left assessors to their own discretion and rectitude, with results that might have been expected. In theory, New Jersey taxed the capital value of land rather than the income or rent it produced. In fact, complained Governor Franklin, "the valuation put by the assessors on the lands throughout a county will, I believe, in very few cases, if any, be found on an average to exceed the value of the annual rent or income." "Many tracts," he was convinced, "are rated at less."[6]

Pennsylvania's property tax was similar to New Jersey's. Both provided their respective colonies with their most important single source of public revenues during the interwar period. In Pennsylvania the general property tax raised over £22,000 in every year of the decade preceding independence, and sometimes much more (Appendix, table 8). During this time, the tax was 18d. per pound of the "clear yearly value" of all estates, real and personal. Pennsylvania taxed unimproved land if it had been surveyed, thus distinguishing the colony sharply from New York and New Jersey, though it shared its neighbors' problem with resourceful citizens and cooperative local officials who sought loopholes in the law. The tax act of 1764, for instance, allowed landowners "a reasonable quantity" of tax-free timberland for "repairs and fuel." The timber allowance was widely abused; excessive exemptions were claimed under it, and "great inequalities" in assessments resulted. With more charity than truth, the assembly blamed "misconstruction" and "want of more clear and explicit directions," and in 1774 it limited fuel and timber exemptions to thirty acres out of each hundred.[7]

Pennsylvania also supplied its assessors with lists of minimum and maximum values for land. The lowest permissible tax on located unimproved land in the colony was 7s. 6d. for each hundred acres; the highest was £1 2s. 6d. Frontier counties with Indian problems got special exemptions. Other rates fell on ferries, mills, forges, livestock, slaves, servants, and unmarried men, who were (if assessments are an accurate guide) thought to be only slightly more valuable to society than horses. But legally mandated rates and the rates actually applied were often very different. And even within particular counties, rates varied tremendously. In Paxton Township, Lancaster County, the tax on William Montgomery's hundred acres and one cow—he listed no horses or servants—was 2s. But David Jones paid £1 on his hundred acres, two horses, and one cow. Most taxpayers in the township owned tracts of between one and two hundred acres, and most paid 7s. or 8s. property tax.[8]

Pennsylvania had a more extensive faculty tax than any other of the middle colonies. All trades, professions, and occupations were rated at the discretion of the assessors "upon the best discovery that can be made of their respective annual profits." "Salaries and lucrative public posts" were included, no doubt because most of them were at the disposal (and in the hands) of the proprietor or his friends. For tax purposes, a public post was rated at four fifths of the amount annually received by the appointee.[9]

Not much is known about Delaware taxation beyond the facts that in the 1760s it included at least one tax of threepence per pound on property and that it normally exempted "unsettled tracts or parcels of land" from colony rates.[10]

Excises were important in Pennsylvania and New York, but not in New Jersey and probably not in Delaware. Both Pennsylvania and New York regularly used the proceeds to reduce land taxes. Between 1767 and 1775 Pennsylvania issued over £90,000 in paper money against anticipated income from excise taxes. By 1775 excises provided between £8,000 and £9,000 a year, collected for the explicit purpose of keeping property taxes low (Appendix, table 9). Until 1768 New York used excise money to redeem its wartime paper. Since the primary fund for sinking those emissions was the general property tax, the excise helped reduce property rates. It was designed to raise from £1,200 to

£1,500 annually for most of the years from 1763 to 1775, but as with most colonial taxes, intention and fact were often far apart. Excises in arrears more than two years, for example, totaled £2,259 in 1773. After 1772 the colony returned excise money to the counties to be used for poor relief, road repairs, and other local expenses, many of which would otherwise have been met by local property taxes or, in some cases, local poll taxes. New Jersey had no excise at all.[11]

Only in New York were import duties a significant source of public revenues. New Jersey had none, and in Pennsylvania the yield was relatively minor. The combined import tax on goods and slaves in Pennsylvania from September, 1763, to September, 1764, was only £1,648. Over £700 of that came from the slave tax, which by 1774 was down to £112 and in 1775 yielded not much more than half that. But in New York, imposts were second in importance only to the property taxes (while they lasted). The duties were collected on rum and other liquors, wine, cocoa, slaves, and dry goods from Europe, East India, and the British West Indies. In the period from 1760 to 1774, income from the duties varied from well over £10,000 in 1760 and 1761 to a low of £3,615 in 1771. The higher figures in the early years grew out of the French and Indian War, when British and colonial soldiers and sailors stationed in New York proved themselves "exceedingly public spirited in the consumption of strong liquors."[12]

New Yorkers, however, were little more scrupulous about paying their own tariffs than they were about paying England's, particularly during Abraham De Peyster's term as treasurer. He was understanding about giving importers, including his son, extra time in which to pay the taxes. This often meant they never paid at all, since De Peyster rarely bothered to take bonds to secure eventual payment. Nevertheless, throughout most of the interwar period the impost brought in about £5,000 a year, and usually more—enough, as a rule, to pay the salaries of New York's colonial officials[13] (Appendix, table 10).

Interest from loan office emissions, a fourth revenue source in the middle colonies, was important to the colonists because the loan emissions provided a circulating currency with which to carry on business and because interest on the loans kept other taxes, especially the property taxes, low. Appeals to England to allow new loan office emissions following the restrictive Currency Act of 1764 stressed their importance as revenue producers. The New York assembly, for example, thought collecting interest from loan office bills "the easiest and most effectual method to enable us . . . to pay off the debts of the colony and provide a fund for future exigencies," without passing new taxes. New York had long had £40,000 in paper out on loan. Between September, 1762, and September, 1764, the colony collected £3,600 in interest. John Watts thought the fund useful, and he told correspondents in England that if New York was permitted any paper money at all under the proposed currency restrictions of 1764, the £40,000 loan office emission should be it. The emission continued from year to year, he explained, more at the insistence of "governors than the governed as it strengthened the hands of government." But the emission died with the new Currency Act, and the colony reaped no additional interest payments until 1772, a year after it let out £120,000 in currency on loan at 5 percent interest.[14]

Loan office interest brought in £9,885 to Pennsylvania's treasury between 1763 and 1768, but the yield declined quickly as the loans were called in. In Delaware the regular expenses of government were usually raised by interest on loan office emissions.[15] In New Jersey such interest had paid for the government before the Seven Years' War, including the governor's salary, a matter of abiding concern to Sir William Franklin. In 1766 he warned English policymakers that their continued refusal to allow a loan emission in his colony would force an increase in property taxes, which is precisely what happened. Not until 1774 did the Privy Council approve a new loan office issue of £100,000 in New Jersey. Franklin expected the colony to make £5,000 a year from it.[16]

Although the region's general property taxes were applied in ways that favored the wealthier landowners, middle colony legislators did not impose upon their constituents one of the most regressive taxes common in New England and the South: the poll tax. In the final years before independence, there were no regular colony-wide poll taxes in the middle colonies (with the possible exception of Delaware), though such taxes were collected by towns or counties for local purposes. Poll taxes were so unpopular in the middle region, and opposition to them so widespread, that candidates for public office sought votes by charging their opponents with secretly planning to impose such taxes once they got into power.[17] And there were a great many votes to be won by making taxation a political issue, especially in Pennsylvania.

By 1763 two well-organized and powerful political parties were locked in a struggle for control of the Pennsylvania assembly. One, the so-called Quaker party, led by Benjamin Franklin and Joseph Galloway, had as its major objective the removal of the Penn family from Pennsylvania government and the establishment of royal government. The Quaker party, more accurately known as the antiproprietary party, drew most of its strength from the old settled sections of Pennsylvania, particularly from the three eastern counties of Philadelphia, Chester, and Bucks. Thanks to gross malapportionment, those three counties held a majority of seats in the assembly, even though they contained by 1763 a minority of the colony's population. Thus the Quaker party dominated the assembly through most of the 1760s.[18]

The proprietary party, on the other hand, served the interests of the Penn family. The proprietary governor, advised by his council and party leaders in the assembly, directed the party's actions. Penn supporters fought as best they could to preserve the prerogatives of the proprietor (to whom many of them were beholden for their own appointments) against encroachment by the Quaker party in the assembly. The proprietary party fought for popular support on election day as hard as the Quaker party did, though not as successfully, and it developed some popular leaders of its own, such as John Dickinson.

Winning a majority of the seats in the popularly elected assembly was important for the proprietary party, but it was critical for the Quaker party, since both the governorship and the council were permanently in the hands of their opponents. Quaker party leaders, therefore, searched constantly for popular issues with which to attack the Penn family and its supporters and to rally votes for their own candidates. The fact that many of the Penn family estates in the colony were tax exempt, and the urgent need to raise large sums of money for defense during the Seven Years' War and the Indian wars that followed, gave Quaker party leaders just such an issue.

The Penn family normally paid no taxes in Pennsylvania on their surveyed but unimproved lands. Since the Penns got first choice of newly surveyed tracts, their land was invariably among the best to be had in the colony and regularly increased in value as adjacent tracts were purchased and settled. The 17,000 acres of Conestoga Manor, for example, rose in value nearly 800 percent between 1726 and 1756, and the increase went wholly untaxed. Beginning in the 1750s the Quaker-led assembly tried repeatedly to tax such land, but the proprietary governors blocked every attempt. The pattern was well established by 1755, when the issue was temporarily sidestepped rather than resolved.[19] The assembly passed a tax bill exempting the Penn lands in return for a "voluntary" contribution from the family of £5,000 for defense. The house did not successfully invade the Penns' tax haven until 1759, when it presented the proprietary governor William Denny with a bill to raise £100,000 by property taxes, "the estates of the proprietaries not excepted." Portions of the law levied a retroactive tax on the Penns' unimproved lands to make up for preceding years during which they had been exempt. Denny signed it, he said, because of General Jeffrey Amherst's urgent pleas for money to maintain an army. Others said he was bribed to sign it. In either case, the Penns were not pleased and they fired Denny and brought the matter before the Privy Council in England. [20]

Quaker party propagandists used the matter of proprietary land taxes so skillfully that by 1758 Thomas Penn was ready to agree that some of his lands, and even his quitrents, ought to be taxed. Penn's agents and the assembly's agent, Benjamin Franklin, worked out a compromise agreement that was embodied in an order-in-council on September 2, 1760. The Penns' "unsurveyed waste" lands would remain tax exempt, but henceforth their surveyed lands, improved or not, would be assessed at a rate no "higher than the lowest rate at which any uncultivated lands belonging to the inhabitants shall be assessed." As a further concession to the proprietor, his unimproved tracts laid out in town lots would be taxed not as town lots but merely as unimproved land (and therefore at a much lower rate). The assembly's agents agreed that the proprietors should have some say in the appointment of tax appeals commissioners and that tax money would not be appropriated without the governor's consent, that is, by mere resolution of the assembly. Franklin and the other agents present promised that they would personally indemnify the proprietors for any damages, should the assembly not honor the agreement.[21]

But antiproprietary leaders were too astute to let so potent a public issue as taxation subside quietly when they were on the popular side and could use it to rally support on election day. So Quaker party leaders ignored the agreements, and under their direction the assembly refused to amend past laws. Thomas Penn ordered Governor James Hamilton to insist on such amendments and to accept no new money bills that did not conform completely to the order-in-council of September, 1760. Deadlock followed. Even when the peace with France brought no peace to the frontier, and Indian raids increased, the deadlock continued. Tax laws could not be passed, and money desperately needed for frontier defense remained unraised. Indian war raged, frontier towns burned, and angry frontiersmen from Paxton Township marched, guns in hand, toward Philadelphia to force the assembly to act, but the governor and his assembly spent their time exchanging messages, each explaining why one could not possibly agree to the other's proposed tax laws.[22]

In fact, outrage over the Penn tax exemptions (they had been significantly whittled away by those parts of the compromise of 1760 the assembly chose to observe) was probably not the main reason the legislature continued to neglect frontier defense through 1764. If sincere Quaker delegates were reluctant to raise tax money that would be used to kill Indians, other antiproprietary men in Philadelphia, Chester, and Bucks counties were equally reluctant to increase their own taxes to pay for frontier defense. Shrilly proclaiming that the stubborn greed of the Penns was the real cause of the frontier's problems was a useful means of directing popular wrath in the outlying counties away from the assembly, and the Quaker party, and toward the proprietors.

This was the situation in 1763, when Thomas Penn grudgingly agreed to replace the beleaguered Governor Hamilton with Thomas' nephew John Penn. John was something of a black sheep in the Penn family, and any appointment that got him out of England and out of sight had great appeal for the rest of the family. His arrival in Pennsylvania was, however, badly timed. He took office just as frontier resentment over neglect and popular resentment over proprietary tax exemptions were rising, and just as the Quaker party launched a new campaign to pry the Penns out of the colony's government once and for all. With the experienced, capable Governor Hamilton gone, defense of the proprietors' interests fell to a young man in his mid-twenties whose own uncle thought him "unschooled in the arts of life or human dealings," a man with little experience in the politics of administration and with a dangerously inflated opinion of the power of his office. Thomas Penn repeatedly warned his nephew that his attitude was "a little too royal." He advised him to stop appointing to office "impudent people that will be always proving we are in the right and the assembly in the wrong" and suggested he steer "a middle course; that is the most prudent method of doing business and adds nothing to the flame of party, when the too open espousing a side, tho' the right one, will add fuel to the fire."[23]

Prudence, moderation, and middle courses held no appeal for John Penn, and he rapidly brought the dispute over taxes to a head in the spring of 1764. Earlier in the year the assembly, responding to General Thomas Gage's pleas for money to mount a campaign to suppress Pontiac's Rebellion, sent the governor a bill to raise £50,000 by a property tax. Penn returned it unsigned on March 8, claiming it violated the agreement of 1760 by over-taxing proprietary town lots and wilderness tracts and by leaving appropriations entirely in the assembly's hands. The house prepared a new bill that met most of Penn's objections and sent it to the governor, who returned it unsigned. Penn insisted that the new bill overtaxed the proprietors' located unimproved lands. The house pointed out that the bill would tax those lands at a rate equal to that on other people's land "under the same circumstances of situation, kind and quality"; hence, the legislators argued, the bill complied with the order-in-council. Penn, however, demanded that the exact wording of the order be used in the new tax law, and the order said nothing about taxing Penn land at the lowest rate on other people's land "under the same circumstances of situation, kind and quality."[24]

The house finally reduced the dispute to a single question. Did the governor mean that "the best and most valuable of the proprietaries' lands and lots should be taxed no higher than the worst and least valuable of the lands and lots belonging to the People?" That was exactly what the governor meant, and he told the house so on March 23, when he again refused to sign the bill.[25]

It was a costly mistake. Penn's uncle in London, who had a better grasp of Pennsylvania politics from three thousand miles away than his nephew did in Philadelphia, recognized it immediately. "If you had stuck to the words of the order in Council and absolutely refused the bill without further argument," he complained after the damage had been done, much "scurrilous abuse" might have been avoided. But it was too late, and anti-proprietary propagandists had a field day. The assembly unanimously refused to amend its bill and filled its journals with attacks on the governor. Did he really "think it just, that because the *worst and least valuable* of the people's lands are rated at five pounds, the *best and most valuable* of the proprietaries' lands should be assessed no higher, when it is well known they select and locate the best in every new purchase before the people are allowed to take up any?" If the governor chose to put "so iniquitous a construction" on the words of the Lords in Council, he could of course do so. The house, discovering a sudden and short-lived reverence for opinions of the Privy Council, would not dare: "respect and decency forbid it." The assembly also discovered a retrospective appreciation for former governor Hamilton, whom it had given trouble enough in his time. Hamilton, the assembly now told Governor Penn, believed that "the money raised for public services should be assessed equally upon all *ranks and conditions* of men, otherwise the highest injustice may be committed under the sanction of law." The house suggested that such "equitable sentiments" had gotten Hamilton fired. Casting anxious eyes toward Paxton Township, the members of the house laid at the Penns' feet all blame for any "ill consequences" of the failure to raise money for the Indian campaign and added, somewhat inconsistently, that the Paxton frontiersmen's march on Philadelphia had probably been a proprietary plot, staged "to awe us into proprietary measures." They piously recommended the inhabitants of the frontier counties to their own efforts, the king's troops, and "the blessing of God" "till his majesty shall graciously think fit to take this distracted province under his immediate care and protection." The assembly followed this with twenty-seven hotly worded antiproprietary resolutions that, among other things, accused the Penns of waiting until people whose safety was their responsibility faced an Indian crisis "with the knife of savages at their throat" to extort unreasonable concessions from the people's representatives.[26]

The dispute began again when the legislature reconvened in May. But assembly leaders, anxious to propitiate western settlers and to unite as much support as possible behind their attack on the Penns, and threatened with a specie scarcity that made the emission of £100,000 in bills of credit appealing to merchants of their own party, gave way finally and sent Penn a bill that met his demands. He refused it and insisted that all such bills amend the supply bills of 1759 and 1760, under which taxes were still being collected, in accord with the order-in-council. The assembly fumed, complained, and traded accusations with the governor but finally capitulated on May 29.[27]

What Quaker party leaders had lost in principle, they recouped in propaganda. The house's messages to the governor were published and circulated throughout the colony along with party broadsides. Benjamin Franklin published lengthy explanatory remarks on the twenty-seven resolves, in case anyone should miss their point. Judging public sympathy for their cause to be at its peak, antiproprietary leaders ushered a petition to the crown through the assembly, asking George III to take over government of the colony. They were overconfident, and the proprietary party, playing on popular fears that the colony's considerable rights of self-government might be lost along with the Penns' proprietary charter, regained much of what it had lost in the tax disputes with the assembly. In the election of 1764 both Franklin and his close ally, Galloway, were defeated.[28]

Nevertheless, John Penn's stubborn refusal to compromise on taxation of his family's estates created much ill will for the proprietors and sowed distrust and resentment broadly across the colony. And it had all been unnecessary. Thomas Penn, early in June, wrote the governor, directing him to defer to the assembly on the land tax "to show our readiness to comply with every proposal that appears in the least degree equitable, and our desire to end the disputes." Besides, he added, "there does appear some equity in their argument." The new instructions reached Philadelphia far too late to do any good. Governor Penn was obliged, finally, to ask the assembly to amend the new tax law, this time in conformity with its original proposals, which he had so recently insisted were unjust and unacceptable.[29]

The assembly had now won almost every substantial point for which it had been contending since 1755, and yet on the brink of nearly total victory, Quaker party members in the house touched off another tax dispute that led to the collapse of their tax reform program. They now insisted that in addition to all the concessions Penn had already made, he agree that proprietary town lots be taxed as such, not merely as located unimproved lands. This blatantly violated the order-in-council, and

Penn refused to agree. Thus no new bill passed. And in fact, the tax laws, though amended twice more before the Revolution, were never changed to conform completely to the assembly's original demands. Notwithstanding all the Quaker party's pious prose and public-spirited rhetoric about lowering the burden of taxes, its overriding concern was evidently politics, not economics; its main complaints were partisan, not substantive. Rather than allow the tax issue to die, it abandoned the chance to secure through a new law the wide concessions it had already won. The Quaker party attacks, however, were not completely without economic substance. Party leaders had hoped, by taxing the Penns' wilderness lands, to force the family to sell them more quickly. In this at least, the Penns' antagonists were successful, and the Penn family began unloading wilderness tracts it thought not worth the taxes.[30]

On the whole, however, the dispute over taxing the Penn lands is a good example of taxation used in the colonies for primarily political ends. The matter would finally be resolved by independence and the end of the proprietorship, but some of the same arguments and principles reappeared in Pennsylvania after independence, when the new state and its revolutionary government began to debate the principles on which a new revenue system should be based.

Although the clash between the proprietors and their opponents colored most of the battles over taxation in prerevolutionary Pennsylvania, there were other deep divisions in the colony that involved taxation and could not be resolved by the mere removal of the proprietary government in 1776.

Two areas of Pennsylvania persistently claimed they were overtaxed: the counties other than Philadelphia, Chester, and Bucks and the city of Philadelphia. Both also complained that they were underrepresented, though this did not mean that a conscious community of interest existed between them. In spite of its complaints, Philadelphia city was relatively well treated by the Pennsylvania assembly. The city, for example, received £8,000 sterling out of a parliamentary compensation grant to the colony and used it for street repairs. The assembly also permitted Philadelphia to extend its poor taxes to include outlying communities, much to the disgust of the areas involved. Nevertheless, the city, like its counterparts in other colonies, was more heavily taxed by the colony than were rural areas. Of the excise taxes actually collected in Pennsylvania between 1763 and 1775, over half came from the city and county of Philadelphia. By 1772 they were paying in nearly 60 percent of the excise revenues yearly. Of the property taxes collected in the colony between 1763 and 1775, the city and county contributed over 45 percent. The city itself paid nearly 25 percent (Appendix, table 11). On taxation, therefore, the city found a natural ally in politically powerful Philadelphia County. Residents of both were convinced that tax evasion by the western rural counties explained their high taxes, and they won the support of Chester and Bucks counties' representatives in 1773, when they demanded and got new laws to prevent such evasion in the future.[31]

Frontier county inhabitants claimed that Indian threats reduced the value of their property and that the minimum assessment on uncultivated land (£5 per hundred acres) was too high, since it assumed a capital value of £100 per hundred acres for land actually worth no more than £20 to £40. In this claim, they were joined by the proprietors' friends and by Philadelphians who owned land in the frontier counties. Settlers in the outlying counties, though, had developed an effective remedy for their tax problems: they virtually nullified the tax laws by undervaluing their property. An investigation in 1764 revealed that the "modes of taxation and assessing the different kinds of property in the respective counties . . . are not so uniform and regular as they ought to be," and the assembly soon adopted more stringent rules for assessments. Lists of taxable property, plus tables of value for taxable property, would be supplied to every assessor. Taxpayers were required to fill in and sign such lists, and faced stiff penalties for false reporting.[32]

The western settlers, seeing in this new arrangement little room for discretion on the part of local assessors, branded the plan troublesome and expensive and demanded a return to the old guesswork method by which "an assessor in each township . . . from his own knowledge or the information of the neighbors could come nearly to the amount of the different kinds of property by each person possessed." Lancaster assemblyman John Ross's constituents were so displeased with the new law that they told him in 1764 that "had they been acquainted with the manner of their being taxed, etc., etc., he never should have sat in the Assembly again for that county." With the support of the Penn family, opponents had the objectionable regulations struck down in September, 1766.[33]

Why the old system was so dear to taxpayers in York, Lancaster, and the other western counties became clear in September, 1773, when a special legislative committee investigating taxes reported that Lancaster, Berks, and York counties had "so far neglected or disregarded the law as to have charged lands and personal estates not higher than the livestock itself would amount to, if rated as the act of Assembly directs." The lowest permissible tax on unimproved land was seven and a half shillings per hundred acres, but the committee found that the average tax on all real estate in Northampton County was three shillings per hundred acres, and in Cumberland County, seven pence per hundred acres.[34]

An earlier investigation of Lancaster County, completed in 1770, revealed something of how it was done. Several county officials were charged with misusing public funds and taking excessive fees. One assessor, Michael Hubly, had been appointed special appeals commissioner by the county, which had no authority to create that post. Hubly held special hearings for residents who claimed they were overtaxed and could not be present at the regular meeting of the court of sessions, which normally handled such matters. To lower the rates of those who claimed to have been overtaxed, Hubly made out certificates of abatement, for each of which he received a fee. He lowered more than one thousand assessments between 1760 and 1762.[35]

In May the assembly finally moved to close some of the loopholes. It ordered all improved land, whether owner occupied or rented, assessed at 60 percent of the annual rent, and nontaxable woodlots limited to thirty acres out of each hundred. It eliminated the ceiling on values for improved land in Philadelphia, Chester, and Bucks counties and commanded that no improved land be valued at less than five pounds per hundred acres. Finally, it left the job of assessment to county assessors, who presumably would be less susceptible than town officials to local personal pressures. In the final vote on the new plan, all but one representative from the three eastern counties and Philadelphia city voted for the bill, while *every* voting representative from the remaining counties opposed it. It passed, nineteen to eight. The measure was clearly intended as tax relief for the eastern counties, but its effectiveness cannot be determined, since the Revolution soon upset the entire revenue system of the colony.[36]

If some western settlers reduced their taxes through collusion with assessors, others paid no Pennsylvania taxes at all, especially in the far western counties that bordered Virginia. Both Pennsylvania and Virginia claimed the same land, and Pennsylvania collectors constantly faced settlers who insisted they were Virginians, who refused to pay a Pennsylvania tax, and who were willing to take up arms against Pennsylvania collectors. In April, 1774, for instance, commissioners for Westmoreland County complained to Governor Penn that they could find no one in the back parts of the county willing to collect taxes, and "the people residing in the back parts, or the greater part of them, absolutely refuse to pay."[37]

In 1772 the assembly tried to close another loophole, this one in the liquor excise law that taxed all sales in any quantity under seventy gallons. Merchants and importers in Philadelphia, however, claimed "a kind of right, from mere custom," to sell wine in lesser amounts without paying the tax, and the excisemen let them do it. The original intention of the liquor excises may have been, as the importers alleged, to "restrain persons in low circumstances from an immoderate use thereof," but by the 1760s the taxes were directed more toward raising revenue than preserving morality. They had the support, for instance, of property owners striving to keep property rates low and of merchant-importers seeking to keep imposts low.[38]

A proposal in 1772 to enforce excise collections touched off a broadside war. Opponents warned that an expanded excise was "the Hydra of corruption and slavery" and would lead to excises on all items of common use. Pennsylvanians would be reduced "to the miserable state of the slavish Parisians to whom nothing remains free but the air and the River Seine." Supporters argued that an excise on the "luxuries of life" was the most prudent and equitable way to raise money ever "invented by the wisdom of man."[39]

During the dispute, however, the issues broadened, and the principles and slogans common to the battle against parliamentary taxation began to be applied to Pennsylvania's internal taxes. One "Civis" warned that the new excise bill would create taxes little different from the "unconstitutional tax laid by Parliament on wines imported into America." What was involved, he argued, was not merely a question of who should pay and who should not. What was involved was nothing less than liberty itself. Those who supported so unconstitutional a tax as the excise, he warned, were the same miscreants who supported the stamp tax and who wished to make Pennsylvanians "slaves and bondsmen."[40]

At the same time, a decade of rhetoric that connected taxation and representation began to have an impact in Philadelphia, as well as in New York and New England. By 1772, Philadelphians began to demand representation in the assembly proportional to the city's population and "the quota they pay towards the support of government."[41] And residents of other middle colonies too were coming to discover close connections between liberty and their own internal taxes.

New York was unique among the middle colonies. In most of them, small freehold farms predominated, but in New York hundreds of thousands of acres in the Hudson River valley, and even beyond it, had been granted through politics, fraud and favoritism over the years to a few families. The great landed families thus established, some of which could trace their holdings back to the original Dutch settlements, firmly dominated politics and society in New York by the second half of the eighteenth century. *Viva voce* voting, landlords' influence over tenants dependent upon them for lease renewals and for credit in bad times, or the simple ability of the wealthy to purchase votes made certain election districts in the colony virtual pocket boroughs of one or another of the great landed families.[42]

By the 1760s the Livingston and De Lancey families had each come to head a loose coalition of manor lords, landlords, merchants, lawyers, and freeholders. Each coalition fought to control the elected New York assembly and the appointed royal council and to influence, whenever possible, the royal governor. But no matter which faction, Livingston or De Lancey, momentarily controlled the institutions of government, a segment of the colonial aristocracy, more particularly the landed aristocracy, always remained in firm control of the colony's legislation and public revenue policies. In the late colonial period, for instance, more than 90 percent of the New York royal council were wealthy men, and three out of four came from long-established families. It was the same in the assembly. In 1769 twenty-one of the twenty-eight seats were held by either great landowners or prominent merchants. Two out of every five assemblymen owned property worth *at least* £5,000, and four out of five owned at least £2,000 worth. One in three was from a long-established wealthy family, and two out of three had been born to at least "well-to-do" parents. Only five members of the assembly belonged to what might reasonably be called the middle class, and they all owned at least £500 worth of property.[43]

It is difficult to draw clear ideological lines between the two factions, although many historians have tried. It has been suggested that the Livingston coalition was held together in the 1760s and 1770s by "fear of Parliament, an appetite for office and patronage, a suspicion of the lower orders," and "a general distaste for taxes on property." Since the De Lancey faction also feared Parliament and the lower orders, and panted after office and patronage as avidly as their opponents, the differences are reduced to two: there were only so many patronage jobs, and each faction supposedly held conflicting views about the proper method of taxing New Yorkers. It has even been suggested that the two factions owed "their intellectual existence" to their "views on direct taxation," which conflicting views made them battle ceaselessly for control of the legislature and of the tax laws. Other historians find the dynamic element of New York politics in a clash between the interests of commerce and agriculture, with the De Lanceys championing the former and the Livingstons the latter.[44]

Such distinctions may have had some validity before 1760. In 1752 the Livingstons did attack a proposed acreage land tax as an underhanded plot of the "monied interest" to drive members of the "landed interest" out of political power by appealing to "those who are possessed of small tracts of land." Robert R. Livingston, Sr., contributed a long lament to the newspapers about the injustice of taxing the land of those whose "ancestors have made the invidious choice of providing for their posterity by the purchase of lands, though reduced to a very frugal and obscure life." He argued that a flat per acre tax on all land was so unjust that it needed no detailed refutation, but he also insisted that taxing land according to its value was equally unjust if applied in any way to unimproved land.[45] City merchants who supported such taxes may have had some difficulty thinking of Livingstons leading frugal and obscure lives, but they had no difficulty recognizing Livingston's arguments for precisely what they were: attempts to preserve the tax shelter of land-speculating manor lords by keeping wilderness lands completely untaxed. Pleas in support of such taxes regularly stressed the injustice of burdening trade (and merchants) with import duties and property taxes on urban holdings while the value of the manor lords' estates grew and went virtually untaxed.[46] It is also true that in the 1760s De Lancey propagandists hunted votes by publicly damning lawyers who doubtless were, it was hinted, Livingston hirelings and who had the temerity to oppose De Lancey men for election to the assembly. Residents of New York City were told that a legislature filled with lawyers would never pass "a law for a land tax, so necessary for lessening the burthen of our taxes; as the interest of the lawyers (they being mostly possessed of considerable landed estates) would prevent such a measure."[47]

Too much has been made of this campaign prose. By the mid-1760s, in any case, it seems clear that the major issue separating the two factions was not internal taxation, but patronage. Peter Livingston warned Robert R. Livingston in 1770 not to be deceived by surface issues in New York politics. The root of the factional struggle was simple: "the De Lanceys are striving their utmost to make our family ridiculous and to keep them out of all posts of honor or profit," he explained, "which is too hard to bear."[48] And it is evident from the actions of the New York merchant community, and of the De Lancey faction during the times it dominated the assembly, that there was far more agreement than disagreement among the politically powerful in New York about the proper way to tax.

The New York merchant community, for example, did not appear particularly upset about the colony's tax laws. From its founding in 1768 until the Revolution the New York City Chamber of Commerce lobbied continually for laws and ordinances favorable to its members, yet it completely ignored the question of domestic taxation. When the royal lieutenant governor of the colony, Cadwallader Colden, described his troublesome legislature as being dominated by "owners of . . . extravagant grants" and by "the merchants of New York," he added that the two were "strongly connected" by "family interest." There were other strong connections as well. Real estate, both income producing and speculative, was the New York merchants' favorite investment for their surplus capital, and they were therefore little more eager to see land, even wilderness, taxed than were the manor lords.[49] Since tenant farmers in New York normally paid the taxes on the land they leased, they found themselves in basic agreement with the manor lords, freehold farmers, and merchant-landowners on at least one point: property taxes were reprehensible necessities, to be tolerated only as wartime expedients and dispensed with at the earliest opportunity.

Party considerations made little difference. A rumored parliamentary land tax of 1764 that frightened the Livingston family would have dealt as heavy a blow to merchant-speculators and the landed De Lanceys. At no time after the De Lancey party's sweeping victories in the elections of 1769 did the legislature seriously consider the reimposition of general property taxes. When the house in 1775 ordered a committee to "consider . . . the most probable means of relieving this colony from the heavy debt it labours under," it specifically forbade consideration of a general property tax. And it was a De Lancey–dominated legislature that ordered excise money plowed back into the counties for poor relief and road repairs, thus lowering local poll and property taxes.[50]

The widespread interest in keeping property taxes out of New York (which meant keeping control of domestic taxation firmly in American hands) cut across party and occupational lines and was an important factor in unifying opposition to Great Britain. When Colden suggested to English policymakers that they impose a permanent land tax in New York, his purpose was only partially to secure a steady income for royal officials. Colden understood that the introduction of such a tax would dissolve the community of interest that lent strength to his, Parliament's, and the king's opponents in New York. Once land taxes became permanent, he expected endless arguments between merchants and farmers, landlords and tenants, and speculators and agrarians over the most equitable definition of taxable estate, over the proper tax rate on cultivated land and on wild land, over the relative justice of acreage and ad valorem taxes. The political possibilities of a permanent land tax in New York were so appealing to Colden, and the consequences for his opponents in the colony so potentially devastating, that he was willing to abandon his own personal aversion to general property taxes. "If the owners of the cultivated lands," he explained to the Board of Trade in 1764, "who exceed the others in numbers beyond any

proportion, shall find that by an equal taxation of all the lands"
—and he meant both cultivated and wild land—"they are to be
freed from unreasonable taxes on their industry," they would
support the royal government.[51] Within a year he got more support for his opinion than he cared for. New York tenant farmers,
with the Stamp Act riots a recent memory, rose against landlords, protesting not only high rents and short leases but having
to pay the taxes on their leaseholds as well.[52]

When De Lancey propagandists sought votes in New York City
by calling for a colony-wide land tax, they advocated a policy
they had little intention of implementing, and they played on a
division in the colony that was more geographic than political.
As in Massachusetts, rural counties' efforts to saddle the metropolis with a heavy proportion of the colony's taxes formed a
consistent theme in New York politics from the 1740s until the
Revolution. The usual pattern of voting on matters of colony-
wide taxation was simple: the rural counties combined to out-
vote New York City and Albany. In 1746 Albany and New York
City narrowly fought off a move in the assembly to force them
to pay nineteen percent and 44 percent, respectively, of all property taxes raised. New York City had its share fixed at one third,
and there it remained until the property tax lapsed in 1768. In
addition, of course, the city collected its own taxes for road repairs, poor relief, and other local services, which amounted to
£5,200 in 1769.[53]

The excise laws discriminated against the city even more severely. Excise laws passed in 1763 and 1764 provided for the annual collection of £1,500, and the city's share was pegged at £954.
Excise taxes from 1765 to 1767 provided for the annual collection
of £1,276, of which the city paid £800. But in December, 1768, the
colony dropped the quota system for excise taxes, which proved
to be a great relief to the city and a shock to some neighboring
counties. The "tax" was converted into a minimum twenty-shil-
ling fee to be paid by each licensed tavern. One Dutchess County
man complained that under the new arrangement his county's
share would jump from its old quota of £40 to nearly £400, for
"in no other county are there so many taverns," and he insisted

that representatives whose incompetence allowed the county to be so taxed should be thrown out of office.[54]

Exaggeration for effect doubtless played its part on both sides of the debate, but in 1773 the outlying counties succeeded in re-imposing quotas on the city and county of New York, which henceforth had to raise at least £1,000 a year by excise. The rest of the colony had to raise only £450. Furthermore, New York had to allot £800 of its excise monies to a charity hospital, which had to receive, free of charge, the sick poor of any county. To the extent that noncity poor entered the hospital, the city subsidized by its taxes poor relief in the surrounding counties.[55]

Faced with such discrimination, New York City politicians complained that their constituents were grossly overtaxed by "a confederacy of all the country members against the citizens of the city, with the exception of only here and there a generous advocate for trade and impartiality." "There is a snake in the grass," warned "Aristedes," pleading for more representation for New York City in the assembly. "The city has been stung by a serpent; she feels the poison in her veins," he continued. The enemy, as he saw it, included Richmond, Kings, Orange, Queens, and Westchester counties, not the frontier counties, and he reminded the latter that the lower counties had been reluctant in the past to vote money for frontier defense. In doing so, Aristedes touched on a long-standing grievance of frontier New Yorkers, who complained, as did their counterparts in Pennsylvania, that the assembly voted insufficient funds for frontier defense and treated the outer settlements as a kind of bloody sponge that was to absorb Indian raids and thus screen the more settled counties and towns. But backcountry New Yorkers put most of the blame for their neglect on "the rich," whom they associated primarily with the city of New York. "They say," reported Colden in 1756, "we willingly pay our share of all public taxes for securing the city of New York and otherwise tho New York has never been attacked and probably never will while the English remain masters at sea. Shall we, they say, who are placed between the enemy and the rich be despised and neglected because we are poor when the money that is necessary for our defence would be no more felt by the rich than a drop of water is in the sea?"[56]

Despite occasional attempts to drag domestic taxation into election campaigns by playing off New York City's interests against those of the outlying counties, it was not a major political issue in New York in the decade preceding the Revolution. But it could remain in the background only if permanent property taxes were avoided. Once admit them, and a potentially explosive situation would be created. Merchants, tradesmen, manor lords, freehold farmers, and tenants would begin to dissolve into contending factions, each battling to define taxable property, and to shape tax policy, in ways most suitable to themselves.[57]

When Benjamin Franklin's illegitimate son William became royal governor of New Jersey, proprietary party men in Pennsylvania recoiled in horror at the thought of *two* Franklins sharing the same continent, much less the same region, with them. They soon learned, however, that the appointment was designed, at at least in part, to check the father's political independence and to make him beholden to the current ministry in England. That plan failed, but in the process New Jersey acquired perhaps the most able royal governor on the continent. He was a master at mollifying legislators while insisting on his own opinions, and under his administration New Jersey remained relatively tranquil during the stormy 1760s. There were Stamp Act riots in the colony, and in 1769 there were riots in northern New Jersey against lawyers, but these problems were not aggravated by the bitter factional fighting that complicated the politics of Massachusetts, Connecticut, Rhode Island, Pennsylvania, and New York.[58] The colony was so free of factional bickering under Franklin that in 1769 it carried out a major reapportionment of its county tax quotas with a minimum of political acrimony. Similar attempts elsewhere, notably in Rhode Island, produced intense factional disputes.

New Jersey's county tax quotas were set in 1751 and had not been substantially changed by 1765, when the colony began a steep slide into depression. Falling land prices and a chronic scarcity of currency compounded the distress. Sheriffs' sales were halted for lack of bidders, and complaints about excessive colony taxes began to be heard along with complaints about the proposed stamp taxes. "Our estates [are] so lessened in value," grumbled James Parker in 1765, "that we are unable to pay the tax we imposed upon ourselves to support the last war."[59]

In May, 1765, then, when Somerset County inhabitants petitioned the assembly for a redistribution of county tax quotas, such a revision was long overdue. "The circumstances of some of the counties are very much altered," the petitioners explained, "by reason whereof the taxes by this time must be very unequal." They complained of "the great odds there is between the taxes in Somerset and some other counties." They were correct. Two counties, Morris and Sussex, had enjoyed a population and economic boom in the years since 1751. By 1790 Morris alone had over 16,000 people, and the two counties combined had more than 35,700. This phenomenal growth was well advanced by 1765, but the legislature at first refused to act. Middlesex County residents petitioned the next year, and Somerset petitioned again the year after that, but the assembly still delayed.[60]

The legislators' reluctance to take up the matter was understandable. The last time they'd dealt with it, in the early 1750s, the resulting battle between the council and the house had raged for nine consecutive sessions. Landed proprietors on the council had been determined to prevent the taxing of unimproved land and had insisted on a land tax based on value rather than mere acreage. The house demanded a tax on all land, improved or not. Eventually, they compromised: improved tracts (presumably those including any improved land) would be taxed according to quality, with minimum and maximum tax values set by law, but unimproved tracts would be left wholly untaxed. Thus the favored positions of proprietary and other speculators were preserved.[61]

When the assembly finally responded to the petitions of Somerset and Middlesex, it carefully avoided altering the *basis* of taxation and made no attempt to redefine taxable property. It merely ordered a new inventory of property, and it provided specific assessments for each kind. There was some difficulty getting local assessors (who were reluctant to see local land values adjusted upward in the tax laws) to turn in reports out of which some sense could be made, but a law establishing new fines for not cooperating ended that problem. In October, 1769, the ticklish task of assigning new quotas was delivered to a house committee composed of representatives from every county. The committee returned a bill, and on November 27 the house passed it without so much as a roll call vote, which any three members could have demanded, and the council passed it the following day.[62]

Under the new law, three counties received substantial quota reductions of more than £220 each: Monmouth, where popular unrest over lawyers' fees and a currency scarcity was most acute; Somerset, the most persistent petitioner for tax reform; and Burlington. Most of the remaining counties received reductions of less than £75 each, and two counties' quotas remained virtually unchanged. The slack was taken up by Sussex and Morris counties, whose rates doubled in strict accord with the new general estimate (Appendix, table 12).

There was little further agitation for internal tax reform in New Jersey until just before the Revolution, when Morris County asked that money at interest be taxed and that debtors be permitted to deduct interest payments from their taxes. These were radical suggestions in New Jersey in 1774, and the assembly killed them quickly.[63] But soon the same demands, and more, would be heard again, and not only in New Jersey.

Despite incessant complaints that taxes were grievous, burdensome, and well-nigh impossible for the people to bear, in the middle colonies they were relatively light (just as they were in New England) when compared with those of the mother country. In Pennsylvania the property tax revenues hit a six-year low in 1775, just as the colonists' struggle with England over taxes reached a climax. By that year, property and excise taxes combined brought in only £31,000 to the Pennsylvania treasury, and imposts added £1,000 more. The per capita rate, therefore, was only two shillings one penny (Pennsylvania currency). At no time from 1763 to the Revolution did the combined tax yield rise above £34,000.[64] Property taxes for redeeming New Jersey's war debt—the largest remaining debt of all the colonies in 1766— were £12,500 (New Jersey currency) per year from 1764 through 1773. They rose to £15,000 in 1774, but it is highly unlikely that the colony collected anything like that amount in the turmoil that preceded independence.[65] Until the Seven Years' War, the normal costs of government in New Jersey, including the civil list, were paid from the interest on loan office emissions, but by the late 1760s these funds too were raised by the general property taxes. According to Governor Franklin, this added at most £1,600 sterling (about £2,700 New Jersey currency) to the annual tax bill. The highest colony tax for the interwar period, then, came to no more than £17,700, or less than three shillings per capita.[66]

To one New Jersey legislator, trying to convince the voters that taxes should be increased to raise the pay of assemblymen, the easy taxes were little short of scandalous. "In England," he asked,

how often have the people, to assist his Majesty in time of war paid four shillings in the pound land tax . . . that is one fifth part of their real estates, besides sustaining the weight of numberless imposts on both their real and personal estates; and at the same time have cheerfully paid the civil list duties and supported the King in a truly honorable manner. How cheerfully do they pay a multitude of taxes, now when they crouch under a load of £140,000,000 sterling? Yet the whole body of Jersey men do not owe a fourth part of one million Proclamation [money], and if they were to support the government in the full extent desired, and continue regularly to pay their other taxes, as by law directed to be paid, they would not part with (to speak very much in the compass) a twelfth part of the annual interest of their estates, and not a three-hundredth part of their present capital.

His voice was a lonely one, although Governor William Franklin, seeking his own pay raise, concurred. The governor argued that while Englishmen paid property taxes in England totaling four shillings per pound of the annual rents, New Jerseyites undervalued their property and paid an average of only sixpence per pound on land and stock in most counties (and some paid an average of fourpence or less). His assembly denied it but then argued that even if the governor's charges were true, they saw no reason to change things. If the English at home "pay higher taxes than we," they asked, "must we ruin ourselves in debt for the sake of paying as high taxes as they do? That is a strange way of demonstrating loyalty."[67]

In New York a brief period of high taxes followed the peace of 1763. The property tax helped reduce New York's unredeemed war-issue paper money from £495,000 in 1760 to £85,000 by 1768.[68] At times, the taxes reached four shillings per pound on the annual rents of New York City buildings, which John Watts thought "tax enough." Nevertheless, New Yorkers at no time paid the variety of taxes their counterparts in England did, and it is doubtful that rates in the rural counties ever approached four shillings per pound of annual rent. In any case, the property tax was no more after 1767, and the colony taxes were limited to imposts and excises, totaling only about £6,500. From 1765 to 1767 New York did retire £134,000 in outstanding treasury bills, but at least half of this was done with parliamentary compensation grants, not tax money. If we assume that half of it was taxed in and add £5,000 for imposts and £1,500 more for excises, New Yorkers paid during those years a maximum per capita provincial tax of four shillings (New York currency).[69]

In each of the colonies, taxes were substantially lowered by subsidies from Parliament. New Jersey received £47,227 sterling (about £79,000 New Jersey currency), which it used to lower taxes for five years. More than £59,000 in subsidies permitted New York to cancel half its property taxes in 1765, 1766, and 1767. Other portions of the grants went to pay for frontier defense, to supply royal troops quartered in the province, and to pay for damages during the Stamp Act riots. Delaware planned to sink its outstanding war debt of £11,000 by a ninepence property tax each year from 1764 through 1768. Parliamentary compensation payments of £6,970 sterling (£11,709 Delaware currency) allowed the colony to cancel almost the entire amount without taxes. In fact, Delaware collected only one threepence rate instead of the planned five taxes of ninepence each.[70]

Pennsylvania's compensation eventually totaled over £51,000 sterling, which was expected to "ease the people much in their taxes." The grants did not noticeably lower existing taxes, though they clearly reduced new ones. The colony used some to retire outstanding paper money, and the remainder to support a charity hospital, to improve navigation, to pay soldiers and quarter them, to repair Philadelphia streets, to provide the commissioners of Indian trade with trading stock, and to reimburse masters whose servants had enlisted in the king's service during the war.[71] The colony, however, lost some of its compensation money in 1760, when Benjamin Franklin, acting as the assembly's agent, invested £4,000 of it in British public stocks, hoping for a rise in price when peace came. When peace rumors proved groundless and Franklin had to sell the stocks at a loss, Thomas Penn suggested that Franklin should be made to pay the colony back personally. The assembly, however, was not about to bankrupt its leading proprietary gadfly, though it was not about to trust him with control of the remaining subsidy money either.[72]

The glaring inefficiency of the middle colonies' tax collection systems further eased the burden on many taxpayers (and nonpayers), and nearly everywhere, huge amounts remained uncollected long after the taxes had been levied. In New York, for example, overdue imposts totaled more than £10,000 in 1771, when the accounts of the late treasurer Abraham De Peyster were audited. Other overdue taxes (not including the excises) amounted to £18,900 by 1774, up from £7,716 in 1762. Overdue excises added £2,250 more to the arrears. By 1770, New York City alone owed the colony treasury £8,680, up from £2,800 in 1762. Some of these debts undoubtedly represented collectors running off with receipts rather than nonpayment by people. In New York, localities were held responsible for thefts by their officials, a prudent precaution when even the new colony treasurer Abraham Lott thought the public funds could be used for his own investments. When the New York assembly audited Lott's accounts in 1772 and found considerably less cash on hand than it had expected, Lott was asked to explain where the money had gone. He replied that he had borrowed about £20,000 of public money to import goods from Europe on his own account. The reason he did not have the money on hand was that the ship carrying his goods arrived from England six weeks late, "by which means . . . other persons who had got their goods before him had the advantage of selling them and so he missed the sale of the greatest part of his goods." So he told the assembly. Lott thought the privilege of using public funds for private investment came with the office of treasurer, and he was miffed about being asked to account for the money, since his predecessor had been doing the same thing for forty years. The colony was still trying to get its money back as late as January, 1775.[73]

Arrears in New Jersey were comparatively low. For example, when the eastern treasurer's accounts were audited in 1772, he reported less than £1,000 in tax arrears. Yet other forms of tax dodging left the colony £60,000 behind schedule in paying off its war debts. The burden was eased still more because the treasury accepted for taxes each year any of the colony's paper money emissions, whether it was the appointed year for retirement of that particular emission or not.[74]

Pennsylvania was also troubled by large amounts that tax collectors would not or, if their complaints are accurate, could not collect and account for (Appendix, table 13). The legislature continually discovered "considerable" deficiencies in tax collections and "large ballances . . . due and uncollected." York County collectors, for example, regularly insisted that they could not collect taxes from nonresident property owners. It simply took too much time and money to track such owners down, when they could be located at all. The records of nonresident collections were so poorly kept, and so far out of date, that the assembly finally agreed there was little hope the money could ever be brought in.[75]

As the colonial years drew to a close and revolution approached, the middle colonies shared tax systems that had already become wheezing anachronisms, shot through with loopholes, fraud, and special-interest provisions. The landed men who wrote the laws made sure the taxes fell gently, if at all, on the great tracts of wilderness land that legislators and colonial leaders speculated in everywhere. The exception was Pennsylvania, where antiproprietary men in the assembly saw both an economic advantage to be gained by shaking the Penns free of their wilderness tracts and votes to be won by taxing, or at least by appearing to want to tax, forest land held against future development. Middle colony legislators shared as well a tendency to shift taxes off property and onto consumption (through imposts and excises) whenever possible, particularly in New York.

The system in each colony and throughout the region depended, of course, on keeping control of the revenue laws in local legislative hands. The interests of the landed wealthy could be protected only if they kept the taxing power firmly in their own hands and out of Parliament's. The New York assembly's strong opposition to the stamp and Townshend taxes sprang in part from the manor lords', and the merchants', deep suspicions that such taxes were but a step toward parliamentary land taxes imposed on the colonies.

The people of the middle colonies accepted the tax laws with little complaint about their form and little challenge to their essential justice, although they complained endlessly about the application of those laws and particularly about excessive assessments and overvalued property. And, of course, the fact that middle colony people rarely challenged the equity of the revenue laws did not mean that they were any less eager to evade them, or any less skillful in doing so when opportunity arose, than other Englishmen were then or than other Americans have been since. That silent acquiescence, however, probably depended on the absence of general poll taxes and upon the low tax levels that prevailed even during and after the Seven Years' War. As Lieutenant Governor Colden pointed out, that acquiescence could not survive a dramatic change in the basic nature of the tax laws or in the amount of taxes collected. If either change came about, then men already unhappy with the existing laws—men on the frontiers of New York, for example, and tenant farmers in northern New Jersey counties—might find enough support to wrest control of the revenue laws from the wealthy. Smaller freehold farmers, and other men whose interests ran for the moment with those of the landed men who filled the legislatures, might find it worth their while, then, to alter the laws and to redistribute the taxes, if the opportunity arose.

In 1776 it did.

CHAPTER THREE

The South

The politics of southern taxation were extremely complex. By 1763 the tax system in each southern colony except Georgia was the result of over a century of development, and each system reflected the particular political and economic conditions of the colony involved. The interests of settlers in the piedmont and mountain South often clashed with the interests of those who lived in the low country. Large planters and small farmers, no matter where they lived, often disagreed about what constituted fair taxation. Occasionally the country interest would unite against the commercial interest, ranging farmers and planters, large or small, east or west, against the merchant community. At other times, merchants and backcountry farmers made common cause against the large planters of the tidewater regions. And in the eighteenth century the distinction between planter and merchant sometimes became unclear as many of the larger planters, particularly in Virginia and Maryland, regularly purchased the crops of their smaller neighbors and operated as planter-merchants.[1]

It is hardly surprising, then, that by 1763 each southern colony relied on a different mixture of poll, property, and commercial taxes to meet the ordinary expenses of government and the extraordinary expenses of war. But this diversity concealed an underlying uniformity: in the South, the tax laws discriminated against the politically powerless and the poor, and favored the interests of men of established landed wealth who normally dominated the southern legislatures.[2] Some colonies achieved this by relying heavily on poll taxes. Elsewhere, acreage land taxes (as distinct from ad valorem land taxes) worked to the low-country planters' advantage, and some southern legislatures imposed both types of discriminatory taxation.

Although tax discrimination in favor of landed wealth took different forms in different colonies, the pattern was evident everywhere. In North Carolina the system was simplicity itself: nearly three quarters of the colony's revenues were collected by poll taxes levied on every white male sixteen or older and on all blacks, slave or free, male or female, over the age of twelve.[3] A liquor import duty accounted for 13 percent more, bringing in about £2,500 in 1768. But poll taxes alone raised more than £8,100 in 1764 and more than £9,300 by 1767 (Appendix, table 14). When public emergency or executive whim created a sudden need for more revenue, the assembly's response was practically reflex: it either laid on additional poll taxes or increased the liquor duties.[4]

In effect, the poll tax on slaves operated as a property tax paid by their owners; otherwise, landed and commercial wealth in North Carolina escaped virtually untapped. In addition, there were special penalties for those too poor to pay their poll taxes. Their personal property could be auctioned off, and if the auctioneers failed to raise enough to clear the tax, the delinquent might be jailed for a month and then sold as an indentured servant, for what he owed plus the cost of keeping him in jail, "to such Person who for the shortest Time of Service will pay the Same." Although the laws provided that paupers might under some circumstances be excused from taxes, sheriffs violated such laws with impunity.[5]

By contrast, neither South Carolina nor Georgia depended on poll taxes for significant revenues before the Revolution. Both levied colony poll taxes only on free Negroes. In Georgia the rate was fifteen shillings a year for most of the period from 1763 to 1770, while the tax on slaves was usually only two shillings sixpence. When the colony lowered taxes across the board in 1763 and again in 1770, it did not lower the black poll tax. By 1773 land and slave taxes hit a ten-year low, but the free Negro poll tax hit a new high of one pound, up 33 percent from 1768. South Carolina poll taxes on free Negroes began during the Seven Years' War and varied considerably from year to year, reaching two pounds in 1765 and falling to seven shillings in 1767.[6]

In Virginia, tobacco export taxes supplemented by quitrents and occasional minor poll taxes paid the ordinary costs of running the colony. When frontier war with the French began in 1754 and the House of Burgesses had to raise money for defense, however, the pattern of discrimination in favor of landed wealth emerged clearly. The burgesses looked on a land tax the way their colleagues in the New York assembly did, as an inconvenient expedient to be avoided if at all possible. In 1755, and only after a year of new poll taxes had failed to raise enough money, they reluctantly imposed the first provincial land tax Virginians had known for over a century. It was an acreage tax that fell on all land equally, regardless of productivity or location, and thus favored those well-established planters in eastern counties who owned the best land with relatively easy access to the sea. Furthermore, the amount raised annually by the land taxes from the first in 1755 to the last in 1768 never equaled the amount raised by the poll taxes. The burgesses expected the wartime poll tax to bring in £10,000 the first year, but the new land taxes raised less than £4,000 the first *two* years.[7] The burgesses planned to raise £34,000 annually from poll taxes between 1763 and 1765 to retire the colony's paper money, but they expected to raise only £19,000 annually during the same period from all other sinking-fund taxes combined (which included the land tax and some tobacco export duties, slave import taxes, and carriage taxes). From 1766 through 1768 they planned to raise £30,000 a year by increasing poll taxes while reducing the yield from all other sinking-fund taxes to £15,000 a year (Appendix, table 15). Thus they expected poll taxes to produce over 55 percent of the sinking funds for the period 1763 through 1765, 66 percent from 1766 to 1768, and 68 percent by 1769 (£24,000 on polls against £6,250 on land and £5,000 on tobacco exports). These figures do not take into account either the extra poll tax (forty-six pounds of tobacco per poll) levied in 1764 to pay for suppressing Pontiac's Rebellion, or other supplementary poll taxes levied in 1766, 1769, and 1772.[8]

Local and religious taxes for support of the Anglican church added still more to the poll tax burden. By 1769, however, the colony's land taxes were gone, sinking-fund taxes had been stopped, and Virginia supported itself again primarily by a tobacco export tax, which raised some £7,000 in 1770. The poll tax yield sank to only £1,300 two years later. Along with an impost on foreign rum, brandy, and other spirits, which raised £1,000 a year, those two sufficed for the ordinary expenses of government.[9]

Between 1763 and 1775 Maryland did not rely heavily on poll taxes for colony expenses, although it did collect a poll tax for the support of the Anglican clergy. Commonly 30 pounds of tobacco a year, paid by all inhabitants over sixteen except white women, it raised over £8,000 sterling a year by 1766. A few minor colony expenses like the cost of printing public laws were included in the county taxes, which were normally poll taxes. The cost of legislative sessions and of supreme court sessions—about £2,400 a year—was also met from time to time by poll taxes, though none was passed from 1763 to 1775, when such bills were paid with new paper money emissions instead. So light was the provincial share of Maryland's poll taxes that of 118,513 pounds of tobacco raised on polls in Worcester County in 1766, less than 1,500 pounds was earmarked for delivery to the province. Nearly 44 percent of the total, some 52,000 pounds, went to local poor relief.[10]

Maryland legislators shared Virginia's aversion to property taxes. Spurred by the shock of Braddock's defeat in 1755, the assembly passed a land tax, one based on acreage rather than market value or income. This brief experiment with property taxes ended by 1764, and between April, 1758, and November, 1763, the land taxes raised only £11,200. Other revenues in the late colonial years came from tonnage duties (£1,330 a year), a tobacco export duty of one shilling per hogshead (£1,300 a year), import duties on slaves, wine, rum, and Irish Catholic servants (£1,200 a year), interest on the colony's stock in the Bank of England (£4,000 a year by 1763), and excises.[11]

By 1763 South Carolina's revenue system resembled those of the New England colonies more closely than did any other in the South. The Seven Years' War and the Cherokee war of 1760 forced the colony's reluctant legislators to tap new sources of public income to meet the crises. They raised existing slave and land taxes, as well as the imposts on wine, flour, and biscuit, and put new taxes on free Negroes, money at interest, annuities, the "wares, merchandize and book debts of persons in trade, shopkeepers and others," and on the "profits of all faculties, professions (the clergy excepted), factorage and handicraft trades, throughout this province." But through it all, the mainstay of the planters' tax protection, the acreage land tax, survived unaltered.[12]

Like Connecticut and other northern colonies, South Carolina used tax policy to encourage the development of local industry. To promote a leather industry, for example, the colony placed a far lower export tax on tanned hides than on raw hides, even though the former were more valuable. A variety of products imported from other colonies paid a stiff import tax, sometimes as high as 20 percent ad valorem, in order to encourage South Carolinians to use homegrown products instead. The most important of the trade taxes were on rum, wine, flour, and biscuit and on imported slaves. A special tax on the first four, for instance, brought in £17,000 (South Carolina currency) between September, 1763, and September, 1764, £16,000 the following year, and £12,000 the year after that (Appendix, table 16). Between 1764 and 1766 alone, £43,340 raised by this tax was used to lower the general property taxes.[13]

The tax on imported slaves, paid by the first Carolina purchaser, began in 1751 at £10 a head, but in 1766, attempting to slow the importation of foreign blacks, the assembly raised it to £100. The tax brought in over £191,000 (South Carolina currency) between September, 1763, and December, 1769 (Appendix, table 16). All told, the various import and export duties annually raised an average of better than £91,000 (South Carolina currency; about £13,000 sterling at the official exchange rate of seven for one) from 1764 through 1770, though the actual yield varied tremendously from year to year (Appendix, table 17).

South Carolina's property taxes resembled those of the New England colonies in what they taxed, but differed significantly in the way they were applied. Of the kinds of property taxed— slaves, land, town lots and buildings, wharves or other improvements on them, stock-in-trade, money at interest, profits from faculties, professions, and the handicraft trades—all *except* land and slaves were taxed according to value. For Charleston residents, this had special significance, for South Carolina tax laws applied a double standard to the city. Not only did many city residents pay taxes on their earnings and on their property, while planters and farmers beyond the city paid only on the latter, but a special set of rules applied to assessments in Charleston. Outside the city, property owners themselves drew up lists of their taxable property and submitted them to parish authorities. In the city, however, special assessors visited homes and businesses, drew up their own lists of taxable property, and made their own judgments about value.[14]

Throughout the 1760s the general property, slave, and faculty taxes fell (though erratically), thus throwing an increasingly large proportion of the tax burden on the imposts (Appendix, table 18). After 1769, when South Carolina passed its last general tax law before the Revolution, almost the entire burden of public revenue fell on the trade taxes.

Sparsely populated Georgia's revenue needs were small, since its government was heavily subsidized by Parliament. Such funds as the colony did raise by taxes (which rarely came to more than £2,000 annually throughout the 1760s) were raised in ways similar to South Carolina's. Georgia taxed exported hides and a variety of imports, but the yield was small. For the rest, Georgia depended on an acreage land tax, a slave head tax, and ad valorem taxes on town lots and buildings, money at interest "by choice," and "all goods, wares, and merchandise imported or brought into this province with intent to sell again, by any merchant, factor, storekeeper or other person whatsoever." Beginning in 1773 Georgia collected 1 percent in taxes from the "salaries provided by the legislature of this province and all public officers and professions except that of divinity." In 1773 the assembly explained—doubtless for the edification of the Privy Council and the Board of Trade, which were less than pleased when American colonies presumed to tax the English goods they imported—that the tax on imports intended for retail sale was "not intended as a tax or duty on goods imported but meant and intended as an assessment on every person's stock-in-trade so that persons in trade, shop keepers and others may contribute equally towards the support of government"[15] (Appendix, table 19).

On the whole, the tax systems of the southern colonies were more regressive and less equitable than those in the middle and the New England colonies, and they departed from the ability-to-pay principle much more openly. As a result, there was greater discontent over taxes in the South than elsewhere, discontent that occasionally led to violence. And there were many more complaints not only about the application of the laws but about the nature of the taxes themselves. Men and groups that hoped to gain by tax reform fought against the legislators who drafted and protected the tax systems that so well served the interests of the great planters. Others who, for reasons of principle or interest or ambition or all three, sought to replace the existing legislative leaders seized on discontent over taxes to rally public support. In every southern colony except Georgia the equity of the tax laws, as well as the fairness of their application, became, long before independence, important political issues. This was true of colonies in which party politics was the rule, as in Maryland, and of colonies in which clearly defined party politics did not yet exist, as in Virginia.

Preservation of Virginia's discriminatory revenue laws depended on keeping control of the House of Burgesses in the hands of the "gentlemen of long-tailed families" and their protégés who had dominated legislative proceedings in the Old Dominion for decades: the Lees, the Burwells, the Randolphs, and the rest. In 1763, that dominance was still very much intact. As late as 1773 half the burgesses owned property worth at least £5,000, 80 percent of them owned at least £2,000 worth, and more than 83 percent of them had inherited their wealth. Behind the capable leadership of men like John Robinson, who held the offices of speaker of the house and treasurer of the colony without interruption from 1738 to 1766, the great planters of Virginia kept tight control of public finance. Not since 1645 had anyone successfully championed the heresy that Virginians ought to pay taxes in proportion to their wealth.[16]

Virginia's planter aristocracy oversaw a smoothly operating apprentice system of political advancement. Ambitious young men were expected to demonstrate their ability and their commitment to orthodoxy by long service in county posts and then in the House of Burgesses before being advanced to positions of real prestige, power, and profit, such as a seat on the royal council, the receiver generalship, or the speaker's chair. This screening process filled the House of Burgesses with like-thinking men of similar backgrounds and interests, reduced the occasional zealous reformer to impotent isolation or self-serving conformity, and made serious reform of the revenue system unlikely.[17]

By the end of the Seven Years' War, however, the context in which the game of politics in Virginia was normally played began to change. Taxes during the war had weighed heavily on people's pockets, and on the public mind as well. The tax increases fell most heavily on the poor in general and on the frontier and backcountry poor in particular. "Taxes on taxes are multiplied," complained the Reverend James Maury from Louisa County in June, 1756, and very burdensome to the "lower ranks of people," especially "as tobacco is the only medium of raising money." Crops had been meager, and since the poor "generally cultivate the meanest lands, so were their crops proportionally short."[18] In addition to bad harvests and high taxes, western Virginians also faced the constant terror of Indian raids. Resentment against the government at Williamsburg became widespread and vocal, not only among those who lived along the cutting edge of the frontier, but also among those who lived in the piedmont country east of the Blue Ridge and who saw repeated Indian attacks strip layers of settlement from the frontier. They watched as thousands fled south to the relative safety of the Carolinas and Georgia, or east into the piedmont.

It was not Indian attacks alone that drove thousands out of the frontier counties. Many who left, as well as many who stayed, were angry because they saw little or no return on the money they sent east year after year for taxes, and in their view the measures Williamsburg took to protect the frontier were halfhearted and hopelessly underfinanced. Western Virginians blamed their problems on the "great men" in the House of Burgesses who were "too wise to be informed" and "too indolent to look about them." With "none of them knowing anything of the back country, our frontiers . . . have been left thus naked and exposed," complained the Reverend Mr. Maury in 1755.[19]

A decade later, the French were gone but Indians remained a real and uncomfortably present danger, and the heavy poll and land taxes levied during the war were still being collected. And as the colony gradually retired its paper emissions, currency shortages grew. "Things wear but a gloomy aspect," wrote Peter Fontaine from Hanover County in July, 1765. "The country is so excessively poor that even the industrious, frugal man can scarcely live, and the least slip in economy would be fatal. There is no money."[20] To top it all off, Virginians had recently learned that Parliament planned to levy a new tax payable in specie, and they feared it would be but the first of many. The usual form of relief, new currency emissions, seemed precluded by the Currency Act of 1764. But by 1765 a few aspiring young Virginians had discovered that a troubled economy and taxes thought to be burdensome could offer a shortcut to power to men willing to play the part of the taxpayers' friend.

Patrick Henry learned the lesson early. In 1758, when poor tobacco harvests drove the price of the colony's leading staple up, the burgesses passed the "Two Penny Act," which, among other things, permitted the counties and vestries of Virginia to pay their tax-supported Anglican ministers in the traditional way (in tobacco) or in cash at the rate of twopence for each pound of tobacco they were owed. Since the short crop had driven the price of tobacco above two pennies a pound, ministers forced to accept cash took, in effect, a pay cut. When the Privy Council disallowed the act, several ministers sued county collectors for what they would have received had the act never been passed. The collectors of Hanover hired Patrick Henry, a young rural lawyer of no particular reputation, to defend them in one of these suits in 1763. Henry thus found himself in the enviable position of defending lower taxes at the expense of the already unpopular Anglican clergy. When Henry got the Hanover collectors off with a one-penny fine after a dramatic speech that attacked not only the clergy but the king and came uncomfortably close to treason, his popularity among the small freehold farmers south of the James River grew. In 1765 they sent him to the House of Burgesses.[21] Thus was Henry's political career launched simultaneously with, and in part because of, his reputation as the taxpayers' friend. The two would parallel each other for the next quarter of a century, and the combination made Henry one of the most powerful men in the state after independence.

Henry arrived in the house at the height of the Stamp Act crisis, just as disagreement over how to respond to it began to erode the amiable rule of the leading burgesses. The crisis created a chance, the first of several, for upstarts like Henry to acquire prestige and power far more quickly than they could have otherwise. But imperial affairs were not the only things on the burgesses' minds in the spring and summer of 1765, and the Stamp Act crisis was but one of several shocks delivered to the commonwealth's traditional leaders.

For several years, the treasurer of the colony and speaker of the house John Robinson had been quietly lending to his associates, and to himself, more than £100,000 in paper money that had been taxed out of circulation and that Robinson as treasurer should have destroyed. In April, 1765, six months after they had complained to Parliament and the king that further parliamentary taxes would reduce the colony to "desolation," the burgesses proposed to tax that money in again in order to cover Robinson's peculations, which were well known to many burgesses but had not yet become public. And they proposed to do it by poll taxes.[22] The burgesses hoped to borrow £240,000 sterling from English merchants to redeem the illegally circulating currency that Robinson had loaned out and to open a loan office. But English merchants, who were having trouble collecting debts through Virginia's courts, doubted the integrity and credit of the colony, and the burgesses had to agree to secure their borrowing with the colony's most dependable source of revenue, the tobacco export tax.[23] They planned to increase it from three shillings a hogshead to ten shillings between 1766 and 1775 and then lower it to six shillings for four years after that.

As matters stood, however, the bulk of the new taxes would have been paid by the larger tobacco planters, directly if they marketed their crops under the old consignment system or exported them on their own account, indirectly in the form of lower prices if they sold to the Scottish merchants in Virginia who were beginning to dominate the tobacco trade. To correct this, the burgesses intended to shift the whole burden from tobacco exports to poll taxes. They proposed that the colony repay planters and exporters an amount equal to the new tax on every hogshead exported, and they planned to raise the money to do it by a new poll tax of three shillings from 1767 to 1769 and three shillings sixpence from 1770 to 1779.

Patrick Henry, as yet ignorant of Robinson's embezzlements, denounced it as a scheme to serve the few, who would benefit from the proposed loan office, at the expense of the many, who would have to pay the new taxes. "What, Sir!" cried Henry. "Is it proposed then to reclaim the spendthrift from his dissipation and extravagance by filling his pockets with money?" The plan passed the house, only to die in the council, where it ran into a strong prejudice against the new taxes and against the loan office plan.[24] No matter to Henry. In the house he carried with him the backcountry counties and solidly established his reputation as the taxpayers' friend. "From this time," recalled Thomas

Jefferson years later, "his popularity swelled apace." Richard Corbin, one of the councillors opposed to the plan, gave a reason for his stand that was less eloquent than Henry's but more succint: "to tax people that are not in debt to lend to those that are is highly unjust."[25]

Richard Henry Lee had long suspected Robinson's dealings, and with brashness unheard of in a burgess barely thirty years old, he had forced an investigation of the treasurer's accounts in 1763. But the speaker's friends dominated the committee appointed to investigate him, and the resulting report was a whitewash. It was not until June, 1766, a month after Robinson died, that the scandal surfaced in the newspapers. The colony's economy was still depressed, tax arrears were growing, and opposition to collections was becoming more violent. Some sheriffs refused even to try to collect taxes in 1765, and several county courts found it impossible to hire collectors.[26] Under the circumstances, the news of mysterious shortages at the treasury provoked an uproar. Aspiring politicians like Robert Carter Nicholas, who had been appointed treasurer after Robinson's death and was politicking hard to win the job permanently, found it prudent to speak publicly of money "squeezed from the people for their taxes." The Stamp Act crisis had focused public attention on the distinction between just and unjust taxes, and discussion soon spread from Robinson's malfeasance to the broader issue of fundamental tax reform. A writer in the *Virginia Gazette*, for example, denounced poll taxes as oppressive and demanded that they be replaced by property taxes so that "none but those possessed of slaves, and other estates will pay the levies and taxes. They are best able and they ought."[27]

After the Robinson scandal the burgesses separated the offices of treasurer of the colony and speaker of the house and created a watchdog committee to audit the public accounts every six months, and to publish its findings, so that, as one irate correspondent put it, we "may be fully satisfy'd how the Money raised by heavy Taxes, and (by most of us) in the Sweat of our Brows, is disposed of." In the winter of 1766 the burgesses also approved a new tax on slaves, to "lessen . . . the levy by the poll."

The following spring they drafted a loan office plan that did not include taxes to bail out Robinson's estate. In 1768, on the same day they asked George III and Parliament to relieve them of the Townshend revenue duties, the burgesses also resolved that "so much of the several acts of assembly imposing the land and poll tax on the inhabitants of this colony, as requires taxes to be collected in the present and succeeding year, be repealed."[28] When frontier troubles and floods forced new taxes the next year, they were laid on legal processes, tobacco exports, tavern licenses, slaves, and carriages because, the burgesses intoned, "it hath been found by experience" that these were "easy to the people, and not so burthensome as a poll tax." When more floods forced the emission of £30,000 in paper in 1771, the burgesses funded it in similar fashion, without new poll taxes. And they began as well to investigate tax collection abuses by sheriffs and collectors, who could, often quite legally, make a great deal of money for themselves by forcing people to pay in money rather than tobacco, or by seizing and selling property for taxes without giving the owner sufficient time to obtain enough tobacco to clear the tax.[29]

The elimination of land and poll taxes for the sinking fund by 1770 made the question of what constituted an equitable tax less pressing for the moment. Nevertheless, the shock of the Robinson scandal further undermined public confidence in the integrity of the colony's traditional leaders, and it helped the careers of Patrick Henry, Richard Henry Lee, and other "young, hot-headed, inexperienced members," as Governor Francis Fauquier called them, who were not disposed to follow the lead of their legislative elders when popular favor might be won by an independent stand, and who showed a disturbing willingness to pander to the prejudices of the "vulgar herd" when it suited their purposes.[30]

Nevertheless, even during the brief spasm of reform that followed Robinson's death, the burgesses did not reject the principle of poll taxes or the principle of taxing land by the acre, nor did they commit themselves to taxation in proportion to ability to pay. But the scandal and the continuing dispute with England over taxes made it inevitable that the question of tax equity would come up again the next time Virginia had to raise large sums rapidly.

Proprietary Maryland had the most clearly defined system of party politics in the South, and party strife shaped its tax system. As in Pennsylvania, a proprietary (or court) party battled an antiproprietary (or country) party for control of the assembly. The similarities between the two colonies were so strong that on occasion antiproprietary men in Maryland simply lifted Quaker party arguments wholesale from the Pennsylvania papers and legislative journals and applied them to the Maryland proprietors. "The Flaming Patriots, or rather inflaming demagogues," complained Governor Horatio Sharpe when his house and council were feuding over a proposed land tax, "made great use of the arguments that have by the Pennsylvanians been urged."[31]

The court party dominated the council, and the proprietor's power to appoint members to it and to the seventy or so other offices in his gift greatly strengthened his party's hand. Cecil Calvert, Lord Baltimore's secretary, thought the patronage power was the very foundation of good government. The "noisy animals" who inhabit the lower house could, he advised a harassed Governor Sharpe in 1761, be rendered "not only silent but tame enough to bear stroking" by the proper use of patronage. Place only trusted men on the council, he cautioned Sharpe, men who would not "blabb everything" and jump the traces on close votes and thus "throw everything into the hands of the people." He warned Sharpe against trying to bribe antiproprietary leaders because their asking price was too high, and every time one was bought off, the people raised another in his place. Far better, buy the votes of their followers, the "middling sort of people of whom the lower House is composed," with the judicious use of the appointive power.[32]

Antiproprietary leaders, cut off from the highest and most profitable public offices and opposed to the proprietor's men for a variety of other reasons, political, personal, economic, and religious, depended for their power on maintaining a majority in the lower house. The country party constantly sought popular issues with which to flay the proprietorship and win public support, and like the Quaker party, it found taxation an excellent issue. But the subject had to be handled delicately, for no matter how much leaders of the two factions were at odds, they shared an important characteristic: virtually all of them were substantial landowners. A sizable majority of the assemblymen owned more than 500 acres each, and many measured their holdings in thousands of acres. In 1765 four out of five owned property worth at least £2,000. Among councillors, the average holding was over 8,000 acres in 1758 and over 7,800 in 1771. Leaders of both factions and both houses were included among Maryland's leading landholders. Proprietary men, like Daniel Dulany, and their bitter opponents, like the Carroll family, were heavily involved in land speculation.[33] Neither group wanted land taxes, and in particular ad valorem land taxes, adopted colony wide. During most of the Seven Years' War, the problem facing country party leaders was to avoid passing new land taxes, but in such a way that the proprietor and his supporters would be blamed for any troublesome consequences.

They found a solution. They saw to it that land tax bills that cleared the lower house between 1758 and 1764 (when attempts to impose new land taxes were abandoned) included provisions that would draw popular support to the country party, yet guarantee that the bills would never become law. The proposed tax bill of 1762 is a good example, since the house passed and the council rejected virtually identical acts twice a year beginning in 1758.[34]

The bill was long, and on the surface it seemed to be a modified version of New England's wide-ranging tax laws, but without the poll taxes. Country party leaders claimed they had merely looked to the "wisdom of their Mother Country" and used "the plan of the land tax in England for their guide." The bill proposed taxing undeveloped land, which was "yielding no present annual profit," though it was "daily greatly increasing in value." All land, cultivated and wild, would be taxed at 5 percent of the "yearly value," which was fixed at 5 percent of the current market value as estimated by tax assessors. It was "reasonable and just," the assembly thought, that the proprietor's land be taxed "in equal proportion" with everyone else's, and so the bill proposed taxing proprietary quitrents and unleased lands. Other kinds of property, including "sterling money in Great Britain," slaves, servants, merchants' stock-in-trade, carriages, ships, and a variety of agricultural commodities, were to be taxed five shillings on each £100 of assessed value. The salaries of "all and every Person or Persons, ecclesiastical or civil, within this Province, having or exercising any Benefice, Publick Office or Employment of Profit," would be taxed at 5 percent of the "clear annual . . . Profit of such Benefice; Office or Employment"—a provision aimed directly at proprietary appointees.[35]

The idea of taxing proprietary land and appointees was popular enough in itself, but the bill of 1762 contained other provisions to make it even more appealing. It exempted from paying taxes anyone who had three or more children and who received public charity, or whose personal estate came to less than £50. Leaseholders whose contracts ran seven years or less would be excused from land taxes and their landlords required to pay, as "if no such Lease . . . had been made." Any debtor could subtract five shillings from the interest on every £100 he owed in order to pay taxes; creditors had to absorb the loss or face prosecution.[36]

All involved understood that these proposals were totally unacceptable to the proprietor and his supporters. The council knew all too well that granting tax assessors virtually unlimited power to decide property values (as the bill proposed) would result in manipulation of assessments to build country party support and empty proprietary pockets. That was happening in Pennsylvania, and the Maryland councillors did not intend to grant "so great a Latitude" to the "partiality of the Assessors." The council's nine consecutive rejections of the plan can have surprised no one. Daniel Dulany believed that the house had taken the council's objections to the original 1758 bill and "literally transcribed [them] into every subsequent assessment bill." Indeed, the plan's proponents never expected it to become law; its purpose was political, not financial. Its supporters, Governor Sharpe explained accurately, had "nothing in view but by offering such Laws as they knew would not pass to lay a foundation for Popularity against the ensuing Election."[37] Country party propagandists replied that the proprietor's stubborn refusal to have his land taxed was behind the deadlock, and the responsibility for not answering the king's call for aid against the French, and for allowing the frontier to burn undefended, must rest with him.[38]

The country party also used popular aversion to poll taxes as an antiproprietary weapon. The house insisted that the council wanted to institute a "grievous unequal and unnecessary" poll tax to pay the salaries of proprietary appointees. The councillors understood the popular distaste for poll taxes and denied the allegations. They accused the house of making "forced Constructions" and "unfair Deductions" from council messages "in order to mislead others," and they mourned the departure of truth and decency from a legislative body that pretended to the rights and privileges of the House of Commons.[39]

The council's various messages to the house had not so much as mentioned poll taxes, but as early as 1757, Governor Sharpe had recommended poll taxes as an alternative to increased land taxes, and he claimed the support of "the superior class of people in every part of the province." Furthermore, he wanted the taxes imposed by Parliament to end his annual brawl with the house over money bills. He suggested parliamentary poll taxes again in 1763, adding that a land tax was out of the question. He thought the poll tax plan might even be popular, were it not for a few malcontents in the assembly who were scheming to "throw things into confusion and thereby to exempt themselves and their constituents from all taxes whatever."[40]

As a result of the deadlock, Maryland contributed less money to the war against France than did any other colony except Georgia and North Carolina. Its only war tax passed in 1756 during the panic following Braddock's defeat. Even in that hour of

fear, several house leaders balked at spending £40,000 for backwoods defense and they inserted into the bill a plan to tax the
proprietor's reserved lands, hoping the council would then reject the whole bill outright. After a suitable period of blasting
the proprietor's sycophants for exposing helpless frontiersmen
to savages' knives, a smaller appropriation might be substituted.
But the weight of public fear could not be ignored. With an
armed mob forming in Frederick County and threatening to
march on Annapolis to expedite passage of a defense bill, a joint
conference committee worked out a compromise, and the £40,000
emission bill became law.[41]

The ensuing taxes were the last new ones passed until the Revolution, and as a result, Maryland had no effective land tax in force
from 1763 to 1775. Even the colony's usual annual operating expenses went unpaid from 1756 until 1766, when they were finally
retired not by new land taxes, but by paper money emissions
that were secured, in turn, by stock the colony owned in the
Bank of England and through the operation of a loan office.[42]

Judged by their goals—to keep taxes, particularly land taxes,
at a minimum and to increase popular discontent with proprietary rule—country party leaders succeeded. During the final
years before independence the country party continually presented itself as the taxpayers' friend. Such tactics had the advantage of consistency: they were not dependent on parliamentary blunders like the Stamp Act to arouse popular support.
Internal taxation was an issue that had a constant political impact on all Marylanders; it could be hammered at again and
again, year after year, no matter what the state of Anglo-Ameri-
can relations. Thus the country party insisted that tavern license
fees go into the public treasury instead of the proprietor's pocket; thus it battled for lower fees for public officers and a reduced
poll tax for support of the clergy.[43] By playing on popular opposition to England's colonial policies and by fanning discontent
over taxes and fees, the country party rose to the peak of its influence shortly before the war for independence began. As long
as a king and a proprietor were available against whom that discontent could be directed, its tactics were well chosen. But with

independence, country party leaders soon found themselves facing the uncomfortable necessity of having to make good their commitments.

Politics in late colonial North Carolina revolved largely around a sectional division between the western counties, peopled mainly by small farmers of Scotch-Irish or German descent, and the eastern region, where a plantation economy, the Anglican church, and a planter aristocracy prevailed. And as in Virginia and South Carolina, the eastern counties' delegates held firm control of the assembly through malapportionment and of local government, even in the west, through their power to appoint directly or indirectly almost all of the colony's county and local officials, from justices of the peace and sheriffs on up. In 1771, for example, the seven westernmost counties had only seventeen members in the house; the remaining counties had sixty-one.[44]

The eastern planters' dominance produced in North Carolina a revenue system that was not only the most regressive in the South but also the most corrupt. The revenue system leaked like a sieve. Taxpayers, particularly from the underrepresented frontier counties, where the Regulators would be most active, complained that fraud and theft by sheriffs and their deputies prolonged unreasonably the taxes to sink the colony's paper money emissions, and the governors of the colony, who were not known for their sympathy to the back counties, agreed. In 1767 Governor William Tryon estimated that only about half the tax money collected in the counties ever found its way into the North Carolina treasury. According to Governor Josiah Martin, tax collectors in 1772 owed the colony £66,000 in back taxes. Since the poll taxes raised about £8,000 a year, at least eight extra years of taxes would be needed to compensate for the loss. And that represented only the amount that all agreed should have been collected and delivered into the treasury. There was more, much more. North Carolina sheriffs, for example, often kept two lists of taxable polls: one, the longer, was more or less accurate; the other, considerably shorter, was sent to the treasurer. Sheriffs were thus held responsible for delivering into the treasury only a sum sufficient to cover the polls on the shorter list. The difference went into their own pockets.[45]

North Carolina did have an auditing system of sorts. The colony was divided into two tax districts, each with a separate treasurer. The northern treasurer, for instance, oversaw twelve counties and, Governor Arthur Dobbs guessed, some 34,000 taxable people. Dobbs had to guess because the northern treasurer had never, to the governor's knowledge, bothered to send a complete list of taxables in his district or to submit a full audit of his collections. Such reports as he chose to turn in to the legislature were ordinarily given cursory examination and accepted by the house. The treasurers owed their appointments to the lower house, not directly to the royal governors, and therein lay the explanation of their dedicated unwillingness to call sheriffs to account. The assembly was composed largely of justices of the peace, sheriffs, county clerks, and other influential members of the local courthouse rings, where real day-to-day power in the counties resided. "The treasurers lenity or rather remissness," Governor Tryon pointed out in 1767, "in the material part of their duty I construe to be founded in the principle of caution, for by not sueing the sheriff in arrear, they obtain considerable weight of influence among the connections of these delinquent sheriffs and which generally secures them a re-election in their offices when expired."[46]

Disgruntled backcountry men not only grumbled about the size and duration of the taxes they paid, they complained that sheriffs used taxes to silence criticism and to increase their own and their friends' fortunes. After 1763 North Carolina suffered a particularly severe currency scarcity, during which sheriffs sometimes ordered hasty sales of property for taxes and then bid it in themselves at bargain prices. Stories of such outrages circulated freely. One told of a sheriff who arrived at a farmer's house to collect a tax and, finding the man out, stripped the dress off his wife, "slapped her on the buttocks, told her to make herself another and sold the dress at auction for her husband's taxes."[47] Governor Tryon was himself attempting, as had Gov-

ernor Dobbs before him, to bring the sheriffs and treasurers
into line and to reform the auditing system. From their different
regions and across a vast social and economic gulf, then, Regulators and North Carolina's governors found themselves working for a common end: to reduce the autonomy of county sheriffs
and the colony treasurers. In the summer of 1768, spokesmen
for the Regulators of Orange County offered Tryon an alliance
when they suggested with tactless straightforwardness that the
local courthouse rings were "to hard for your excellency as well
as for us" to handle alone. They offered to support Tryon's reforms.[48]

But the kind of support the Regulator counties could offer—
petitions to the assembly and perhaps a few votes from western
representatives—was not likely to accomplish much, and Tryon
knew it. Like its neighbor to the south, North Carolina had a
grossly malapportioned legislature. Four coastal counties in the
north, for instance, each had five representatives in the assembly, while the much larger and more populous western counties
of Rowan and Orange had only two each. "It is become very
apparent to the inhabitants of the western country," wrote Governor Martin in September, 1774, that they "must be ever governed" by the eastern counties, even though their population was
four times as great.[49]

The same was also apparent to Governor Tryon, who knew
that any serious attempt at reform would mean a prolonged,
unpleasant, and personally costly conflict with his assembly. To
secure for himself as peaceful and as profitable a governorship
as possible, Tryon let the Regulators' offer of an alliance lapse
and never pushed his reform proposals to the point of open rup-
ture with the house. Instead, he contented himself with periodically raising a ritual banner or two in the name of reform. The
punchless bills that resulted were the sort the assembly could
live with comfortably: they sounded significant and they signified little. Even such watered-down measures as the house did
accept came only after violence began to grow and the legislators
thought a gesture toward honesty prudent. After 1766, for example, they made treasurers responsible for all money owed the

colony by any sheriff whom they failed to sue within six months of his default on collections. In fact, however, no North Carolina treasurer in this period was ever taken to task by the legislature for failing to sue a delinquent sheriff. A diluted auditing plan did pass in January, 1771, but it kept real power in the assembly's hands and thus meant little. As late as 1774, sheriffs were still regularly collecting tax money from people certified as paupers by the courts and therefore legally exempt from paying.[50]

It would be difficult to exaggerate the importance of tax fraud and corruption on the part of sheriffs and collectors in fomenting the Regulator movement. In addition to the abuses already mentioned, sheriffs often made the taxes even more burdensome by charging excessive fees for those who violated arbitrary payment rules. In 1768, for instance, Sheriff Tyree Harriss of Orange County announced that he would accept tax payments only at five specified places and times, and would charge anyone who paid him at any other time or place an extra fee of two shillings eight pence. Since the poll tax for that county was ten shillings eight pence, Harriss' penalty increased the tax in some cases by 25 percent. Harriss posted his notice at the same time reports reached the county of new taxes to be levied to build Governor Tryon an executive mansion. The two grievances combined gave rise to "what was commonly called the mob," and greatly strengthened the Regulators in that county.[51]

That such corruption was among the primary causes of the Regulator movement in North Carolina is undeniable, but the Regulators' criticisms of North Carolina went much deeper. They or at least their spokesmen understood that even if all the corrupt sheriffs and collectors were replaced by scrupulously honest men, the colony's revenue system would still be discriminatory and regressive as long as general poll taxes remained a substantial part of it. Is it just, asked a resident of Mecklenburg, that a man "worth 10,000 £ pays no more than a poor back settler that has nothing but the labour of his hands to depend upon for his daily support?" A few shillings in taxes might seem trifling to gentlemen "rowling in affluence," complained petitioners from Rowan and Orange counties in 1768, but "to Poor People who must have their Bed and Bed-clothes yea their Wives Petticoats taken and sold to Defray [taxes], how Tremenjous judge must be the Consequences: an only Horse, to raise Bread by or Only Cow, to give Milk to an helpless Family by which in a Great Measure are Otherwise Supported, seized and sold."⁵² To end oppression of "poor Inhabitants . . . by reason of disproportionate Taxes," Anson County petitioners demanded nothing less than a revolution in the colony's revenue system. They wanted the right to pay their taxes in farm commodities; they wanted a new paper money emission, funded not by new taxes but by a loan office. Most important, they demanded that the poll tax be replaced by an income tax so that each man might pay "in proportion to the proffits arising from his Estate." Herman Husband made the same point graphically in 1770. "The Publick taxes," he wrote, "is an unequal burden on the poor of this province, by reason the poorest man is taxed as high as the richest. Allowing the taxes to be all necessary, yet there ought to be some regard had to the strength of the beast, for all asses are not equally strong. We ought to be taxed accordingly to the profits of each man's estate."⁵³

The demand for commodity payments was met in part in 1768, ironically through passage of a tax law to raise money to suppress the Regulators. And in December, 1768, the assembly moved to eliminate some of the sinking-fund taxes in order to keep in circulation what remained of the colony's paper currency.⁵⁴ But the North Carolina legislature never seriously considered substantive tax reform, and the Regulators' call for a more equitable distribution of taxes went unheeded in North Carolina before the Revolution.

In 1771 Governor Tryon and a low-country army crushed the Regulators at the battle of Alamance Creek. The Regulator movement in general, however, and the unsuccessful effort to reform North Carolina's revenue system in particular, convinced many discontented North Carolinians that the source of their most pressing problems lay in Edenton, not London. It was not "any reflection on the king, to say, the poor are oppressed," explained

Husband in 1770, "for he don't make our laws." And some were beginning to see that the principles the colonial legislatures invoked so freely against parliamentary taxation could have internal applications as well.[55] The grievances that had given rise to the Regulator movement continued after its demise until revolution unexpectedly opened the door to reform. After 1775 the colony's backcountry men and the poor discovered that although their greatest asset, their numbers, carried little weight in time of peace, it gave them great influence in a time of war and revolution.

In South Carolina the great planters of the lowlands dominated the legislature more completely than they did anywhere else in the South. In 1765, for example, all the members of the South Carolina House of Commons owned at least £2,000 in property, and two out of three owned more than £5,000 worth. Large sections of the interior were wholly unrepresented or at best were virtually represented. So rigidly had westerners been excluded, so tightly had the planters of St. James–Goose Creek and other eastern parishes restricted the distribution of assembly seats, the legislature could be accurately described as "an exclusively eastern body."[56] The tax system these men devised was unquestionably less regressive on the whole than that in North Carolina, but it still clearly served the interests of the great planters, particularly through the imposition of acreage property taxes rather than ad valorem rates. Demands for reform came primarily from the two areas of South Carolina that were badly underrepresented in the assembly and whose interests were therefore poorly served: the piedmont backcountry and the city of Charleston.

As in North Carolina, backcountry discontent had drifted dangerously close to rebellion in South Carolina by the late 1760s. In 1767 Governor Charles Montagu reported "tumultuous risings" in the back areas, and the colony faced a Regulator uprising of its own. Regulators complained about a lack of law enforcement in the backcountry, which made their homes, property, prosperity, and their lives insecure, and about the complete absence of courts in the interior, which meant a trip all the way to Charleston, at great expense, for any legal action involving more than twenty pounds.[57] Even the low-country planters who filled the assembly agreed these complaints had merit, and when reports of Regulator mobs massing to march on Charleston struck fear into them, they acted. After several delays caused by the Townshend Acts crisis and years of the assembly, the governor, and the Board of Trade squabbling over the distribution of patronage under a revised judicial system, a new circuit court bill that dealt with many of the backcountry's complaints became law.[58]

But South Carolina Regulators did not limit their demands to court reform. They also called for accurate surveys of parish lines, for public schools, for more effective antivagrancy laws, for roads built at public expense, for extended bounties on up-country hemp, flax, and flour. And they said "that the tax upon lands up in the frontiers, which are of very little value, ought not to be as great as upon lands of great value near a market." In short, they wanted property taxed ad valorem. A legislative committee, appointed to study Regulator petitions in 1769, eventually recommended the creation of new parishes in the piedmont, extended hemp and flax bounties, publicly supported teachers to educate "a certain number of poor children," and court reform. Although the house rejected, delayed, or adulterated most of the recommendations, they had at least received a hearing. No mention was made, however, by the committee or the house, of the demand for tax reform.[59]

South Carolina was unique among the southern colonies in that it had the region's only major commercial port and city, Charleston. In the 1760s Charleston was booming, and improvements designed to make it an even more attractive entrepôt were either planned or under way, including better navigation aids and transportation facilities, and a new exchange building.[60] Despite its evident prosperity, the city nevertheless suffered from the same urban problems that plagued New York, Philadelphia, and Boston: the heavy expense of poor relief and legislative tax discrimination.

Poor rates in Charleston soared after 1763 as the indigent drifted into the city from all parts of South Carolina and from North Carolina and Georgia. By the winter of 1766, the poor-house, paid for by a city property tax and forced to serve not only the city's poor but sailors as well, was filled to over-flowing and could no longer accept those seeking admission or those the city sought to commit. In November, 1766, Charleston vestrymen and churchwardens complained that the city's burden of poor relief had become intolerable. The city had spent £1,200 on poor relief in 1747, but it spent £6,100 in 1763 and £6,500 in 1766, much of it raised by special city taxes in addition to what Charlestonians and the rest of the colony paid for the support of the transient poor.[61] City spokesmen often demanded that poor relief be put "on such a Footing that every Part of the Province may bear an equal Proportion thereof."[62] In 1767 a seven-man house committee, which included four city representatives, reported that Charleston's support of the poor was "grievous and burthensome . . . and is now become intolerable" and recommended that poor relief be paid for by the colony as a whole. The rural-dominated assembly, however, deciding that the problem needed more study, appointed a new committee of seven, this time including only one city representative. The new committee reported in April. It too noted the rapidly rising number of poor people in the city and cited a variety of causes: the failure of wardens to send newly arrived paupers back to their home parishes; the ease of establishing residency (and therefore a claim for public support); the tendency of many poor German, Irish, and French Protestant immigrants who had been imported to populate the frontiers, to stay in Charleston; the fact that many British soldiers and sailors who died in the war or departed after it, left behind women and children, who became public charges; the large number of sailors thrown out of work "during the late stagnation of trade and business occasioned by the British Stamp Act"; and the prodigious and alarming number of tippling houses in the city. To deal with all this, the committee made several recommendations that did *not* include support of Charleston's poor by means of a colony-wide property tax.[63]

The house accepted the report and ordered a bill prepared in conformity with its recommendations. But the house deleted the one suggestion that promised to cost the country parishes substantial money, that paupers arriving in Charleston be swiftly returned to their home parishes. A bill finally became law in April, 1768. It extended the time needed to establish residency (and therefore a right to city charity) from three months to twelve, and it authorized construction of a new poorhouse and hospital, to be funded by existing imposts on wine, rum, and other commodities. These measures did little to solve the problem. The "poor from all parts of this extensive province, and other parts of the world," explained the Charleston grand jury in 1771, continued to "crowd into Charleston daily," and the city's taxpayers and their spokesmen continued to complain.[64]

Charleston's complaints involved more than just the poor rates, for South Carolina's revenue laws discriminated openly against the city in general and against the commercial community in particular. Before 1759, for instance, the law required Charleston (the only place in the colony where ad valorem property rates were collected) to raise 20 percent of the general provincial tax revenues. Originally the 20 percent limit may have been a floor below which the planters did not intend to let city contributions fall, but as Charleston prospered it began to seem more like a ceiling above which Charleston's contributions could not rise. In 1759 city delegates in the assembly arranged a deal with the house: they would agree to the removal of the 20 percent ceiling if the house would pass an act "for the equitable and impartial taxation of all estates throughout the province, according to the value of each estate in like manner, as the Charles Town Estates were made liable to." In brief, they wanted exactly what the Regulators wanted a decade later: a general ad valorem property tax to take effect throughout the colony. The house quickly removed the ceiling on Charleston's share of the provincial revenues to be raised, and the city's proportion of the funds raised promptly shot up to 26 percent. By 1765 it had risen to 28 percent (Appendix, table 20). But when it came time to complete the agreement, the country representatives reneged; and when the ad valorem general property tax came before the house, they defeated it.[65]

In 1770, irate Charleston taxpayers again petitioned the assembly for relief. They pointed out that only Charleston residents paid taxes on the full value, annually reassessed, of their land, improved or not, as well as on the full value of their stock-in-trade, profits, and salaries. Everyone else paid property taxes on the basis of "ancient" valuations that, they claimed, generally presumed good land beyond the city limits to be one fifth its real value. Slaves in the rural parishes were presumed, for tax purposes, to be worth £200 each when in fact they brought, on an average, better than £300 each. The result was a one-third tax saving for rural slave owners. Charleston residents who paid taxes on their land and slaves also paid on the profits arising from them, as well as their own efforts "under the head of profits in trade, faculties, &c., whereas the planter in the country pays no tax at all on the profits of his own labour or faculty, or the profits of his Negroes however great such annual profits may be." A man who had £7,000 invested in property or stock-in-trade in Charleston in 1770, complained petitioners, paid ten shillings for each £100 value, a total tax of thirty-five pounds. But a man who invested £7,000 in land outside Charleston might pay as little as seven pounds property tax.[66]

The treatment of the petition shows clearly how firmly the low-country planters controlled the house and how rigidly determined they were to prevent tax reform. As soon as Christopher Gadsden presented it, someone moved to dismiss it out of hand, without so much as the courtesy of a reading. The house instead sent the petition to a committee, which reported back on March 2. The committee declared that a "more equal method of taxation than what has been hitherto adopted" was "not only desirable, but practicable and necessary," and recommended a colony-wide ad valorem property tax. It suggested a £50 increase, for tax purposes, in the estimated worth of Negroes and exemption from the faculty taxes for merchants, clerks, tradesmen, journeymen, and overseers. In the subsequent debates and votes, the house rejected every recommendation except the proposed increase in the estimated taxable value of slaves. That proposal it refused to consider at all.[67]

As elsewhere in the South, demands for changes in the colony's general tax policies were widespread during the decade before independence and were capable of unifying, at least potentially, such disparate groups as backcountry Regulators and wealthy Charleston merchants. But the strong grip of low-country planters on the legislature ensured that in South Carolina, as elsewhere, meaningful tax reform would have to await either a revolution in the internal distribution of power in the colony or a crisis severe enough to cause the dominant political force to barter reform in one area for support in another.

Prerevolutionary Georgia consisted of little more than a strip of thinly populated land bordering the Atlantic coast and parts of the Savannah River. Heavily subsidized by Parliament and desperately dependent on the protection of the British army, Georgia could not afford the luxury of baiting the British lion, and it lacked the well-defined political factionalism that enlivened public life elsewhere in the colonies. Its political life was, however, far from quiescent, and insofar as domestic taxation created political disputes, they often reflected the kinds of problems common elsewhere in the South. The colony's treasurer, for example, was accused of incompetence at best, embezzlement at worst. When tax collections were £4,000 short in 1773, there seemed some basis for the charges, and the acting governor James Habersham accused the assembly of covering up for the treasurer by delaying a long-overdue audit of his accounts.[68] The usual problem with people concealing taxable property plagued Georgia as it did the other colonies. Its assemblies, like those elsewhere in the South, took whatever opportunities arose to lessen the land taxes by shifting the burden to import duties or by tapping funds from the colony's loan office.[69]

In the winter of 1769 the lower house of Georgia discovered that the principle of no taxation without representation could be useful as more than a debating point with England. The house demanded that four recently organized parishes be granted representation in order that they might be taxed constitutionally. Governor James Wright was unsure whether his instructions permitted him to increase the size of the assembly, but he promised to have the matter cleared up as quickly as possible. Why the assembly chose to force the issue at this particular time is not entirely clear. Unrepresented parishes had been taxed before in Georgia without noticeably disturbing the conscience of the house.[70] It is unlikely that the parishes involved were clamoring to be taxed, and representation per se was not the critical point, for when Governor Wright finally got permission to allow the four representation in 1770, they sent no delegates to the assembly until the Revolution.[71]

Part of the answer probably lay in the colony's financial problems. Like most of the other southern colonies, Georgia suffered from a severe currency shortage. A paper emission had been disallowed by the Privy Council in 1766, and merchants, complaining of the scarcity of money, demanded that the colony's circulating currency be tripled. In 1768 Secretary Habersham estimated that Georgia had in circulation no more than £7,000 sterling worth of currency, which he thought "much too little." When the house brought the matter of representation up again in February, 1770, it threatened to approve no new tax laws unless the governor backed down, which he could not do. The house eventually discovered a means of relieving the currency scarcity more suitable than using the representation issue as a convenient pretext for not passing tax bills. The tax act of May, 1770, exempted the four parishes, but more important, it authorized the treasurer to issue certificates of public indebtedness to the colony's creditors, which certificates were receivable for public taxes until they might be called in and exchanged for money raised, eventually, by new taxes. What it all amounted to was an emission of some £3,355 worth of non-legal tender currency.[72]

If the house's original intention in raising the matter of representation was to suspend taxes, it achieved that a year later, when Governor Wright and his temporary stand-in, Habersham, disputed the house's right to choose its own speaker. As a result of the adjournments and dissolutions that followed, no tax laws passed and no new taxes were collected in 1771 or 1772.[73]

The southern colonists complained to England that they were overburdened with taxes no less shrilly than did other colonists, yet on the whole, southern taxes between the Seven Years' War and the Revolution declined. The declining rates did not, of course, necessarily disturb the inequities in the taxes that were collected.

Virginia's 1764 taxes were the heaviest of the period, yet the per capita rate came to just over two and a half shillings, exclusive of the tobacco poll tax. That levy, forty-six pounds, brought the total per capita rate to about ten shillings. From there on, it was all downhill. The tobacco poll tax never again rose above nine pounds.[74] The sinking-fund poll taxes were lowered in 1765, and both land and poll taxes on that account were eliminated by 1768. Three subsequent paper emissions were funded by carriage taxes, legal fees, slave imposts, and the tobacco export tax, and by 1770 quitrents and the tobacco export tax sufficed to cover the normal annual expenses of government.[75]

Maryland was also relatively well off. After the land tax ended in 1764 the remaining imposts, tobacco duties and the small colony poll tax raised at most £7,000 a year, or about one shilling for each white inhabitant. Adding the tax for support of the Anglican clergy raised the total to about two shillings threepence. Direct taxes for support of the colony government, then, amounted to no more than fivepence per capita.[76]

South Carolina's tax act of 1764 authorized a levy of about two pounds (South Carolina currency) per capita, or less than six shillings sterling at the official exchange rate of seven for one. Various trade taxes added another two shillings sterling to the total.[77] But from 1765 on, the direct taxes were never again half as high, and after 1769 they disappeared completely, when the house and council deadlocked over the legality of the colony's £10,500 contribution to John Wilkes. No tax law passed from 1770 until the Revolution, and the colony relied wholly on its trade taxes. Despite the initially high per capita figure in South Carolina currency, the taxes were scarcely backbreaking when compared with those collected in England. For the most part, the colony enjoyed prosperity and substantial economic growth between 1763 and 1774, and David Ramsay looked back on the period as one of "inconsiderable" taxation.[78]

The pattern of declining rates did not hold in Georgia, where taxes rose during the period 1763 to 1770. Still, exclusive of the trade duties (which were negligible), the annual total was never more than £3,375 sterling, or just under four shillings sterling per capita. No taxes at all were passed in 1771 or 1772, and the high assessment the following year (£5,172 sterling) covered more than one year's expenditures.[79]

The chaos of North Carolina's revenue system makes it impossible to arrive at a per capita tax figure that means much. A figure based on the amount of money turned in by collectors would, for example, certainly be far too low. Suffice it to say that the tax rates generally declined during the period 1763 to 1771, when the colony refunded its debt and issued more paper money, whereupon the taxes rose to perhaps their highest postwar level. Whether these new taxes were collected any more faithfully or efficiently than the old ones is doubtful.[80]

Parliamentary compensation payments that substantially lowered taxes in the New England and middle colonies were much less important in the South because the southern colonies raised less money and fewer soldiers for the king's service against the French during the Seven Years' War. Maryland's parsimony in that regard was notorious both in England and in the colonies. Because of North Carolina's isolation and poverty, England expected (and got) little from it. The colony received £7,000 of the £50,000 granted the southern colonies in 1757, and probably some smaller payments later, which the house planned to use "in aid to the taxes."[81]

Compensation money depended on the number of soldiers raised for the king's service, and militia raised by the colonies to fight Indians on their own frontiers did not count. As a result, South Carolina, which ultimately spent well over £200,000 sterling on the war and war-related expenses, received back only £12,000 sterling, nearly all of it before 1760. Georgia was too weak to provide for its own military security, much less aid the king's expeditionary forces. The heavy sterling payments it received from Parliament were outright subsidies rather than in return for services. In 1767 the subsidy totaled £3,986, about equal to the cost of running the colony for one year. Such subsidies continued after the Declaration of Independence, though they went to the royal rather than to the rebel government.[82]

Only in Virginia did compensation payments play an important role in tax relief. The colony used a £30,000 grant to ease tobacco export taxes, to reduce Virginia's interest-bearing debt, and to lower slave taxes. Such grants eventually permitted the cancellation of four years of a planned five-year one-shilling poll tax.[83]

The southern colonies stood second to none in the awesome inefficiency of their collection systems. Faulty land surveys helped Georgians evade payment and doubtless contributed to shortages in the treasury accounts that totaled £1,200 to £1,400 annually between 1768 and 1771. Those amounts were more than one third of the taxes Georgia hoped to raise during that period.[84] In providing generous subsidies to the young colony, Parliament underwrote to some extent the tax evasions of its citizens or the peculations of its officials, or both.

Large deficiencies marred Virginia public finance as well, exclusive of Robinson's embezzlements. Eleven counties owed the treasury over 68,000 pounds of tobacco in back taxes in 1762.

That year, the legislature tightened assessment procedures and raised fines for concealing taxable property in order to end the "great frauds . . . committed by the sheriffs in collecting the taxes."[85] The attempted reforms did little good. In the summer of 1766 the treasurer Robert Carter Nicholas complained that "very large arrears, some of many years standing," were still due from collectors for the land, poll, carriage, and tobacco taxes. The committee appointed to settle the public accounts following the Robinson scandal reported, in December, 1766, that sheriffs and other collectors owed the colony "a considerable sum" and that several of them had not bothered to render *any* accounts for several years. Arrears from land, poll, and carriage taxes alone totaled £55,750 in 1768, though they declined steadily after that. They were down to £34,151 by 1770 and £20,748 by 1772.[86]

North Carolina's revenue system was so inefficient and corrupt that for the period 1748–1770, sheriffs wound up owing the treasury more than they collected and turned in. By 1772, arrearages for the poll tax reached £66,000, two thirds of which Governor Martin abandoned all hope of ever recovering.[87]

South Carolina found itself in a rare position in 1764, when a house committee discovered that the tax law of 1760, designed to raise £181,191, had actually brought in £14,000 too much. But collections under the 1761 law were short almost £36,000, and those for 1762 were short almost £20,000. The committee put most of the blame on the collectors.[88] In September, 1766 some thirty-six collectors still owed money for the previous year's taxes. Twenty-five still owed for 1763, nineteen for 1762, and seven had not yet paid in taxes supposed to have been collected in 1761. By 1767 the surplus on the 1760 account had risen to £16,435 as late collections came in, but shortages for 1761 and 1762 still totaled more than £32,400. When the treasurer Jacob Motte died in 1769, he owed the public £48,975. The colony had similar problems with its customs collectors. William Harvey, the Port Royal collector, let his accounts run two years without an audit, and before he died, he admitted owing the colony £6,864, though several members of the assembly thought his estimate far too modest. In the midst of a dispute with the public treasurers and the governor concerning tax abatements, the house found that the treasurers had allowed various "gentlemen in trade" to fall far behind on the commerce taxes, for which indulgence the merchants paid the treasurers interest on what they owed.[89]

Maryland discovered "very unequal collection of the excise in the different counties" in 1762, which it attributed to strict collections in some counties and "extraordinary negligence" in others. A detailed report on overdue taxes submitted to the council showed arrears due on a wide variety of taxes, some going back to 1756. Anne Arundel County land tax collectors, for instance, had paid nothing from September, 1761, to March, 1763, nor had the county excisemen. Later audits showed the problem to be growing, though in view of the chaos and terror Pontiac's Rebellion brought to the western settlements, it is not surprising that frontier Frederick County sent no tax money to the treasury for 1763.[90]

In many ways, southern attitudes toward taxation in the years following the Seven Years' War reflected those farther north. Southerners agreed that it was important to keep control of their taxes firmly in local hands lest "all the variety of ways and means of raising money in Great Britan will soon be in practice here."[91] As in the North, controlling political elites established and defended tax systems that favored their interests, though occasionally, as in Maryland, men with no real interest in substantive reform championed it in the name of the people when votes might be won by doing so. And in the South as in the northern colonies, each colony contained some men who were convinced of the inequity of existing laws and eager to change them. As England and the colonies edged toward civil war, and colonists from Boston to Charleston rioted against the stamp tax, the Townshend Acts, and the customs service, Americans learned anew the power of the mob, and a growing number realized that violence could also be used to oppose a local tax deemed unjust. Rebellion against royal authority provided excellent training for resistance to local authority as well.

The South Carolina Regulator movement, wrote Peter Timothy, owed its origin to "Greenville's Hellish idea of the Stamp Act, when some from Charlestown persuaded these ignorant back settlers" to organize in opposition to the act. "This brought them together," he reported, "and now they look into other matters."[92] The lesson was driven home in Maryland in 1765, when one Colonel Cresap organized the Fredericktown Sons of Liberty, "many of them with guns and tommahawks," and threatened to march on Annapolis "in order (as they express themselves) to settle the disputes betwixt the two Houses of Assembly" over paying public creditors the debts long owed them. The truth was, Governor Sharpe explained, that the success of the Stamp Act riots led the people "to think they can by the same way of proceeding accomplish anything their leaders may tell them they ought to do."[93] South Carolina's William Bull spoke for many in 1773, when he warned that through participation in riots and resistance to English taxes, the people had "discovered their own strength and importance" and would never again be "so easily governed by their former leaders."[94] And in the South especially, those same people were discovering, along with their power, needs that did not always coincide with those of their former leaders. One such need was tax reform.

As revolution approached, the two reforms most often demanded were the reduction or outright elimination of poll taxes and the replacement of acreage land taxes with ad valorem property rates. When southern revolutionary leaders faced independence in 1776 and the uncertainties of the war that lay beyond it, as they cast about for ways to raise unprecedented sums by public taxation, all the while trying desperately to solidify popular support for the rebel cause, they were forced to deal with complaints that had gone unanswered for decades and to respond to demands they had previously ignored. The South's traditional political leaders, who were already fully aware of the political and economic advantages to be gained from controlling public finance, were about to learn firsthand that "the transforming hand of Revolution" could set free social aspirations, economic desires, and political ambitions long held in check.[95]

PART TWO

The Sovereign States

War involves in its progress such a train
of unforseen and unsupposed circumstances
that no human wisdom can calculate
the end. It has but one thing certain,
and this is to increase taxes.

Prospects on the Rubicon (1787)
—THOMAS PAINE

Introduction

The outbreak of war in April, 1775, and the Declaration of Independence in July, 1776, made intercolonial unity a matter of overriding importance for American leaders, but their success depended as well on unifying popular support for the revolutions *within* each state, in many ways a more difficult task. After July, 1776, rebels from New Hampshire to Georgia at least had a common enemy in England and a common goal in independence. But within each colony, rebels often divided sharply over what direction the Revolution should take, over which colonial policies and practices should be retained, and over which institutions should be preserved, altered, or eliminated. Some rebelling colonists saw in the potential for social and political change that accompanied the collapse of the old empire, and in the creation of new states and constitutions, an opportunity to win reforms they had not been able to win before. Others in the rebelling states saw in that potential a serious threat to social and political stability, to the preservation of property rights, to the war effort, and to their own political and economic interests. The struggle in each state to determine the course of the Revolution after independence— to define, through legislative policy and practice, what the Revolution was, what it meant in each state— was fought in the provisional revolutionary assemblies and the new state legislatures. The issues ranged from grand questions of intercolonial policy, such as the proper relation of the states to Congress, to more mundane matters, such as the distribution of taxes within each state.

Ironically, in 1776 the new states found themselves facing a crisis similar to the one faced by England in 1755, a crisis that had led Parliament to adopt some of the very policies the colonists rebelled against. Now the new state legislatures had to find, and quickly, the money to carry on a war of national survival. All the new governments faced the problem of raising sufficient funds to establish their independence, though each state was (as each colony had been) unique and each responded to the problems of revolutionary finance in its own way. Yet out of their varied and sometimes contradictory experience, several trends emerged, more clearly in some states than in others, but trends that were, on the whole, common to them all.

First, the rebel legislatures found that by declaring independence they had not escaped the conflicts over taxation that marked the late colonial years. A common enemy may have driven thirteen diverse, self-interested, and stubborn colonial assemblies to work together, but the common threat did not necessarily eliminate long-standing rivalries and differences within each colony. These old disputes had to be resolved or somehow bypassed before effective revenues could be raised to fight the war. Frequently the revolutionary assemblies appeared to think that the national revolution was secondary to local imperatives and to the revolutions in the states.

Second, the war raised new problems for all legislatures and created new rivalries and new interest groups, complicating the search for equitable and efficient tax systems.

Third, the rebel governments in all sections soon faced widespread popular opposition to tax collections, opposition that ranged from petitioning and remonstrating through tax withholding to attacking assessors and collectors, and rioting. Rebel legislators had to keep the anticipated public reaction in mind as they debated tax laws, and this often reduced the efficiency of the ones they adopted. Sometimes out of fear of armed resistance, sometimes merely because the newly formed legislatures were more sensitive to popular pressure than the old ones had been, sometimes because they were unable to enforce the laws in the face of popular opposition, the legislatures tolerated inefficiency and evasion in tax collections that seriously crippled their ability to raise money, soldiers and supplies.

Fourth, there were in most states during the war movements for tax reform that sought to bring under taxation income, property, and wealth that had previously gone untaxed and to reduce or eliminate taxes popularly thought to be unfair, unequal, and discriminatory against the poor and the many as opposed to the rich and the few. Not all attempts at reform were successful, and of those that were, not all were permanent. But the battles in the states between those who favored the old colonial tax laws and fought to preserve them after independence and those who were discriminated against by the old laws and fought to change them formed one dimension of the developing political struggle within the new nation as a whole and within each individual state.

CHAPTER FOUR
New England

The American Revolution changed the structure of New England taxation very little, but it altered the politics of New England taxation dramatically. The politics of taxation in the late colonial years had not been primarily "class" politics and had involved conflict between rich and poor only incidentally. But the financial crisis brought on by the war highlighted, as never before, the inequities of the laws and drove many New Englanders (especially those in the interior farming towns) to the brink of ruin. And after 1777 the politics of taxation in New England often ranged the poor and those facing ruin against the wealthy and those prospering from the war. The former demanded tax reform, such as the elimination or reduction of poll taxes, and tax relief, such as suspension of collections or acceptance of farm commodities in payment. The latter argued for specie collections, strict enforcement, and high poll taxes. Debates over taxation began almost immediately upon the organization of provisional revolutionary governments in the rebelling states. For the most part, the men who directed those governments in New England, and who drafted their laws, successfully checked efforts to reform in any fundamental way the old colonial tax systems, especially in Massachusetts. In no other New England state was the demand for tax reform and relief greater, and in none did it receive a less sympathetic response from government.[1]

Long before the war began at Lexington and Concord, Massachusetts towns and counties seized control of the colony's revenue system so that taxes could be used to serve the Revolution rather than the royal military government. As early as August, 1774, a Worcester County convention directed towns to stop sending taxes to the colony treasurer, and by the end of September, conventions in Suffolk, Hampshire, and Plymouth counties had done the same. When the provincial congress finally ordered towns to stop payments to treasurer Harrison Gray, it merely ratified a decision already made locally across the colony.[2]

But revolution did not bring reform to Massachusetts taxes. The new state's leaders—men like Samuel Adams, John Adams, and John Hancock—quickly made it plain that no matter how radical they may have been with respect to parliamentary taxation, they had little intention and less desire to reform the old colonial revenue system in Massachusetts or to purge the new state of poll taxes. In fact, the war and the financial crisis it brought induced representatives of the prosperous eastern commercial farming towns to unite with representatives of the eastern trading towns and seaports in order to block reform and to preserve, or even extend, the inequities of the old colonial revenue laws. In October, 1774, the provincial congress, setting the policy it would follow throughout the war, "strongly recommended" that towns continue collecting the usual taxes in the usual ways. When the congress issued £26,000 in bills of credit the following May, it directed that taxes to retire the money be levied as usual on polls, estates, and faculties and collected in the familiar manner.[3]

The revolutionary government of Massachusetts would have preferred not taxing at all during the first years of the war. The people were, after all, in rebellion against oppressive English taxes, or so all claimed, and some members of the General Court were afraid that heavy American taxes might produce still another rebellion, this one directed against the new revolutionary government.[4] And heavy war taxes might mean the end of the quiet acquiescence with which most people had greeted their colonial taxes. Such fears were not idle, for as the taxes rose to previously undreamed-of levels the inequities buried within them became more and more evident, and the colony divided into brawling, self-interested geographic and economic factions.

In the first uncertain days of rebellion, with loyalties still untested, the new state could not afford to risk the internal divisions that heavy taxes were expected to produce, and so the first legislatures adopted a policy finally chosen by nearly all the colonies: they issued huge amounts of paper currency but delayed the taxes needed to support it. The General Court printed £100,000 in August, 1775, for instance, but put off until 1778 the first tax to redeem it. Taxes to redeem another £75,000 issued in December, 1775, were delayed until 1781, and funding taxes for some of the £295,000 issued during 1776 were not to begin until 1784. Between August, 1775, and December, 1776, Massachusetts issued a total of £470,000 in legal tender paper, supported by little more than hope of winning the war and the promise of future taxes if the hope became a reality.[5]

By 1777, however, it was clear that the war would be long and expensive, and the General Court could no longer avoid the troublesome problem of taxing an independent people. The revolutionary assemblies that addressed the problem were still filled with country men from country towns, but they often disagreed among themselves about public finance. When delegates from the prosperous eastern farming villages joined with delegates from trade centers like Boston and Newburyport, however, together they were virtually unstoppable. As the war dragged on and taxes climbed, delegates from the eastern villages and trade centers united to stop tax reform, to establish high poll taxes and thus reduce the burden on property, and to convert the state's paper debt into a specie debt supported by specie taxes—to develop, in short, a revenue system that catered to the commercial and creditor interests as opposed to those of debtors and subsistence farmers. Occasionally the poorer rural interior towns and the commercial eastern farming towns combined to vote against the merchant community, as when they tripled the assessments on income from trades, professions, and commissions in October, 1775, and when they later adopted an excess war profits tax and reimposed liquor excises and imposts.[6] But for the most part, the delegates from the subsistence farming towns of the interior remained in a minority in the General Court, and their constituents paid the price of their weakness in higher taxes.

In 1777 the General Court began to formulate the conservative economic policy to which it adhered throughout the war. It declared the first revolutionary paper emissions to be no longer legal tender and announced that after December, 1777, they would not be accepted for taxes, though some exceptions were later permitted. And at the same time, the General Court began to levy massive taxes to reduce the amount of paper currency in circulation. In January, 1777, it ordered collection of a £109,000 tax that, except for the tripled assessment on merchants' incomes, virtually reproduced the old colonial revenue system. A £314,608 tax law followed in October, and another of £254,718 in March, 1778. By January, 1780, the General Court had authorized taxes totaling $40,781,000.[7] Eventually Massachusetts imposed heavier taxes than any other rebelling colony and collected many of them, particularly after 1781, in specie rather than in quartermaster's certificates, soldiers' pay certificates, or commodities, all of which were commonly accepted elsewhere.

The new taxes soon produced the kind of divisions earlier legislatures had feared. The massive levies and the assembly's deflationary policies united the interior rural towns against the coastal trading and eastern farming towns, which had relatively easy access to currency and specie with which to pay taxes; the interior towns, isolated from major markets, did not. Although the amount of the state poll tax was fixed and therefore presumably the same for an interior farmer and an eastern one, in practical terms that often was not the case, since the former had to expend more in produce or labor to obtain the specie and currency he had to have to pay the tax. And since one third of the new taxes fell on the polls, a tremendous share of the load was carried by the poor and middling sort, wherever they lived and whatever their occupations. They had been willing enough to accept poll taxes before the Revolution, when such taxes were low and relatively easy to pay, but the war changed that. By

1781, provincial taxes were more than ten times higher than they had been in 1774. Local taxes soared as well. Braintree's local taxes, for example, came to only £150 in 1774, but three years later they had increased ten times to £1,500, and by 1778 the town was £4,000 in debt.[8] The new taxes shattered the unity of the revolutionary movement in Massachusetts and helped divide the state into factions that were not reunited until afer Shays's Rebellion and the ratification of the United States Constitution in 1789.

Demands for reform followed hard upon the new tax and funding programs adopted in 1777 and were important motives behind the attempts to draft a new state constitution that began in Berkshire County early in the war. By 1778 many who demanded a new constitution were beginning to see a clear connection between existing property qualifications for voting and the revolutionary government's reluctance to reform the tax laws in general and to reduce the poll taxes in particular. The greatest burdens, Northampton voters complained, fell on the common people, "especially in time of war." And why? Because when the General Court considered taxes, "owners of a large property, generally upon such occasions strive to get the polls' share as high as they can; for they are fully sensible that it is their interest that the polls' share should not be low, for the higher that is the less will remain on the estates, and they conduct in the case accordingly." Should not the common and poor people "have some weight also who will always be subjects of legislation and taxation?" Was it just that "these poor adult persons . . . are always to be taxed as high as our men of property shall prevail to have them set, and their low pittances of day wages be taken to lighten the burden on property?" Would the independent government of Massachusetts, they asked, "treat these polls precisely as Britain intended and resolved to treat all the sons of America?"[9]

It was a good question, and after heavy taxes began in 1777, more people began asking it. Dorchester voters complained that members of the General Court were "all men of considerable property" who preferred to "lay too great a proportion on the polls, and by that means ease their estates and bring a heavy burden on those who have no power to remove it." The injustice was obvious, they explained, since no one could deny that "taxation and representation ought to be inseparable." The issue could hardly have been drawn more clearly. Other protesting towns warned that revolutionary actions justified by English oppression were equally available to those suffering from American oppression, for "unlimited passive obedience & Non-Resistance to any human power whatever is what we are now contending with Great Britain & to transfer that power to any other Body of Men is equally dangerous to our Security & Happiness."[10]

The two issues—democratization of government and tax reform—were also closely related for the men who opposed the movement for a new Massachusetts constitution. Such men, like John Adams, were often the ones who fought the drive for tax reform, and they saw the connection between property qualifications for voters and for officeholders and taxation as clearly as did their opponents but from the opposite direction. Eliminate property qualifications, they warned, and the poor men thus enfranchised and raised to office would "vote away the money of those that have estates." Theophilus Parsons put the conservatives' point succinctly: legislative majorities, he wrote, "should include those who possess a major part of the property of the state."[11]

The Massachusetts constitutional convention agreed, and the constitution of 1780 provided that no man might sit in the house of representatives unless he possessed a freehold estate worth £100 or other taxable property worth £200, and none might be a senator without a freehold estate worth £300 or other taxable property worth twice that. These precautions, John Adams and the convention explained, would keep power beyond the reach of "men who will pay less regard to the rights of property because they have nothing to lose." The members of the convention then made certain that there would be little significant reform under the new government. The existing tax system, including the poll taxes, was incorporated into the constitution itself. "The public charges of government or any part thereof," the new document decreed, "shall be assessed on polls and estates, in the manner that has been hitherto practiced."[12]

The constitution of 1780 precluded the elimination of poll taxes by any means short of constitutional amendment, but it left open the possibility of lowering them, and after 1780, tax reformers continued to demand that property and income provide more, and polls less, of the general revenues. They had little success. With the adoption of the new constitution, the eastern traders' and commercial farmers' alliance triumphed and quickly exploited its victory. Soon after the convention declared the new constitution ratified, even though it had not received the requisite number of favorable votes from the towns, the General Court attacked inflationary prodebtor policies that survived from preconstitution days. By the end of 1781 the legislature had refinanced the state debt, on terms extremely favorable to public creditors, and through specie taxes had provided for the eventual payment of the principal and interest in specie. The new funding system of 1781 thus passed the benefits of refunding to private and public creditors and rested the burden of the plan on the state's middling and poorer inhabitants, particularly on those in the interior counties, where specie was hard to come by.[13]

The advocates of poll tax reform had been so thoroughly whipped in the constitutional convention and in the General Court that the proportion of general tax revenues raised on polls actually increased after 1780. Before the Revolution, polls provided about one third of the total, and the provisional government after independence seemed content to keep things as they were. In February, 1779, for instance, the General Court authorized town assessors to lower the state poll tax within their towns until it brought in no more than one third of a town's provincial taxes. But the one-third poll tax ceiling was not included in tax legislation passed after the adoption of the constitution of 1780, and without it, the percentage raised on polls began to climb. More important, the burden on polls was proportionally greater in the less prosperous rural regions than elsewhere. In 1778, for example, polls accounted for 19.6 percent of the tax revenues raised in Suffolk County (which included Boston), 34 percent in Plymouth County, and 55.7 percent in western Berkshire County. By the end of the war (1784), the figure for Suffolk was 26.1 percent; for Plymouth, 40 percent; and for Berkshire, 43.7 percent. In other words, the poll taxes caused the greatest hardship in precisely those areas that were low in taxable wealth.[14]

The General Court, furthermore, tolerated loopholes in the law that helped shift taxes onto polls and off property. Before 1777, values built into the assessment acts assured that property would be rated at about one third of its market value. But by the spring of 1778 the assembly had dropped from the laws specified values for real property, leaving assessments up to assessors, who were to judge on the basis of current market worth. In theory, the new system would bring tax assessments into line with real values, but in fact, the assessors gave to real property the same two-thirds undervaluation previously secured by the laws. The system benefited owners of the most valuable land, and the heavy undervaluation of prime agricultural and other property was one reason polls were forced to carry so much of the tax load.[15]

By the end of 1780 the legislators' efforts to curb inflation and currency depreciation through heavy taxes were having an impact. As taxes rose, currency was withdrawn from circulation, making it even more difficult for many to pay the remaining taxes. After 1780 the burden fell more and more on the remote interior towns, and after 1781 the bulk of the tax complaints that regularly arrived in the legislature came from them. Soaring local taxes, which were also levied on polls and estates, further increased the burden on the poor and on the smaller farmers in the interior towns, and unrest followed. Taxes created the most discontent in Massachusetts, but creditors flocking to the newly opened state courts to collect old debts, the repeal of the legal tender laws, and the government's active attempts to collect taxes that had earlier been allowed to stand in arrears added to the problems of Massachusetts debtors and subsistence farmers.[16]

The trouble had been building since the first heavy war taxes of 1777. Robert Treat Paine then complained that the war taxes fell with uncommon severity on the common people, and he urged that some way be found to shift them, or at least some of them, to the wealthy. As early as the spring of 1779, Timothy Dwight warned that "the movement which forces small farmers to sell their real estate for the purpose of paying taxes will produce a revolution." Even Alexander Hamilton (no friend to lax collections) conceded that in Massachusetts, taxes were so heavy that "there were real marks of distress among some classes of the people."[17]

Governor John Hancock recognized the problem in 1781, when he told his assembly that tax reform was a matter of "particular importance to the internal peace and good temper, and consequently the safety of the commonwealth." The General Court, however, offered only piecemeal adjustments that did little to alleviate the problems. In November, 1781, and in 1782 it adopted an excise tax on wine, rum, brandy, tea, and coaches (primarily luxuries) and it increased imposts in 1783.[18]

Faced with heavy specie taxes they could not pay, debtors and others in several towns fell back on the revolutionary tactics they had used in the struggle with England: conventions and mob violence. In the spring of 1782, Governor Hancock reported "extremely alarming . . . disturbances" in Hampshire County. In Worcester County, protesters held two conventions to demand that farmers be allowed to pay taxes in commodities, and mobs rioted at tax sales and seized property from auctioneers to return it to the owners. At Taunton in July, 1782, a mob threatened anyone who dared bid for property at a tax sale.[19]

Unlike other state legislatures, the Massachusetts General Court, dominated by hard-money men, refused to go beyond token reforms in response to complaints, and conditions grew progressively worse. In 1782 Joseph Hawley reported that western Massachusetts, and perhaps the whole state, was ripe for a new revolution, and later he warned that the distress was spreading rapidly among the "middling people," who had heretofore supported government but who were now beginning to be "more distressed than the real poor." By the end of June, 1782, Hawley was near panic. He warned that there was no longer a threat of revolution in western Massachusetts, there was a revolution in fact. He advised against trying to put it down by force—the disaffected were too numerous—and he warned that it would be folly even to try to collect taxes without an army raised from the other states.[20]

Massachusetts newspapers reported publicly what Hawley wrote of privately. On October 24, 1782, for example, the Salem *Gazette* told of "an insurrection" in Berkshire County. One Enoch Marvin owed money to a Pittsfield man, and a deputy sheriff seized the debtor's yoke of oxen. Before the team could be appraised and auctioned off, Marvin and several friends "rescued the cattle." The sheriff issued warrants for their arrest and raised a posse to bring them in, but in the meantime Marvin and his friends called for help and got it. Thirty local farmers, having sworn to "resist all sheriffs and collectors in the levying Executions and collecting taxes," surprised the posse and "began a battle with clubs and staves." A leader of the mob, Thomas Lusk, and his brother advanced toward the high sheriff, "each armed with a heavy bludgeon cut for the purpose." Finally, twenty-one rioters were captured, tried, found guilty, and fined.

The rioters were quieted in 1782, but their grievances were not dealt with that year or the next, and the disaffection reappeared. In April, 1782, Hawley wrote a long letter, analyzing the problems of western Massachusetts and suggesting solutions. All certificates of public debt, particularly those given to soldiers in lieu of pay, must be made receivable for taxes, he warned, or the people would pay no taxes at all, and "there will not be men enough here to compel them to it." "If such people once make a stand," he predicted, "and absolutely refuse to pay their taxes, as you may be assured they are on the point of doing, there is no power short of continental and French soldiers that can compel them to it." This was not, Hawley wrote, "wild conjecture and guessing but events are at the door." The very people who had protected the local courts against rioters and tax delinquents were themselves "on the point of turning to the mob."[21]

Hawley's warnings and others like them were ignored, and after the war Massachusetts' tax system was if anything more regressive, more discriminatory, and farther from the ability-to-pay principle than it had been before. The revolutionary government refused to adopt either substantive reforms or short-term tax relief, and the problems that underlay the conventions, protests, and riots continued unabated. The General Court remained unresponsive during the depression that followed the peace in 1783, and those same problems grew worse, finally laying the foundations for Shays's Rebellion in 1786. Other New England governments faced the same problems, but although they were almost as reluctant as Massachusetts to reform their prewar tax systems, they were generally more willing to respond to public protests with some reforms and with short-term tax relief.

New Hampshire began war taxation sooner than the other New England colonies did. In July, 1774, an illegal session of the general assembly, meeting in a tavern, authorized a tax of £200, each town to pay in proportion to its share of the regular provincial rates. And in May, 1775, the provincial congress authorized a £3,000 tax to pay for raising and supplying an army.[22]

But as the probability of a long war and of independence grew, the revolutionary government prudently decided not to test its popularity by levying heavy taxes. Many New Hampshire men opposed independence, and Tory propagandists warned them— accurately, as it turned out—that independence would bring at least a tenfold increase in taxes. Would people prefer, asked "Junius" in January, 1776, "to be independent and pay 15 dollars tax, or to be in the condition we were in in 1762 and pay one?"[23] Even more disturbing, several New Hampshire frontier towns quickly challenged the new government, just as western towns in Massachusetts challenged the provisional government at Boston. The New Hampshire frontier towns complained that control of the government remained exactly where it had been before the war—in the hands of Rockingham County delegates, who represented the interests of the southeastern coastal and commercial farming towns. The protesting towns objected to property qualifications for voting and accused the provisional government of taxation without representation. Claiming that they were in a state of nature and were thus absolved of all obedience to the new government until they voluntarily agreed to a new constitution more in line with their understanding of the principles of the Revolution, the western towns touched off a debate over constitution writing that was not resolved until the end of the revolutionary war.[24]

Rather than endanger the fragile, uncertain unity of the rebellion in New Hampshire by trying to collect heavy taxes from a people accustomed to low levies, a people already too eager to challenge authority, the state's new leaders chose instead to issue paper money and to delay funding taxes until (in some cases) the 1790s. Taxes to redeem £20,000 issued in January, 1776, for instance, were to run from 1783 until 1786, and those to sink another £20,000 emitted in July were to begin in 1789 and run until 1792. Such taxes as the provincial congress did authorize, however, did not deviate from the assessment and collection practices of the past. New Hampshire's first state law guiding assessors, for example, virtually reproduced the old colonial assessment laws.[25]

By the end of 1777, however, New Hampshire began to tax heavily. The legislature authorized £40,000 to be raised on polls, estates, and faculties by the following March. By 1778, taxes reached £80,000; by 1779, £700,000; and by 1780 they had soared to £2,160,000. But at the same time, the government worked to make the levies somewhat more equitable than they had been before and more acceptable to backcountry taxpayers. In 1776 the new provisional government partially corrected the chronic undervaluation of commercial property in the colony by increasing valuations on improved land nearly 50 percent.[26] And in 1777, just as the heavy war taxes began, the assembly ordered a new general estimate, to bring assessments more into line with the actual distribution of wealth in the state, and it placed a tax on unimproved land—a reform the house had advocated twenty years earlier and the council, defending the interests of proprietors and land speculators, had rejected. Beginning in 1777, revolutionary New Hampshire taxed unimproved land at the same rate as money at interest, thus recognizing and taxing the increase in value of wilderness lands held for speculation. For the first time, this source of wealth and profit was included under the general tax laws.[27]

In 1780 the assembly lowered the value of polls for tax purposes from twelve shillings to ten, thus reducing the amount of money raised on polls in proportion to that raised on property. Finally, the new government responded to demands backcountry towns had been making for several years by permitting them to tax land owned by nonresident proprietors for the general province rates, country rates, and the special war taxes and to sell the land of any nonresident proprietor from whom they could not collect.[28] Town selectmen and assessors promptly began to tax nonresidents' land (in many cases, more heavily than residents' land), to condemn it for nonpayment, and to sell it at auction for a fraction of its worth. In the view of many settlers, loading taxes onto nonresident proprietors merely paid them back for the tax immunities they had long enjoyed, and raised tax money without further raising residents' rates. And through seizures and sales, land was made available at bargain rates to actual settlers. Nonresident proprietors complained, of course, and eventually discrimination against them became so blatant that the assembly again restricted the towns' taxing powers. The restrictions, though, were often ignored, and the tax haven that speculators had enjoyed in New Hampshire was effectively destroyed during the war. At the same time, the assembly redistributed taxes somewhat by adopting new luxury taxes on wines, rum, and brandies.[29]

Such reforms became necessary as the war drove taxes to levels not even Tories had predicted. Peterborough, for example, paid only £29 in provincial taxes in 1775, but by 1780 it paid over £15,000 (and 5 percent of that in specie). Even if inflation is taken into account, the town's taxes had increased more than thirteen times over what they had been before independence. The new taxes brought increasing trouble with taxpayers who could not pay, and with collectors who could not or would not collect, especially in the frontier settlements. By 1781, tax refusals, delinquencies, and malfeasance had driven arrearages statewide to nearly £400,000. Some towns tried to avoid paying by not electing assessors or collectors. With the offices vacant, they reasoned, the taxes could not be collected. In April, 1781, the assembly countered by making the property of each individual in a delinquent town liable for the whole amount the town owed and by authorizing state and county treasurers to sue any two or more residents of a delinquent town, "as they shall judge proper," and to seize and sell their property for the town's taxes. The unfortunates so chosen could then sue the rest of the town to recover their losses plus damages and expenses.[30]

The new war taxes eventually drove some interior towns to the point of rebellion. In 1780, residents of Conway explained the particular problems of backcountry settlers everywhere in New England (and in the rest of the states as well). This "is a Frontier Town," they explained to the New Hampshire legislature,

> Ninety Miles distant from Sea-Port, Fifty Miles whereof are through a Wilderness almost uninhabited; that the great Distance from Market, & Badness of Roads (especially in the Winter Season) render the Transportation of Produce, & Other Articles of Commerce exceeding difficult & costly; that your Petitioners have no other Means to raise Money but by the Common Produce of the Land, & transporting the Same to Market, and for the Reasons aforesaid, the neat Proceeds thereof are not more than one Third Part of the current Price at Market; that the incidental Casualties & Charges of settling a new Township, together with the Distresses of the present War, have rendered your Petitioners extremely poor.

In all the town, they claimed, there was not enough money to pay even one quarter of the taxes demanded of them. Under such circumstances, many began to ask a question that would be asked with greater frequency and growing urgency throughout the states after 1783: with what justice could the revolutionary governments seize and sell for taxes the land and homes of men who had fought to establish those governments? "We are a frunteer place," explained the all but illiterate selectmen of Bath, "whear we have often ben cold out in Scouts &c &c," and "mose of us ben more or les in the war for sence the commencement." More than half "the inhabitance of this town," they added, "do not Raise thare provision and are abliged to work for it by the Day in other towns and tharefor unable to cultivate thare one lands and many have no land attole." Under such conditions, their taxes could not be paid, and they begged for relief. The town of Bedford, in the Merrimack Valley, echoed another complaint that might have been heard anywhere in the backcountry from Georgia to New England: its money went east in taxes and disappeared without visible benefit to the community and without any accounting. Bedford demanded that the state's legislative journals be published regularly and sent to the towns, "to the Intent we may know what we Pay our Money for."[31] In January, 1781, forty-three western towns in the Connecticut River valley, complaining that they were overtaxed and underrepresented, met in convention at Charlestown and resolved to secede from New Hampshire and to join the embryonic state of Vermont, whereafter many of them refused to pay any more New Hampshire taxes. Even those who opposed secession thought the disaffected towns were being taxed more heavily than their primitive and isolated condition warranted.[32]

The western towns were certain that such overtaxation was the direct result of malapportionment. But what constituted fair representation was a matter of debate. The Revolution swept away the colony's malapportioned legislature and substituted one based roughly on population. In many colonies, such changes benefited the western regions at the expense of eastern ones, but not in New Hampshire, where the bulk of the population lived in the southeastern towns. As far as the western towns were concerned, the new distribution of representatives among the towns left control of the assembly largely where it had been, in eastern hands. Western towns with fewer than one hundred freeholders had to combine with other towns in order to be represented at all, which they considered a violation of the principle of no taxation without representation. They demanded instead representation by towns rather than by population.[33]

New Hampshire's constitution, adopted in 1776, produced legislatures that spoke clearly for rural interests. The majority of the members, however, were from commercial farming towns that prospered during the war, and they had no great desire to adopt laws or policies that would, in their view, damage the state's commerce. In 1780 and 1781 the assembly, adopting an economic policy similar to Massachusetts', refunded the state debt on terms favorable to creditors, provided for specie taxes, and ended the legal tender status of previous paper emissions. But the assembly cushioned the shock of this deflationary policy with short-run relief measures such as abating some poll taxes and occasionally accepting commodities in payment. In January, 1782, for instance, the assembly adopted a £110,000 general poll and property tax, but resolved to accept in payment specie, treasurer's certificates for interest on the public debt, or several kinds of paper, as well as commodities, including beef, rum, and flour. And after March, 1782, soldiers' pay certificates were acceptable in lieu of specie as well.[34]

These relief laws did not, of course, solve New Hampshire's economic problems, and by the end of the war, towns were inundating the legislature with pleas for tax suspensions, more paper money, and laws making commodities a tender for private debts as well as public taxes.[35] Eventually, as a postwar depression drove farm prices down, the rumblings of discontent that so frightened Joseph Hawley in Massachusetts appeared in New Hampshire as well, and by the 1780s the state faced an incipient Shaysite rebellion of its own.[36] Nevertheless, the Revolution and the heavy taxes that came with it created conditions that made possible important reforms in the old colonial revenue system. Among the reforms that had not been politically acceptable before were an increase in the assessed value of improved land, new taxes on unimproved land, a reduction in the poll taxes, and extended taxes on nonresident proprietors. Taken together, these changes left New Hampshire's revenue system at the end of the war more in line with the ability-to-pay principle than it had been before. And demands for reforms continued long after the peace.

English armies never invaded New Hampshire, and once the British withdrew from Boston, Massachusetts was spared invasion and occupation for the remainder of the war. Rhode Island was not so fortunate. British forces captured and occupied Newport and the surrounding territories in 1777 and, from there, struck out to raid Rhode Island's mainland towns and to disrupt its seaborne commerce. By occupying Newport, the British altered the pattern of Rhode Island politics permanently. Revolution, war, and invasion all but destroyed Newport as a major commercial and political center and did away with the vestiges of the Ward-Hopkins factional divisions. After British occupation, Newporters had either to flee and become refugees or to remain and become at best passive collaborators of the royal military administration or at worst outright Tories. In either case, their political influence virtually disappeared for a time, as did the economic strength on which much of that influence rested. War damage in Newport alone totaled nearly £125,000 sterling, and the city's population fell almost 40 percent during the struggle. Newport did not return to its prewar population level until the nineteenth century. Other southern towns, subject to British raid or capture, suffered nearly as much.[37]

The conflict did, however, quickly establish a new basis of factional politics in Rhode Island. The rivalry between rural agricultural towns and the commercial centers, which had occasionally complicated politics before 1775, became a major division in state politics, and by 1783 it had become central to debates over economic policy and taxation. It remained the focus of internal politics until after Rhode Island ratified the United States Constitution. In fact, the conditions created by the Revolution and independence made the split between farmer and merchant, town and country, deeper and the resulting struggles over taxation more bitter than either had been before.

At first, the Revolution brought little change to Rhode Island's government or taxes. The new state did not even draft a constitution. It simply carried on under its old colonial charter after removing the embarrassing presence of a king's name on that document by just crossing it out. In Rhode Island, as in nearly every colony, legislators at first tried to keep as many of the old familiar laws as possible, to hold as closely as they could to the old familiar procedures. They hoped, for instance, to raise money by taxing the usual things—polls, estates, and the income from faculties, trades, and professions—in the usual ways, and they even planned to base assessments on the prewar general estimates.[38]

It was not possible. With trade disrupted by British blockade and raiding and with war expenses soaring, the towns demanded a new general estimate that would reflect changes since 1767 and "the present state of affairs" so that taxes could be distributed fairly. Accordingly, in October, 1776, a legislative committee began preparing recommendations for a new distribution of public taxes. But revising general estimates was a tough and lengthy process, even in the best of times, which these were not, and the new revolutionary government tried to put off the potentially divisive task as long as it could by raising money through paper emissions and borrowing. The war paper emission of September, 1776, for instance, contained no funding provisions, nor were funding taxes adopted when the assembly decided to borrow £30,000 in December, 1776, and another £50,000 in February, 1777. Another loan of £40,000, approved in late December, 1776, pledged a tax on polls and estates within two years sufficient to redeem the debt plus interest, but the legislature could cancel the tax if it thought collection "impracticable"—hardly an iron-clad guarantee of redemption.[39] Once war taxes began, the divisions feared by the government developed rapidly, and to some extent the assembly fell again into its old habits. It appointed committees to take new general estimates, then revoked their authority, then appointed new committees, then passed taxes on the basis of old estimates, along with promises to make refunds and additional assessments where necessary, once new estimates were completed. The towns also began (as they had in the colonial period) to pay taxes according to whatever recent estimate they most favored, and to refuse to pay or to pay only reluctantly, and with loud complaint, according to those estimates they did not favor.[40]

Substantial war taxation began in March, 1777, when Rhode Island passed its first general state tax law of the Revolution. It called for collection of £16,000 and was a patchwork of expedient compromises hastily thrown together. But the law established two important precedents. It included no significant tax reforms, no major restructuring of the poll and general property taxes of the late colonial period. And it provoked the first major clash between the rural towns and the port of Providence over taxes.

By the time the law passed, Rhode Island faced invasion. The assembly was committed to a new general estimate of taxable property and polls, but the taxes were needed for defense immediately. To avoid delay, Providence delegates agreed to accept an arbitrary addition of £100,000 to the town's 1767 assessed valuation. In return, they got a pledge that the increase would not be used as a precedent for later taxes and would be altered to conform to the new general estimate once it was completed. But after getting Providence to accept a higher share of state taxes, the country towns were not disposed to reduce that share, their delegates' pledges notwithstanding. The £32,000 tax of August, 1777, left Providence's proportion unaltered and the £100,000 added valuation undiminished. The tax law passed in December retained three quarters of the arbitrary addition, and the February, 1778, law retained half of it.[41]

Providence assemblymen roared out in complaint. The added £100,000 was, they argued, purely "conjectural" and "manifestly unequal," and they reminded the assembly, without much effect, of its pledge that the addition would not be admitted as precedent. They looked upon the violation of that pledge as a raid by country farmers upon the pockets of Providence merchants and craftsmen. "It's an old maxim," they explained, "that mankind are not to be trusted where they are interested against you, and it is equally true that they are not to act in matters whereof they are ignorant." Since the assembly was both "interested against" Providence and ignorant of the true distribution of taxable wealth in the state, the arbitrary, excessive taxation of Providence was unconstitutional and a violation of the principles of the Revolution, for it savored much of "those capricious and arbitrary measures of raising money from their subjects adopted by absolute monarchs." Instead of paying the disputed portion of its 1777–1778 rates, Providence ordered its treasurer to pay only what the town would have paid if the 1767 estimate had been followed, and directed him to go to jail rather than pay any more. Not until the assembly agreed, finally, to the long-demanded new estimate did Providence pay in the money it had withheld.[42]

As the Revolution progressed, however, it was the mainland country towns that began to complain about unjust taxation and the commercial towns that seemed to them privileged. The war forced the mainland rural towns of Rhode Island to assume a large proportion of the war costs, far heavier than that shouldered by similar towns in New Hampshire, Connecticut, or even Massachusetts. British invasion and occupation in Rhode Island devastated the economy and eroded the tax base. The new state lost nearly 12 percent of its population in the struggle, and for several years some of the most prosperous towns—Newport, Middletown, Jamestown, New Shoreham, and Portsmouth—were eliminated from the tax rolls completely. The government not only lost the taxes from the occupied or often-raided towns but also had to tax the remaining towns for money to care for refugees. Some of the towns involved did not go back onto the tax rolls until well after 1780.[43]

As early as 1778, travelers reported that Rhode Island taverns and farmhouses were "full of complaints" about the "enormity of taxes which they said must very soon ruin them." By the spring of the following year, Governor William Greene, a well-to-do merchant himself and for the most part an advocate of fiscal orthodoxy and sound finance, feared that Rhode Islanders were reaching the limit of what they could pay. So expensive had the war become, he told Rhode Island's delegates in Congress, that of the £76,000 in taxes collected in the last six months no more than £100 "passable money" remained in the treasury. The "burthen" he warned, was becoming "heavier than the inhabitants can bear."[44] By 1780—the year Rhode Island added £420,000 to its existing £360,000 tax program in an ill-fated attempt to comply with Congress' plan to refinance Continental currency at forty to one—towns were refusing to cooperate with collectors and assessors, and rural residents were refusing to bid on their neighbors' property when its was auctioned for taxes. The problem became so serious that the assembly authorized sheriffs to carry condemned property to other towns, where presumably strangers would bid for it seriously. Some towns reappointed collectors and assessors notoriously lax about their work; others tried to avoid taxes by not appointing those officers at all.[45]

As the rates rose dramatically and inexorably, many Rhode Islanders began to question both the equity of the levies and the justice of the political system that produced them. In 1777, for example, the residents of Scituate demanded (unsuccessfully) that representation in the assembly be based on population and the proportion of taxes a town paid to the treasury. They expected such reforms to produce a more equitable distribution of taxes in the state, and they realized—just as reformers in Massachusetts did—that there was little hope of redistributing taxes without first redistributing power in the general assembly. Scituate, for instance, ranked third in population and eighth in taxable wealth, according to the general estimate taken in 1777, and it had two representatives in the assembly. But Portsmouth, which, according to the general estimate of 1782, had about one third of Scituate's population and ranked twenty-fourth in taxable wealth, had four representatives. As the taxes soared the rural towns complained that there was a direct and obvious connection between the overrepresentation of certain towns and their relatively low assessed valuations, just as there was between the underrepresentation of towns like Scituate and

Gloucester and their high taxes. By the third year of the war, the problem of fairly distributing taxes led the rural towns into the movement for constitutional reform, exactly as had happened in Massachusetts. In fact, from the rural farming towns' point of view, success in the war made their problems worse and the inequity of the taxes more pronounced. By 1782 the British had withdrawn from all the occupied towns except New Shoreham (on Block Island in Long Island Sound), and that meant that Newport was again represented in the assembly with all of its six delegates, even though it now had only a fraction of its former population. Other prosperous captured towns, which had a low proportion of voters to delegates, were back as well. In 1782, for instance, Jamestown (Newport County) had one representative for every 173 residents, while Gloucester, an interior rural town in northwest Providence County, had one delegate for every 1,396 residents.[46]

As in Massachusetts and New Hampshire, the aggrieved towns began to apply the principles of the Revolution as they understood them to their own situations, and it is scarcely surprising that they saw a direct connection between taxation and representation or that they argued that there could not possibly be equity in one without equity in the other. "Taxation and representation," explained delegates from four towns, "ever ought to go hand in hand, an idea an American ought never to depart from." If the Revolution meant anything at all, explained representatives of North Kingstown and South Kingstown in 1779, it meant that "taxation . . . ought to be free and voluntary and equal upon every part which receives protection, agreeable to the abilities of the individuals or towns at large who receive benefit thereby." And, they added, "whenever that ceases, uneasiness and discontent prevail, and sooner or later that government, which imposes unequal assessments upon the inhabitants must be imbroiled in trouble and difficulty."[47]

"Agreeable to the abilities of the individuals": thus did the North and South Kingstown delegates incorporate the ability-to-pay principle into the principles of the American Revolution, and thus did they, by implication at least, warn that an American government violating those principles might find the same "trouble and difficulty" an English government had faced. The warning, unheeded, became prophecy.

By May, 1781, so many town treasurers were in jail for failing to collect their quotas that the assembly released them all to give them a chance to make collections, an expedient it had to adopt several times during the war. Towns complained endlessly that they could not pay. South Kingstown reported in January, 1782 "one universal scene of distress" because people were so "greatly oppressed and burthened with taxes." Their livestock had been seized and sold and their livelihoods threatened. The assembly's attempts to tighten collections only made things worse. Collectors, for instance, normally seized personal property, not real estate, for taxes, but in May, 1781, the assembly authorized them to sell land owned by delinquent taxpayers in four towns because there was "not sufficient personal estate" to pay the rates. And in June, 1782, the assembly ordered assessors to condemn and sell landlords' land if the tenants, who were responsible for the taxes, did not have enough real or personal property in their own right to clear the tax.[48]

There was a certain grim irony in the situation. Rhode Island's poorer farmers, craftsmen, and tradesmen, tenants and freeholders alike, faced losing their livestock, their tools, their very livelihood, and in some cases their homes and land (if they owned them), all in the name of paying taxes to a revolutionary government that had been born in a struggle against arbitrary and excessive taxes. But if the situation was ironic, it was also explosive. By the spring of 1782 some towns in Washington County (formerly Kings County) began taking steps against the Rhode Island government that were uncomfortably similar to the actions preceding rebellion against England. In April, delegates from several towns met in convention at South Kingstown and petitioned the general assembly for revised election laws and for tax reforms. Every town in the county supported a call for a constitutional convention to revise the charter, but the assembly refused to act.[49]

Finally it came to violence. The discontent and sullen anger, which had flared in Massachusetts and New Hampshire, now appeared in Rhode Island as well. Furious farmers, who faced losing their property at tax sales, rioted. Even more frightening, the Rhode Island troubles showed that the disaffected in New England were beginning to cooperate across state lines, that hard-pressed farmers from Connecticut, Massachusetts, and Rhode Island were beginning to organize and to march to each other's aid against tax collectors and sheriffs.

In the autumn of 1782 several Gloucester farmers "rescued" some cattle that had been seized by the sheriff of Providence County for taxes. The rioters were eventually arrested, and it developed in the course of the investigation that several men from Massachusetts were involved. Deputy Governor Jabez Bowen wrote to Massachusetts Governor John Hancock, describing the alarming situation. Hancock may have been annoyed at the novel suggestion that Massachusetts men were corrupting Rhode Islanders (most Bay Colony people thought corruption generally flowed the other way) or his pride may have rebelled at corresponding with a mere deputy governor. In any case, Hancock never replied, and the situation deteriorated. The arrest of the Gloucester rioters merely made things worse, for a new mob, composed of men from Massachusetts and Rhode Island, attacked the jail in which the rioters were being held and freed them.[50]

By February, 1783, the rioting had become serious enough that the assembly could no longer ignore it. The members demanded a full investigation and ordered Governor William Greene to write to Governor Hancock and "acquaint him with the disorderly and riotous behaviour of sundry of the inhabitants of the towns of Uxbridge, Douglas, Dudley," and other Massachusetts towns "in coming into this state and violently rescuing certain prisoners from the civil authority." They wanted Hancock informed also of "the unlawful assemblies which are frequently had of sundry disaffected and evil-minded persons living in the towns aforesaid, the towns in this state, and the state of Connecticut, adjacent to said towns, for the purpose of obstructing the collection of taxes."[51]

Greene wrote to Hancock on February 28, and added more to the story. The ringleader of the raid on the jail had been "one Tourtellot," who had since been arrested and jailed. The angry farmers, Greene now reported, were holding meetings with "an avowed design to release Tourtellot, and to put a total stop to the payment of taxes." They were giving out "the most daring menaces," and they came from Connecticut as well as Massachusetts and Rhode Island. They had become so bold, Greene went on, as to post notices for a public meeting to be held in Gloucester to make plans. The high sheriff of Providence County, accompanied by "a sufficient armed force," broke up the meeting and captured fourteen of the conspirators, six of them Massachusetts men. Both Greene and his assembly asked that the states cooperate to suppress such challenges to all government," which "might lead to the most unhappy consequences."[52]

There were some who saw the problems building far in advance. "It will be good policy," Nathanael Greene explained to Samuel Ward in December, 1775, just as the war began, "to render the poorer sort of people as easy and as happy under present circumstances as possible, for they are creatures of a day, and present gain and gratification, though small, have more weight with them than much greater advantages at a distance." A good politician, he continued, "will consider the temper of the times and the prejudices" of the people when he takes "measures to execute any great design."[53] Greene's advice was well suited to the situation after 1780. It was all very well to tell the rioters in Gloucester (or in Massachusetts, the great valley of Virginia, or the Pennsylvania hill country) that in the long run they and their nation would benefit from the strict enforcement of high taxes, but they faced the immediate loss of their property and livelihoods, and they acted accordingly.

The revolutionary government of Rhode Island never did respond fully to the demands for fundamental reform that came from the protesting towns, but it did enact a series of tax reform and relief measures that, taken together, brought the new state's revenue system closer to the ability-to-pay ideal than it had been, making the system somewhat easier to bear. War tax laws, for instance, commonly exempted soldiers from poll taxes, which was prudent, to say the least. And by 1780, tax laws regularly permitted local assessors to "consider the circumstances of the poor, in their respective towns, and exempt from the poll tax such as they think unable to pay the same."[54] The assembly briefly permitted each town to determine for itself the size of its poll taxes. The tax act of February, 1778, established a £32,000 poll and general property tax, to be "assessed upon the inhabitants of this state, [and] to be levied on the present possessors of land." The law set the poll tax at sixteen shillings, payable by all men over twenty-one except ministers and soldiers, but it gave the towns the power to "reduce the poll tax to such sum as they shall think fit, so far as affects the inhabitants of such town." Since the towns could not lower their tax quotas under the law, any town that chose to lower its poll taxes had to make up the difference by the property tax. The experiment lasted less than two years. By 1780, Rhode Island had abandoned the local-option poll tax and reestablished a uniform statewide poll tax, though there were local exemptions for those too poor to pay.[55]

In spite of its postwar reputation for irresponsible finance, the revolutionary government of Rhode Island tried, at least until it rejected the congressional impost plan in 1781, to comply with Congress' requisitions and the various schemes to save the Continental currency and the nation's internal credit. And yet, by the end of 1780, the assembly had reluctantly recognized that heavy taxes, the disruption of trade, and a growing specie scarcity made it impossible for many to pay, however much they may have wanted to. And thereafter, Rhode Island never held to a specie standard in taxation quite as rigidly as did Massachusetts. Rhode Island accepted a wide range of paper including soldiers' pay certificates for taxes and began granting multiple tax extensions to towns and pushing the "final day" for various collections back farther and farther.

The £20,000 specie tax adopted in June, 1783, is a good example. It was originally to have been collected by December,

1783. In October the assembly made half the tax payable in supply certificates rather than specie. In February, 1784, it put the final collection date off until May, and in May it gave collectors another month after the close of the legislative session, to complete their work. In June the assembly ordered sheriffs to stop suing town treasurers for the tax until two months after the session ended, but resolved that the final day would not be postponed again. But in August, collectors received still another extension.[56]

In November, 1782, with the Gloucester riots fresh in mind, a ways and means committee recommended to the assembly that "a considerable sum might be raised" by excise taxes on "those articles which are generally consumed by the rich and affluent." Such items, the committee argued, "should be rated as high as they will conveniently bear, that the industrous farmer and mechanic may be relieved." In February the legislators laid excises on a long list of luxury items, including wines, brandies, snuff, sugar, chocolate, silver, gold, coaches, jewelry, silks, and mirrors. In less than a year, however, they abandoned luxury excises in favor of a 2 percent tariff on all imported goods grown or manufactured in a foreign state.[57]

To the extent that the tariff held down subsequent poll taxes, it was an important reform, for the imposts (passed on to consumers through higher prices) were linked roughly to ability to pay. The poor and the middling sort, who had farms to work but little specie to spend, obviously could not purchase much (or so the argument went), while the wealthy and well-to-do could and they would thereby pay a greater proportion of the tax. Hard-pressed rural towns quickly saw in the state impost plan their best hope for reducing poll and property rates. Seven towns in Washington County met in convention in April, 1784, to denounce Rhode Island's tax system as inequitable and oppressive and to demand that the tariff on imports be raised to 5 percent. Seven other towns concurred, but assembly spokesmen for the commercial towns and the merchant community held the increase to only 5 percent.[58]

Rhode Island's one major tax reform during the revolutionary period, the impost plan, had important consequences for both the state and the new nation. The state's commercial and farming towns were driven farther apart as the latter came to see in high state tariffs a way to avoid the heavy poll and land taxes and to shift the burden to the more prosperous port towns. And many in the poorer rural towns saw a threat in the Continental Congress' efforts to win the impost power for itself. If Congress got that power, they reasoned, and Rhode Island thereby lost the income from its state tariffs, the poll and property taxes must inevitably rise. And some feared as well that once Congress got the power to tax in any form, it would impose a federal land tax and a federal poll tax.[59]

Except for the impost, though, the Revolution had little impact on the structure of Rhode Island's tax laws: the old colonial general property and poll taxes remained the mainstays of the revenue system throughout the war. But the Revolution created conditions that altered the politics of Rhode Island taxation beyond recognition. The equity of the revenue laws—the inherent fairness of the general poll and property taxes—had been accepted before 1775 with little visible protest, as had the colony's charter and the uneven distribution of votes in the assembly. Taxes were low, the burden relatively light, and most complaints from the towns spoke not of inherently unjust laws but of just laws unjustly applied. But the massive war taxes, far heavier than anyone had expected or feared, threw the inequities of the laws into bold relief, and the quiet acquiescence with which Rhode Islanders had treated their colonial taxes began to evaporate. As the war progressed, legislative struggles over taxes became, more and more, battles between merchant and farmer and, in a broader sense, between the wealthy on the one hand and the poor and the small farmers on the other. The war taxes lay behind much of the drive for political and financial reform in Rhode Island after 1776, and the divisions that grew out of that struggle remained at the center of Rhode Island politics during the troubled decade that followed the peace in 1783.[60]

Revolution both unified Connecticut and divided it. Like Rhode Island, the new state continued under its old colonial charter after independence and underwent only minor changes in leadership. Governor Jonathan Trumbull, who had first been elected in 1769, remained in office through the war until 1784, when he retired at the age of seventy-three.[61] But unlike Rhode Island, Connecticut remained largely free from invasion and so did not have the problem of shifting taxes from occupied towns to the remaining rebelling ones, or of reapportioning taxes among many devastated towns when the British withdrew. Yet for all Connecticut's political continuity and homogeneity, the war and war taxes created bitter political divisions that had little to do with the prewar political alignments. Debate over revenues ranged merchants against farmers and (as the taxes rose) the poor and struggling of whatever occupation against the prospering and wealthy.

Connecticut mobilized rapidly for war under Governor Trumbull's direction. Within a month of the battle of Lexington, Connecticut was on a war footing, with soldiers en route to the Continental army at Cambridge, supplies accumulating (at an unexpectedly high cost), and one fourth of the militia called up.[62] To pay for it all, Trumbull's revolutionary government issued £50,000 in currency in May, 1775, another £50,000 in June, £50,000 more in July, and another £110,000 in June 1776. The entire sum was to be retired by annual taxes on polls, property, and faculties, beginning in May, 1777, the year after the last of the prewar sinking-fund taxes lapsed.[63]

But after long years of easy rates indifferently enforced, Connecticut's people were ill prepared for heavy taxes rigorously collected. The state had problems with collections almost immediately and had to deal with serious discontent over taxes early in the war. By the end of 1777, newspapers carried collectors' pleas to taxpayers to settle accounts. "Gentlemen," pleaded collector Samuel Holliston in December, 1777, "what shall I say to you? I have advertised three times. . . . I have flattered and invited for a long time. . . . Yet all to no purpose; this will be the last time, for your rates are now on interest and I must collect them immediately, be it Whigs or Tories." As happened elsewhere, towns underrated their taxable wealth, and state and local officials worked out, when they could, mutually profitable ways to alter assessments. Sometimes the laws themselves made evasion simple. A tax adopted in 1779, for instance, provided that each man should pay a tax on the cash he actually had on hand on August 20. Merchants and others in the commercial community simply made certain that they and their cash were elsewhere when the grim day came, and thus avoided the tax. Eventually the assembly revised the law.[64]

From the first, Connecticut tried to head off serious trouble from the two groups that felt the weight of the war taxes most heavily and complained the loudest: the army and the poor. In May, 1776, after the council of safety reported "great uneasiness" among Connecticut's Continental soldiers because they had trouble collecting their pay, the assembly ordered collectors not to collect taxes from soldiers away on duty but to await "a more convenient season." And in December the assembly told collectors "not to enforce the collection immediately on such as are not now of sufficient ability to discharge the same." In 1778 the state abated the poll taxes of Continental soldiers for the duration of their service, and by the war's end, tax laws regularly permitted assessors to abate the taxes of those too poor to pay, provided such abatements totaled no more than 5 percent of a town's taxes. And Connecticut eventually adopted, as did most states, tax rebates for towns that suffered British raids, and accepted for taxes a variety of state and Continental currency emissions and certificates of debt, including army supply and pay certificates.[65]

Heavy war taxes began in 1777 and were rapidly followed by demands for fundamental tax reforms and complaints that "men of superior interest and property" dominated the government and were blocking reform because they knew it would "sensibly increase their own taxes." In short, the equity of the tax laws, questioned but rarely before independence, began to be challenged loudly once the war began. Connecticut taxes were supposedly based on the ability-to-pay principle, and by 1778, petitioners began to demand that supposition and reality be brought at last into line. The existing taxes were "very unequal," New

Haven's delegates said, because they violated the ability-to-pay principle. "Many men of small estates and large families," the town complained, "who can barely maintain themselves and their families from one end of the year to the other, pay larger taxes than some of the most affluent fortunes." The house tax, for example, took no account of whether a building was new or old, in good repair or dilapidated, or was in the country or near a town. "The poorest sort very sensibly feel the burden" of such discriminatory taxes, the petitioners warned, and "it will very soon become intolerable."[66]

During the war, Connecticut became an important supply center for armies fighting elsewhere, and when British occupation closed the ports of New York and Newport, and British blockade restricted trade at Providence and Boston, the Connecticut commercial community (which had long struggled in the shadow of neighboring seaports) began to grow. By 1780 it had become a powerful force in the state legislature.[67] Nevertheless, in 1777 the assembly that grappled with tax reform was still largely agrarian, and it responded to demands for reform in ways pleasing to farmers and alarming to merchants. In August it directed assessors to list money at interest, less what a man paid interest for, in the tax lists at 6 percent of the principal, and imposed an excess war profits tax on traders who hoarded goods and raised prices to "make great gains to themselves." The same law, declaring that all persons ought to be taxed "in proportion to the value of their estates *and* annual incomes," expanded the faculty tax and provided that tradesmen, merchants, professionals, artisans, and all others on the faculty tax should pay not only for the "clear annual profits" of their professions but also for their "polls and rateable estates . . . any law, usage or custom to the contrary notwithstanding."[68]

Principles were one thing, however, and practices another, and such piecemeal reforms did little to mitigate the most regressive holdover from the colonial period, the poll tax. Demands for fundamental reform continued and grew louder as the taxes grew heavier. Towns complained that in spite of some reforms, the burden of the war still fell with intolerable severity on small farmers and on the poor. Norwich petitioners wanted the state's patchwork revenue system of several different tax rates and methods of assessment for different kinds of income, property, and wealth replaced by one uniform system of assessments so that the value of a man's "whole estate" might be added up and his taxes apportioned accordingly. As early as the fall of 1778, when disgruntled taxpayers called a convention in Litchfield County to demand changes, collectors reported being threatened with death "or worse" by rioters if they tried to collect, and some had to ask for military protection. In October a Norwich town meeting denounced the poll tax as an "insupportable burden on the poor" and, seeing the same connections between taxation and representation other New Englanders did, charged that oppressive taxes continued because property qualifications for voting rendered powerless precisely those people the poll taxes distressed the most.[69]

In January, 1779, Connecticut legislators began another reform program that struck directly at some of the old inequities and that moved the state closer to the ability-to-pay standard. The assembly halved poll taxes for men between sixteen and twenty-one and ordered unenclosed wilderness land put into the tax lists for the first time at 5 percent of its market value. This undoubtedly cost all farmers something, but it cost speculators and owners of large tracts more than it did subsistence farmers and small resident owners. The assembly also levied a tax on all money over £50 in anyone's possession on August 20 and expanded taxes on luxury items like carriages, gold and silver plate, and watches.[70]

Taken as a whole, the reforms reflected the growing conviction among the farming towns that the merchant community's tax havens, which had been acceptable enough during the low taxes of the late colonial years, were acceptable no longer. But for many, even these reforms did not go far enough because they were "not done . . . upon that general principle which as we apprehend, is the only equitable one" for collecting taxes: the ability-to-pay principle. The new laws, even with all the reforms included, Norwich argued in March, 1779, were still "inconsistent with the first principle of equity" because they applied a double standard. Farmers' property, such as cattle and swine, was assessed at virtually full market value, but money at interest went into the lists "not according to its value but according to profit." A cow, petitioners complained, and £100 loaned out at interest were both income-producing property. Why should the cow go into the farmer's ratable estate at or near full market value, while money on loan went into the merchant's ratable estate at only 6 percent of its value? By current law, they pointed out, six yearling pigs were rated at £6 (£1 each), and £100 loaned out at interest was also rated at £6 (6 percent of the principal). The law thus presumed six yearling pigs to be as valuable as £100, which was ridiculous and unfair. One standard, they insisted, ought to apply to all incomes and all property. The Norwich town meeting that made these demands ordered its proceedings published and sent to every town in the state.[71]

The reforms of 1778 and 1779 were more cosmetic than substantive, for poll taxes continued to bring in about one third of the general tax revenues. Poll, improved land, and livestock taxes together brought in more than 90 percent of the revenues, while building taxes, faculty taxes, rates on luxury items, wild land, stock-in-trade, money at interest, and several other taxes combined brought in less than 10 percent[72] (Appendix, table 22).

The assembly continued to get bitter complaints about the inequity of the revenue laws, and it continued to make marginal reforms in line with agrarian demands until 1780. In May, 1779, for instance, legislators cut by two thirds the taxes on money at interest and money in hand, but raised taxes on merchants' stock-in-trade 150 percent. They also increased the number of "classes" into which land could be divided for tax purposes, thus permitting assessments to reflect more closely the relative value of each tract. They reformed the house tax, basing assessments on the type of construction (brick or wood), the condition of the house (in good repair or "decayed by age"), and the number of floors and square feet of space. Finally, they adopted new taxes on warehouses, as well as on stores and traders' shops, none of which had been taxed before the war. But barns remained tax free.[73]

Such reforms alarmed the Connecticut merchant community and helped drive merchants into active politics. By 1780 the state's merchant and commercial interests had mounted a successful campaign to increase their influence in the legislature, which was soon reflected in changing tax policy as the assembly began to undo some of its earlier reforms. In May, 1780, it eliminated the tax on stock-in-trade and abolished the graduated house tax to return to the older system. These changes produced a new wave of agrarian protests and a new round of charges that farmers were being bled dry by the property taxes and the poor by the poll taxes, while those on the faculty rates escaped lightly.[74]

By the spring of 1782, Connecticut faced the possibility of violence over taxes. "Will the people any longer sit quietly" under these oppressive taxes? asked one newspaper essayist. "Will the farmer be content" while the "merchant or man of faculty" reduces him to "as abject a condition as those in some of the northern parts of Europe where a peasant, a farmer, is in little better repute than a slave?"[75] In the spring of 1782, with rioting over taxes already threatened or occurring in Rhode Island and Massachusetts, the implications of that kind of rhetoric were painfully clear.

Those who defended the existing revenue laws, and the low rates on merchants' property, generally portrayed themselves as defenders of order and stressed the importance of obeying the law. They portrayed tax reformers as secret Tories, out to create dissension and division for their own dark purposes. "A Lover of Order," writing in the *Connecticut Gazette* in April, warned against "the excessive fondness for innovation and change" that was unfortunately so "universally prevalent" during the Revolution. Unreasonable demands for change kindled "the flames of discord" and encouraged "opposition to the government," and all who made them aided the enemy. Furthermore, he argued, if indeed money, stock-in-trade, and commercial property (particularly ships) were but lightly taxed in Connecticut, then that was as it should be, for of all the different kinds of property in the world, these were inherently the least valuable. Money could be lost in a depressing variety of ways, he explained. Merchandise could be destroyed by fire or flood. Ships could sink. But land was permanent and immovable, and no matter what man or nature did to it, it endured and could be worked again. Hence land, being eternal or nearly so, was inherently far more valuable than transitory things like ships, warehouses, and the goods that crowded merchants' shelves, and therefore land should be more heavily taxed.[76]

If order was the rallying cry of those who opposed reform, justice was that of those who demanded it. "A Lover of Justice" condemned those who pretended the debate over tax reform was between Tory and Whig. The dispute was really between "the man of middling circumstances and all that follow husbandry for a livelihood" and those who lived by trade and had "the greatest share of clear profits." Connecticut's tax laws, he contended, were arranged like "an unfinished building with a good roof and upper works, but without walls, apartments or inside work below, so that none but those in the upper rooms are screened from the inclement weather." Only reform would lead to "equal justice among the several classes of people," and only equal justice could preserve peace, restore order, and "quiet the people."[77]

The legislature responded as it had before, with piecemeal reforms that in the end made relatively little difference. Late in the war, it established minimum tax assessments for lawyers, doctors, merchants, and those in "any mechanical part or mastery such as blacksmiths, shoemakers, tanners, goldsmiths or silversmiths" and directed assessors to add to those minimums "in proportion to their situation and profits, according to the best judgement of the listers." Finally, just as the war ended, the assembly laid an excise on imported luxuries like wines, brandy, snuff, chocolate, sugar, fine fabrics, and jewelry, which outraged many merchants.[78]

Revolution, then, brought to Connecticut some tax reform. Poll taxes were substantially lowered for men under twenty-one, tax abatements for the very poor were a regular feature of the laws, the state reached out to tax more effectively expensive luxury imports and some kinds of commercial property, and revised land taxes more accurately reflected property values. Yet Connecticut ended the war with a revenue system that still fell far short of the ability-to-pay standard, which remained its theoretical foundation. Poll taxes still brought in nearly a third of the revenues, just as they had before independence, and whole categories of income-producing property (particularly merchants' stock-in-trade) were still protected by powerful lobbies in the assembly. Because of the shockingly high taxes that followed independence, however, the equity of Connecticut's revenue laws became a matter for serious debate between rich and poor, and between farmers and merchants, as it had not been before 1775. And those debates and the political divisions that underlay them and in part resulted from them grew increasingly important after 1783.

CHAPTER FIVE
The Middle States

The advocates of fiscal orthodoxy and of the old colonial revenue laws were successful in holding tax reform to a minimum in the New England states, but they were less so in the middle states. Nearly everywhere in the middle region, the dominance of the groups that had directed the colonies' tax policies was severely shaken by the Revolution, and in New York it was all but destroyed. Popular pressure soon forced from the new revolutionary governments either substantive tax reforms or substantial concession in the way old taxes were administered. To many, such changes seemed a natural and desirable application of the principles of the Revolution, particularly a principle expressed in newspaper essays, pamphlets, and letters more frequently as the war continued: *Salus populi suprema lex*—("the welfare of the people is the supreme law"). But for other, more conservative men, like Alexander Hamilton, James Duane, and Robert Livingston of New York, Robert Morris of Pennsylvania, and William Livingston of New Jersey, the same reforms and concessions seemed more the result of democracy run wild, more the perversion of revolutionary principles than their fulfillment. For such men, the lesson of revolutionary finance in the middle states was that the sovereign states were too responsive to public whim and the shortsighted prejudices of the majority and too prone to sacrifice sound principles to popularity. For those who thought this way, lessons were drawn most clearly in New York.

Few of the provisional revolutionary governments that began forming soon after Lexington and Concord faced greater problems than did the provincial congress of New York, for in few states was support for royal government so strong. Most of the southern counties of New York were Tory in sympathy, as were the Mohawk Valley and Lake Champlain frontiers and the tenant farmer communities on the great manors east of the Hudson. Ultimately, England found 25,000 American colonists willing to fight for their king and country, and it found half of them in New York.[1] The provincial congress that met in the spring and summer of 1775 feared that any attempt to levy a war tax would alienate still more people and might be met with "popular disgust . . . or opposition." In May the congress told its delegates in Philadelphia that supporting the war by taxes in New York, was, for the moment at least, "clearly impossible." Instead, the provisional government "borrowed" money from the old colonial treasury and looked for other ways to finance resistance without general taxes. It asked the Continental Congress for loans and sought unsuccessfully a special dispensation from the Continental nonconsumption agreements so that New York merchants could sell (and the provincial congress could tax) imported tea.[2]

By August it was clear that piecemeal measures and stopgap expedients would not be enough, and a ways and means committee recommended a tax of £30,000 to be collected "in the usual manner," then thought better of it and slashed the amount to £15,000. The size of the tax was secondary, for before the congress could collect any general tax, however small, it faced another problem that threatened not only to alienate Tories and neutrals, but to set Whig against Whig. Since it intended to raise the tax "in the usual manner," the congress would have to assign a tax quota to each county. Rural delegates insisted that New York City receive its usual quota (one third of the tax to be raised). City residents had complained about their quotas for years, and now that they faced British invasion, their support for the congress was critical and their complaints could not be lightly passed over. And city delegates loudly opposed continuing the old apportionments, first imposed in 1755, especially since the colonies' agreement to boycott British goods and shut off trade with England had crippled the commerce that was New York City's lifeblood. Assigning quotas to the city and counties promised to touch off long and bitter debates, and produce, as one observer put it, "great heats."[3]

"Great heats" were the last thing the revolutionary government of New York could afford in 1775 and 1776, and the congress tried again to sidestep the problem. It authorized £45,000 in paper money, to be funded by a tax beginning in 1776, and decided to leave the quotas "to be determined when this Congress meets again." But in December the congress again refused to assign quotas and instead asked the Continental Congress for a loan big enough to make the paper emission and the funding taxes, and therefore the quotas, unnecessary. The first installment of the funding tax already approved, however, would be due in March, 1776, and if the New York congress intended to collect it on time, the quota question could not be delayed while the Continental Congress made up its mind about the loan. The provincial congress therefore shoved the whole problem farther into the future by suspending collection of the first tax until 1777. When the hoped-for Continental loan fell through in January, 1776, New York went ahead with its paper money issue but left the tax suspension unaltered.[4]

John Jay, representing New York at the Continental Congress, fumed at the delay and urged the provincial congress to impose a tax quickly, "rather with a view to precedent than profit." When New York issued another £55,000 in paper in March, 1776, and put off funding taxes to 1779, Jay again wrote to complain. A moderate levy, he thought, would "be bourne without a murmur."[5] In Philadelphia, temporarily remote from the day-to-day realities of New York politics, Jay did not understand that a question of precedent, not size, was holding things up. Provincial congressman Alexander McDougall of New York City set him straight. McDougall too wanted taxes to begin, he explained, but he voted for delay because "the country members seem bent on saddling us with one-third of the colony expenses." The policy of delay continued into the summer of 1776, when the provincial congress issued another £200,000 without resolving the quota problem. The new emission rested only on a promise of support from "this convention or some future legislature of this state," a pledge that seemed little more than a hope as General Howe readied his army to invade New York.[6]

By the time New York finally began to levy general war taxes, most of the lower counties had fallen to General Howe, and so the problem of New York City's quota disappeared for the moment. But by that time as well, a political upheaval had occurred within the remaining rebelling counties. The more conservative Whig leaders, such as Robert R. Livingston, John Jay, and Philip Schuyler, who had shepherded New York's new constitution to adoption in 1777 and who had hoped to create by it a government "measurably centralized and measurably aristocratic," had lost control of the new legislature. They soon began to see, as Walter Livingston put it, evidence of "the levelling principle." And when the legislature began to levy general war taxes in March, 1778, their apprehension grew for the legislature did so in anything but the usual manner.[7]

From the first, the newly established assembly of New York adopted tax laws that struck hard at interests the old colonial assemblies had protected. The war tax adopted in March, 1778, included a reform the great landholders had fought successfully for decades, an ad valorem tax on land, both improved and unimproved. Cultivated land and wilderness land alike would be taxed at the same rate—threepence per pound of the value in 1775, as estimated by popularly elected assessors. Some things did not change. Wartime leases, for instance, regularly required tenants to pay the taxes on the land they occupied, but the new law did eliminate one of the manor lords' and speculators' most lucrative exemptions when it brought much undeveloped land onto the tax rolls for the first time.[8] The new revenue law signaled clearly that in public finance at least, New York had indeed undergone a revolution, that a new government had been established that would be more responsive to the middle-class and poorer farmers of the Hudson Valley and the frontier counties, and significantly less amenable to the wishes of the great landed families, than the colonial government had been.

With the state's main source of revenue, the imposts, virtually cut off by British occupation and with five southern counties, which contained about 65 percent of New York's prewar taxable wealth, in British hands, the new government not only expanded property taxes, it also tried to raise revenues in other ways that would not alienate the farmers and tenants who composed most of the population still not under British control. The assembly thought merchants, government officials, and the wealthy in general politically safe targets for new taxes. The new laws made taxable 75 percent of public salaries and the profits of any "traffic, trade or profession," and other regulations shifted some taxes off poorer Whigs. All family men, for example, with personal estates worth less than £300 were excused from the personal property taxes, as were Continental soldiers serving for three years. Other laws doubled taxes on Tories and on neutrals who refused to swear allegiance to the rebel government. And the legislators, many of whom had themselves been chased out of New York City by British invasion, exempted men whose property or income had been so damaged by the war that "a tax on their remaining property . . . would be an intolerable burthen." And at the same time the legislature reformed the general property tax, it imposed an excess war profits tax. Anyone suspected of having made £1,000 or more by "trade, merchandise, traffic or manufactory" since September, 1775, had to report his earnings, swear to them by a special oath, and pay a 5 percent tax on them beyond his other taxes.[9] The law sought to penalize traders who did business with the British in occupied New York, and merchants who profited from shortages by raising prices, but for some New York leaders, already concerned about the new land taxes and their "levelling" implications, the excess profits tax seemed ominous. They looked upon it as a dangerously radical experiment, an attack not on profiteering but on wealth. Robert R. Livingston condemned it as an unprecedented violation of individual rights, and Chief Justice John Jay argued that it violated the state constitution by requiring some men (those who had made over £1,000 in trade since September, 1775) to pay higher taxes than others. The council of revision agreed with Jay and rejected the law, but the assembly overrode the council's veto.[10]

The following winter, the assembly struck again at war profiteers, men who, "taking advantage of the necessities of their
country, have, in pursuing their private gain, amassed large sums
of money to the great prejudice of the public." Such men should
"pay an extraordinary tax," the legislators thought, and they
granted tax assessors virtually unlimited power to rate profiteers. The council, again at Jay's behest, rejected the tax. Grant
assessors this power, it warned, and "all security for property
will be at an end," and "people would hold their estates not by
the Constitution and law of the state, but the mere will of the
legislature and mercy of the assessors." The assembly agreed the
law was too vague, and the council's veto stood, but Jay's victory
was short-lived.[11] Within a year, the assembly took the same procedures that Jay saw as undermining the sanctity of property,
and did not want applied even to war profiteers, and applied
them to all New Yorkers still beyond the reach of England's
armies.

Late in 1779 the assembly altered the tax system again, drop-
ping fixed ad valorem rates on property and reimposing the old
colonial system of tax quotas for each county. The assembly did
not return entirely to New York's old colonial revenue laws,
however, for it did not direct assessors to apportion taxes merely according to "estates real and personal." Instead, assessors
were told to distribute taxes among individuals within their
counties "according to the estates *and other circumstances and
ability of each respective person to pay taxes collectively considered.*"[12] Thus the new law gave to the popularly elected assessors virtually unchecked power to rate not only property but
income from trade, manufacturing, labor, or professional services and non-income-producing wealth as well. According to
Alexander Hamilton, who despised the new plan, the assembly's
public motive for adopting the law was "a desire for equality. It
was pretended that this could not be obtained so well by any
fixed tariff of taxable property as by leaving it to the discretion
of persons chosen by the people themselves to determine the
ability of each citizen." Hamilton suspected that the real motive
was to saddle Tories with massive taxes, but the assembly's "pre-

tended" reason may have had more truth to it than Hamilton cared to admit, for not only Tories suffered under the new law. If the manor lords and great landowners expected the return to quotas to restore the exemptions they had enjoyed, they were soon expensively disappointed. The new law did not specifically exempt unimproved land, and assessors, looking warily ahead to the next election, often chose to retain the reforms of 1778, in particular the tax on woodlands. James Duane, for instance, was surprised and angry when he learned that assessors were including his woodlands in their calculations of his ability to pay. And Robert R. Livingston and others complained about assessors who insisted on collecting taxes from them for property they owned in counties other than the ones in which they lived, but with the assembly in the hands of men aligned with Governor George Clinton, men who spoke for the middle-class farmers of the state, there was little they could do but complain. That the great landowners were paying taxes to New York's revolutionary government that they had never paid before is clear from the long, grumbling letters they wrote to each other, to public officials, to their lawyers, and occasionally to Governor Clinton (who politely replied that he could not help them).[13] Robert R. Livingston insisted to anyone willing to listen that his taxes were "O MONSTROUS!" and that his neighbors kept their own levies low by raising his beyond all reason and justice or, what amounted to the same thing, by electing assessors who took special delight in taxing Livingston land. His mother, Margaret Beekman Livingston, appalled by her tax bills and forced now to deal with assessors and collectors who had little sympathy for her problems and no great respect for her family, begged God to deliver her from "the persecutions of the lower class" and from the tax assessors that class elected.[14]

The remnants of New York's landed elite thought tax reform had gone too far by 1779, but as the taxes continued to rise— between October, 1779, and July, 1780, for example, the assembly approved taxes totaling $10,000,000—other New Yorkers became convinced reform had not gone far enough. "A Real Farmer," writing in the *New York Journal* in the winter of 1779, demanded that the revenue laws be reformed still more to protect middle-class and poor farmers. "The security of American liberty," he explained, "requires a more equal distribution of property than at present," and he thought tax reform the best way to arrange it. Although the old colonial elite complained about taxes under the revolutionary government, by 1780, newspaper essayists, political candidates' speeches, and the actions of the legislature all attested to the growing impression in the minds of many that the Revolution was too much a rich man's war fought and paid for by the poor and the middling sort.[15] By 1780 the old rivalry between the upstate counties and New York City had reemerged in the assembly, and that added to the discontent. Even though the lower counties, including the city, were in British hands, their representatives continued to sit in the assembly and to vote. But since taxes could obviously not be collected in the occupied counties, the full financial burden of the war fell on the upstate counties. More than 95 percent of the £3,000,000 collected in the state between July 1776, and October, 1781, came from Albany, Dutchess, Ulster, and Orange counties.[16] With their own and their constituents' property "safe" behind British lines, the "refugee members" of the legislature clamored for high taxes and rigid collections and fought (generally without success) the various tax relief measures proposed by the upstate delegates, including more paper currency emissions and the confiscation of Tory estates. Spokesmen for the rural counties and angry crowds of taxpayers complained that if it was unjust for men to be taxed without being represented, then it was equally unjust for men to be represented without being taxed. That parliamentary taxes upon the colonies were unconstitutional because the members of Parliament would not feel the effects was a commonplace in the colonies by 1775. The three hundred men who attended a protest meeting on Livingston Manor in January, 1781, argued that the same principle ought to apply to the New York assembly.[17] Because of the continued presence in the legislature of refugee members, who represented districts under English control, many upstate farmers questioned the legitimacy both of the heavy taxes they were asked to pay and of the government that imposed them. Some farmers, outraged as well by rising taxes, took steps that seemed all too familiar to those New York leaders who recalled the beginnings of the struggle against Parliament.

By 1781, New York faced the same danger Joseph Hawley warned about in Massachusetts—popular violence over taxes directed against the new government. Taxes were far too heavy, Robert Livingston warned Gouverneur Morris in January, 1781, and "the people are clamorous. The whole county of Dutchess have chosen precinct and county committees to instruct their members. Some districts in Albany have gone further and chosen members for a state convention." Ten days earlier he had warned George Washington that the people's "discontents begin to break out in complaints against their rulers, in committees and instructions which cannot but serve to weaken the hands of government." It would be "highly imprudent," he continued, for the government in New York to risk its "authority by making any new demands." By March, Governor Clinton reported that high taxes and the state's and the Continental Congresses' inability to pay their debts were producing "many alarming commotions," and unless something was done quickly, he expected "very serious consequences." A few saw in the growing protests the beginnings of a leveling rebellion. A worried Thomas Tillotson (one of Livingston's in-laws) thought "the people want nothing but to be a little more impoverished to prepare them for it," and he expected the rebellion to strike first "at the tenanted estates." New specie taxes on luxuries presumed to be the unmistakable signs of wealth—coaches, chariots, carriages, clocks, watches, slaves, and gold and silver plate—did little to calm the fears of the wealthy and well-to-do.[18]

Under such conditions, the efforts of Robert Livingston, Egbert Benson, Philip Schuyler, Alexander Hamilton, and others to roll back the reforms of 1779 and to remove "ability to pay collectively considered" as the basis for assessments failed repeatedly, though they kept trying. The crux of the problem for these men was the combination of ability-to-pay assessments and popularly elected assessors. The assessors and collectors did not enforce the laws rigidly, explained Hamilton, because they did

not want "to risk the displeasure of those who elect." Where paying taxes was something people were "not very violently devoted
to" anyway, as Hamilton wrote, the results were all but inevitable: massive tax arrears and discrimination against unpopular
men and groups, and in particular against the wealthy, the man-
or lords, and Tories.[19]

Hamilton and his supporters' solutions for New York's problems were simple. First, they wanted assessors and collectors
appointed rather than elected. "The further off we can remove
the appointment of collectors from popular influence," Robert
Morris explained, "the more effectual will be their operation."
He thought this especially important with respect to taxes
passed for the benefit of the Continental Congress, since New
York collectors, faced with competing demands from Congress
and their own legislature, tended to satisfy the latter first even if
it meant using money collected for the Continental receiver. Second, Hamilton wanted to replace New York's ad valorem general
taxes with poll taxes and acreage land taxes. Wealth, he noted
elsewhere, could not be accurately measured, and therefore the
only practical basis for tax assessments was "land and numbers."[20]

The alternative, much less preferable in Hamilton's view, was
to increase the efficiency of New York's existing revenue laws.
But even that ran head on into the legislators' strong reluctance
to disoblige their constituents by enforcing the tax laws rigidly.
And therein Hamilton, Livingston, Schuyler, and others, who
later formed the nucleus of New York's Federalist party, saw
the defect of the new state government drawn in bold relief: it
was too responsive to popular pressure to be run efficiently or
fairly. The tax laws both Hamilton and Livingston thought
"radically vicious" could not be changed because, they believed,
popular elections filled the assembly with men too willing to
tolerate lax enforcement, too ready to traffic in "what will *please*,
not what will *benefit* the people," too anxious to "screen" themselves at election time by "intriguing with the assessors" between
elections. They were like Governor Clinton's ally Abraham Yates,
who continuously assured the voters who returned him to office

that "they are too poor to pay taxes." Despite long-standing arrears, in 1782 Hamilton could not recall one collector who had
been prosecuted for malfeasance.[21]

Large arrearages began to accumulate almost as soon as the
first tax law passed. In fact, New York collected only about one
third of all the taxes levied from 1777 through June, 1781. The
assembly would not act, complained Livingston in April, 1781,
because it contained too many farmers, too many men who, unlike himself, lacked "the habit of business and the vigor of mind
that is necessary to build a firm and permanent system. They
are (to speak in their own stile) lazy farmers who would rather
be perpetually stopping holes in their bush fences than building
good stone walls."[22]

In many cases, however, the taxes simply could not be paid.
"I tenck," wrote a Newburgh man, echoing a complaint that typi-
fied much of the state, "it will not be in the power of the collector to collect the whole as some of the persons taxed are not
worth half the sum they are taxed." By the summer of 1782, even
Hamilton agreed that no amount of effort at any level, and no
conceivable revision of the laws or assessment rules, would enable New York to pay all that the war and the Continental Congress demanded. Nevertheless, he was certain the state could do
more than it had done, and he blamed Governor Clinton for the
arrears that continued to build. Clinton, he said, pandered too
much to the populace, flattering them and championing their
demands, however impolitic, "especially when a new election
approaches." Yet Hamilton had to admit that when Clinton
moved to enforce collections, his popularity suffered, just as
Hamilton's ally General Philip Schuyler risked his popularity by
supporting high taxes vigorously collected.[23]

Clinton was a soldier as well as a governor and he knew the
importance of raising money to fight the war. Well-to-do himself,
he was no backwoods radical, and when Hamilton launched an
all-out attempt to enforce collections and alter the assessment
rules in 1782 and 1783, Clinton offered cautious support. Yet
even the popular governor felt trapped by the same pressures
that Hamilton decried, and he especially feared pushing his war-

weary and tax-burdened populace into open rebellion. Thus Clinton, who thought accepting commodities for taxes an "expensive and bad expedient" and who would have liked to end the practice in his state, found he could not. Taking commodities for taxes, he explained to Robert Morris, had originally been justified as "a matter of ease and convenience to the people," and the practice could not be dropped without "increasing the discontent" that was already "too generally prevalent." New York's delegates in Congress warned in 1781 that "our inhabitants feel themselves so aggrieved that prudence forbids any further attempts on their patience."[24]

Beyond a law eliminating the most glaring frauds used in the counties to avoid taxes, such as not electing assessors and collectors at all, Hamilton's drive for change accomplished little. A committee appointed at his behest to study "a more effectual system of taxation" spent much of its time bickering. In the fall of 1782 the committee finally agreed to recommend a land valuation act and poll taxes, but the session ended before the committee reported, leaving "everything afloat." When the new assembly met in February, an attempt to replace "ability to pay collectively considered" as the basis of assessments with the value of estates real and personal failed by a vote of twenty-four to fifteen. The resulting tax law of March, 1783, left unchanged the essential features of the war reforms, which had rendered taxes (in Hamilton's view) "voluntary" and barely worth the cost and bother of collection.[25]

Hamilton's unhappy experience as Continental receiver for New York reinforced his growing conviction that the national government must have the power to levy direct taxes on individuals, especially poll and land taxes, and the authority and power to collect them. His experience with revolutionary taxation in New York helped convince him and others that the thirteen independent states had been crippled by a "general disease" called democracy.[26]

But what Hamilton and the future Federalists saw as a fatal weakness others saw as a saving strength. Where Hamilton saw New York's government truckling to the ignorant and self-interested, others saw a government responding to the needs of its people. Where Hamilton appealed to the laws of fiscal orthodoxy and national interest, legislators chosen by the common farmers of upstate New York appealed instead to the principle *Salus populi suprema lex* and to their belief that the first concern of the government of New York must be the welfare of New Yorkers. Where Hamilton saw a government irresponsibly neglecting to collect taxes, others saw a government responding to economic and political realities by not imposing impossible levies on a state suffering British invasion and occupation. The autonomy and independence of New York, which Hamilton thought an unfortunate outgrowth of the Revolution and a flaw to be corrected, others thought a prize to be defended against all challengers, English or American. After all, the Revolution and the popularly elected independent state government it established reformed the state's tax laws, bringing them closer to the ability-to-pay standard than they had ever been. And at the end of the war, the reforms of 1779 were still intact, despite persistent attempts by Hamilton and representatives of the great landed families and the merchant community of New York to undo them.

Reform accompanied revolution in New Jersey too, although the changes were less dramatic than in New York. New Jersey had no major metropolis, and so the delegates who established the state's first provisional revolutionary government at Trenton in May, 1775, did not have to resolve a dispute between urban and rural interests before they began taxing. New Jersey was a wholly rural colony and carried on most of its trade through the "foreign" cities of New York and Philadelphia. And unlike New York, New Jersey at the beginning of the war had general colonial property taxes in force and county quotas, whose equity was generally conceded, already established. It was relatively easy, therefore, for the provincial congressmen to impose a tax, quotaed on the counties in the usual way, with a minimum of debate and disagreement. This they did in June, 1775. The £10,000 levy adhered closely to the old colonial forms except that committees of safety in the towns were to collect the money and pay it to county revolutionary committees rather than to the colonial treasury. The congress hoped people would pay willingly, or at least punctually, but many New Jersey colonists were apparently no more eager to pay new American taxes than they had been to pay new British ones. The response to the tax was so poor that within months the congress began debating ways to force payment, and in October it ordered county collectors to seize and sell the property of delinquents. As late as the fall of 1777, "considerable sums" remained unpaid and the congress was still trying to collect.[27]

New Jersey had no great commercial center to divide its government, but there were other divisions that could not be ignored. West Jersey, for instance, harbored an influential Quaker population that opposed the collection of war taxes on religious grounds, and several New Jersey counties were hotbeds of Toryism.[28] By the fall of 1775 it was clear that the tax passed in June was producing opposition and dissension where the provincial congress desperately needed unity and cooperation. The royal governor William Franklin reported that attempts to collect the revolutionary tax had caused "confusion and disturbance." Some colonists refused to pay, and others agreed to pay the congressional tax or the regular New Jersey colonial tax (then being collected) but not both. When the provincial congress met in October, 1775, to discuss a second war tax, it opted for a policy of fighting now and paying later. The congress feared, with some reason, that new taxes would alienate still more people. By November, 1775, people all across the colony were grumbling that New Jersey was being asked to pay too large a share of the Continental Congresses' expenses. By January, 1776, some began to organize associations to oppose tax collections by pledging members not to bid on property at tax auctions. Shortly after independence, provincial congressman Samuel Tucker warned that "taxes to any very great amount would be highly imprudent at this time."[29] By delaying taxes until the colony was so deeply implicated in the Revolution that it could not turn back, Tory propagandists later complained, rebel leaders had deliberately deceived people into believing independence could be had at bargain rates. Looking at the situation from the perspective of 1780, one Whig saw the decision not to levy new taxes in 1776 as "a masterstroke of policy."[30]

The provincial congress wanted to avoid imposing new taxes for other reasons as well. By the fall of 1775 the congress knew that new taxes would touch off a debate over tax reform and that many who approved of the congress and the Revolution and who were willing to support them by paying taxes, were not willing to pay taxes in the old familiar ways. On October 6, a petition arrived from Hunterdon County, in East Jersey, asking that money at interest be taxed in any new war levies. Two weeks later the "farmers of Essex" made the same request and also asked that "lawyers and mechanics" be taxed. Similar demands made in 1774 by several East Jersey counties had been ignored. But now they had to be heard, since the most vigorous support for resistance to England came from East Jersey.[31] And at the same time, some began to demand that the revolutionary government adopt other reforms, such as taxpayer suffrage, which the congress did not particularly want to debate on the eve of independence. It was simpler, for the moment, and safer to delay new taxes. The congress first tried to borrow money from the Continental Congress, and when that failed, it issued £30,000 in paper but put off the first tax to support it until 1784. However, the members prudently did not slam the door to reform. They declared that the 1784 tax should be levied in the usual way, "provided that some equitable expedient" for sinking the paper money "by a more easy method to the inhabitants of this colony, shall not be agreed upon in the meantime."[32]

Interest in tax reform could not be shunted aside that easily. Too many people, particularly in East Jersey, saw in the Revolution an opportunity to win new reforms, and they made the most of their chance. On February 1, 1776, Essex County's second petition, demanding that "money at interest and other effects may bear an equal proportion of the taxes," arrived at the provincial congress. Five days later a similar petition from Middlesex County arrived, and one from Morris County came in the day after that. By February 13, two more (from Middlesex and Essex) had arrived, and one week later the town of Piscataway asked "that some more equal mode of taxation may be prescribed," and in particular "that money at interest be taxed." On February 9, fifty-nine New Brunswick petitioners had made the same request. Such a reform, they argued, would "Prove a Great Easement to the Lower Class of Men on whom the Burthen will fall the heaviest; many of whom to keep their familyes in Imploy has borrowed money to buy Lands and now pays tax for their Lands and Interest for the Money while the man of Estates Goes free."[33]

Under pressure, the congress agreed to some reforms, but it also tried to delay implementation for a decade. It authorized £20,000 more in paper currency but put off until 1787 the first sinking-fund taxes for it and for the £30,000 authorized in October, 1775. The same ordinance, however, directed assessors to tax unimproved land, even if such land was not part of a developed tract. Thus the Revolution in New Jersey, as in New York, destroyed an important tax haven for wealthy landholders and speculators, the wholesale exemption of wilderness land. Furthermore, the ordinance told assessors to rate "all mortgages, bonds and notes at interest."[34]

Taxes under the new rules were not to begin until 1787, but New Jersey could not avoid imposing taxes during the war, and the debate over reform flared up again. There was little open opposition to taxing unimproved land, and most of the debate centered instead on the money at interest tax, which included a tax on farm mortgages. Between 1766 and 1776, New Jersey citizens took out more than four thousand mortgages worth over £950,000. The annual interest payments, at a moderate rate of 6 percent came to £57,000. Not only did that amount go wholly untaxed, it was more than three times the colony's annual general taxes.[35]

Opponents of the money at interest tax condemned it as impractical, unprecedented, unjust, and a thinly disguised attack upon the wealthy by the poor. Nothing should be taxed, argued " T. W." in the *New Jersey Gazette*, "but what is visible," and that did not include paper debts, bonds, and mortgages, with which the public had "no right to meddle." The tax would probably be popular, he conceded, but popularity alone was a poor justification for conducting wild and dangerous experiments. "Would not a law for dividing the wealth of the state equally among the inhabitants be just as popular," he asked, "or perhaps more so?" He warned that if the legislature placed the idea of equal distribution of property before the public, there would soon be "legions of advocates for it." Raise the notion of leveling by this tax, he predicted, and New Jersey would quickly see its beggars "smack their lips." The tax would doubtless please "those amongst us who behold their superiors in life with an envious eye, and right or wrong, would gladly drag them down to a level with themselves. But this levelling spirit should never be indulged. It is always dangerous in civil society, always destructive of order and government."[36]"A True Patriot" warned that unless irresponsible taxes such as the money at interest tax were abandoned, the "respectable citizens of America" would soon "behold many men . . . whose fathers they would have disdained to have set with the dogs of their flock, raised to immense wealth."[37]

Advocates of reform countered with arguments typical of the reform movements throughout the newly independent states. "Property of whatsoever kind, ought to bear its proportional part of the taxes," explained "A Farmer," and there was no reason men whose wealth was in money rather than land, whose income came from interest instead of agriculture, should escape taxation. There was nothing unprecedented about taxing money at interest, claimed "Equal Taxer"; other states did it as a matter of course. The only reason colonial New Jersey had not was that the "monied gentry" had been influential in the colonial government and had "cast the burden off themselves and on their poorer neighbors." But no more. Independence and the Revolution had changed all that. What T. W. really objected to, Equal Taxer continued, was not tax reform so much as the Revolution itself: "Alas! poor soul, the revolution and independency sticks in his weak stomach! Let him vomit or choke!"[38]

T. W.'s claim that revolution had reduced the power of the wealthy in New Jersey was correct. Well-to-do or wealthy men had held 75 percent of the house seats before independence, but in the assemblies chosen under the new state constitution, common farmers soon held two thirds of the seats. These new assemblymen quickly made their influence felt. On March 26, 1778, under the new state constitution New Jersey adopted its first general tax law that was designed to be imposed immediately, not far in the future. It substantially altered the basis of taxation in the state and included some important reforms. By 1778, New Jersey had become a major battleground in the war, and the assembly abandoned the county quota system (it was restored in December) and imposed general property taxes directly upon individuals.[39] The law told assessors to determine the pound value of every man's estate and to collect a tax of two shillings in the pound. It is clear from the law that "pound value" meant presumed income rather than actual market value. Developed land, for instance, and houses, mills, and other improvements were to be assessed at 5 percent of the "real and saleable value thereof." Unlike New York, New Jersey circumscribed the power of its assessors by incorporating in the law minimum and maximum values for several kinds of taxable property and by imposing fixed taxes on some kinds of property, such as livestock. Merchants might have their shops and stock-in-trade rated at no less than ten shillings but no more than twenty pounds.

The new statute included three major reforms. First it directed assessors to rate all unimproved land at one thirtieth of its market value, thus bringing wilderness land under immediate taxation for the first time. Second, the law imposed some direct taxes on luxuries—five shillings on riding carriages; fifteen on chaises; and twenty on coaches. "Finally, all mortgages, bonds, bills and notes upon interest" would be assessed at "one thirtieth of the principal thereof." This substantially undervalued money at interest, which normally returned more than 3.3 percent a year, but it nevertheless brought a new category of income-producing property onto the tax rolls.

These reforms were important, and the last had been bitterly opposed, but as taxes continued to soar farmers around the state continued to complain that nonagricultural property and wealth were not carrying a fair share of the load. Some advocated a tax on money as the best possible ability-to-pay tax, since obviously only those who had money could pay the tax.[40] One of New Jersey's delegates at the Continental Congress, William Houston, warned that something should be done to distribute taxes more equitably. "There is," he wrote, "one clear and obvious principle on which all taxation ought to be rested, and if it could be laid as the groundwork and extend through our tax laws, payment would not only be practicable but light and easy; it is that every man be called upon to pay in exact proportion to his ability, all things considered." Other states had extensive faculty taxes, he continued, so why not adopt one in New Jersey too?[41]

Under continued popular pressure, the assembly further reformed the laws in June, 1779, by adopting a faculty tax. Edging toward New York's "ability to pay collectively considered" standard, the law told assessors to "dilligently enquire and examine into the circumstances and ability" of each person since the war began, together with present annual "profits, emoluments and advantages" stemming from "business, occupation, trade, art or profession," and to tax them accordingly. The law also granted assessors special powers in "extraordinary" cases where strict conformity with the letter of the law would not yield equitable assessments. They could then increase a merchant's or a moneylender's assessment, for example, until it was "proportionable to the assessments laid upon lands."[42]

By 1780, however, New Jersey's tax reform movement had spent itself, and more orthodox interests began to reassert their influence in the assembly. In December, 1779, legislators withdrew the assessors' discretionary power to equalize assessments of farmers and nonfarmers in extraordinary cases. By the spring of 1781 the money at interest tax had disappeared from the laws, probably because all New Jersey farmers, large and small, needed credit to rebuild, and many, both prospering and poor, thought the tax made credit hard to get. But in the absence of money at interest taxes, new luxury taxes were imposed on gold and silver plate, clocks, and watches. In May, 1783, a new drive to tax income not already taxed failed. Nevertheless, the assembly approved several tax relief policies at the same time it was drawing back from continued tax reform. It consistently slashed the governor's requests for high taxes. When William Livingston asked for £500,000 in new levies in 1779, the assembly approved £100,000. Livingston asked for £600,000 in 1780, but the delegates gave him only £100,000, thereby reinforcing his belief that the legislators were frightened of "disobliging their constituents."[43] In June, 1780, the assembly decided to accept for some taxes quartermaster's and commissary's certificates, as well as notes issued by county contractors, and in the summer of 1781 it made a long list of farm commodities acceptable for taxes.[44]

On the whole, New Jersey's tax laws worked surprisingly well during the Revolution. There were some problems with arrears and faulty collections, but these were inevitable in a state that quickly became a battleground. Nevertheless, at a time when New York and Pennsylvania were struggling to collect one third to one half of the taxes they passed, New Jersey collected almost 90 percent of its taxes and avoided most of the rioting and resistance that endangered New York and the New England states.[45] New Jersey at the end of the war had a smoothly functioning revenue system that no longer taxed income from mortgages and loans, but did tax unimproved land and such luxuries as gold and silver plate, watches, and riding carriages, a system that came appreciably closer to the ability-to-pay standard than it had before independence.

Delaware had relied on interest from its loan office emissions and parliamentary compensation grants rather than on taxes to pay expenses in the last years before independence. That heritage made it particularly difficult for the state's revolutionary government to raise money. Whig leaders feared wholesale desertions to the king's colors if Delaware's new loyalties were tested too quickly or too sharply. When the war began, therefore, the assembly did not impose new taxes, but instead held to its traditional and familiar methods of raising money. In September, 1775, it issued £30,000 in bills of credit to be loaned out at interest on landed security for up to sixteen years. Delaware imposed no war tax until February, 1777, when it adopted a light one. It issued £15,000 more to be loaned out and another £10,000 in paper to be spent for defense, the latter to be raised by collecting a £664 tax annually in each of the state's three counties. Thus Delaware preserved for a time the old colonial assumption that each county was equally able to pay and thus should assume one-third of the tax burden.[46]

The assembly's caution was no less shrewd in Delaware than it had been in New Jersey or New York, for in none of the rebelling colonies was support for the Revolution shakier during the first years of independence. Tory sympathizers were everywhere, and they were only too eager to exploit discontent over taxes. In 1780 some Delaware men threatened rebellion against the new state government "to beat down the tax laws and make the rich pay as much on the pound rate as the poor." They took up arms "against the Whigs," they said, "because taxes was too high, and no man could live by such laws." With trouble like that brewing, heavy taxes before 1778 would not have been wise, nor could they have been effectively collected. "In times like unto the present," wrote a troubled George Read, "the assent of very many is necessary to public measures."[47] Read, the state's vice-president, also worried about Delaware's Whigs, many of whom were applying to their own assembly the rhetoric that had been directed against Parliament, and were drawing from it disturbing conclusions. For years, colonists had been told that they had not only the ability but the responsibility to judge the king and Parliament and to determine whether taxes were constitutional. Levies popularly thought to be unjust, such as the stamp tax, had been disobeyed and effectively nullified, and revolutionary leaders and propagandists had applauded. But now, Read complained, people were beginning to apply the same principles to American government, the same rhetoric to the Delaware assembly. "A great mistake among many of us," he explained to Thomas McKean in March, 1778, "has been to set at naught such acts of legislation as do not exactly tally with our own sentiments; this has a fatal tendency at all times, but particularly at the present, making each individual a judge of what he ought and what he ought not submit to."[48] The assembly's reluctance to impose new taxes frustrated Read, even though he understood the reasons for it. Delaware's elaborate caution and long delay in taxing finally moved some of the more fiery rebels to denounce the assemblymen as hirelings of the king and secret enemies to independence.[49]

The rhetoric of revolution interfered in other ways with raising money. When Continental soldiers were sent into Sussex County to suppress Tories and interfered in legislative elections, the county was unrepresented for several sessions. With one third of the state unrepresented, new taxes were out of the question, Read explained, since "according to the American creed, representation is necessary for taxation."[50]

When Delaware finally adopted substantial war taxes in May, 1778, the old colonial arrangements quickly came under attack. The revenue law of May, 1778, assigned every county the usual one-third quota of the money (£120,000) to be raised. A presumed equal ability to pay among the counties may have been acceptable enough during the years of light or nonexistent general taxes, but not when massive war taxation became the rule. By February, 1779, complaints forced the assembly to act. "Some doubts have arisen," the assemblymen explained, "whether the equal proportion . . . to be raised within each of the counties of this state is the just and proper quota of each county according to the present ability of its inhabitants to pay the same." To resolve such doubts, they appointed a special commission to tour the state and to prepare "an estimate and valuation of all the real estate within the same, having regard to quantity, quality and circumstances attending the same."[51]

By June, 1779, equal county quotas were dead, casualties of the Revolution. A new law to raise $495,000 assigned 36.4 percent of the taxes to New Castle, 33.3 percent to Kent, and 30.3 percent to Sussex. The assembly, admitting that even this new distribution was "not so equal and just" as it might have been, ordered another general estimate and directed assessors to rate "the persons and estates agreeable to the profits arising thereon." The law also exempted from some taxes Continental soldiers, the poor, those with many children and small estates, and widows and imposed an excess war profits tax on "all such as may have been fortunate in trade or concerned in speculation or engrossing since the commencement of the present war."[52]

Once the presumption of equality among the counties fell, squabbling over each county's proper share followed. In December, 1779, delegates from Sussex and Kent joined to raise New Castle's quota to 38 percent and to lower Sussex's to 28 percent. All agreed that Sussex was the poorest and should pay the least. New Castle's delegates wanted to split the remaining taxes equally with Kent, but Kent's delegates outbid New Castle's for the support of Sussex. The lowest share proposed for Sussex by New Castle's delegation was higher than the share Sussex eventually paid with the support of the Kent delegation. And it was Sussex votes that enabled Kent to stop all New Castle's attempts to lower its own taxes at Kent's expense. The quotas established in 1779 remained substantially unchanged for the rest of the war.[53]

The tax reforms that followed independence in Delaware were not nearly so dramatic or far-reaching as they were in other colonies, and perhaps for that reason they were not so bitterly fought. Nevertheless, the war did force the state to revise its revenue system so that it at least attempted to distribute taxes among the counties according to their ability to pay.

In Pennsylvania, revolution and independence finally accomplished what two decades of maneuvering by Benjamin Franklin and the Quaker party had failed to accomplish: the removal of the Penn family from Pennsylvania politics and government. The internal revolution in Pennsylvania that accompanied independence and the end of the proprietorship altered the state's politics permanently and ultimately created two strong new political parties. The first to emerge, the Constitutionalist party, drew most of its strength from the interior and western counties, which dramatically increased their power in the Pennsylvania constitution of 1776 and in the legislatures that followed.[54] As its name implied, the party supported Pennsylvania's revolutionary constitution of 1776 and the unicameral legislature it created. The opposing Republican party drew most of its support from the Quaker party's old stronghold, the three eastern counties of Philadelphia, Chester, and Bucks. Republicans were opposed to the constitution of 1776, which they thought dangerously democratic, and especially to the unicameral legislature. They fought for constitutional change, bicameralism, and a stronger executive and in general represented the interests of the commercial farming towns in eastern Pennsylvania and of the merchant community in Philadelphia and elsewhere.[55]

The two parties also differed on economic policy, the confiscation of Loyalists' property, the conduct of the war, and the treatment of Loyalists and neutrals, and the disagreements produced hard-fought contests at the polls, sharp battles in the assembly, and bitter newspaper and broadside debates. But in Pennsylvania, tax reform did not become a major subject of partisan political struggle. The major tax reform campaigns of the late colonial period sought to bring the Penn family's estates and income under the general tax laws, and thus the central issue in prewar tax debates disappeared at independence. Final disposition of the proprietors' lands took years, but there was no longer any question after 1776 of ever again preserving vast areas as a tax haven for one family. Furthermore, the Penn lands aside, Pennsylvania had perhaps the least regressive and most equitable tax laws (judged according to the ability-to-pay standard) of any of the new states. At the beginning of the war, Pennsylvania had no general poll taxes in force and had ad valorem property rates that taxed much of the state's unimproved land. Thus two key provisions that reformers in other states often had to fight to win, and that appeared elsewhere as a result of the Revolution, were already part of Pennsylvania's general revenue system before independence. The two parties did, however, disagree sharply over many aspects of tax policy, in particular over the wisdom and justice of using taxes to enforce political conformity and to punish those who did not support the Revolution with proper enthusiasm. Even before independence many Whigs demanded punitive taxes on neutrals and those who refused to fight, which demands were strongly supported by the Pennsylvania militia.

Proprietary Pennsylvania did not have a permanent militia, but by June, 1775, the hastily formed revolutionary militia boasted nearly 20,000 men and included, according to some leading citizens, an alarming number of poor people, especially in the units in and near Philadelphia. This Whig militia, which generally supported the Constitutionalist party, was at first Pennsylvania's sole defense against British invasion, and along with the local committees of safety, its only effective police force. For a time, then, the militia and the militia committees that spoke for the soldiers had enormous influence. The sudden acquisition of such power by an uncertain multitude worried some Pennsylvania Whigs so much that they began to be "almost as much afraid of success in this contest as being vanquished."[56] That fear, expressed so succinctly by Arthur St. Clair, became an ever-present fact of life for Pennsylvania's leaders throughout the war for independence and helped shape the policies of the new revolutionary government.

The government's sensitivity to popular pressure, particularly to the militia's demands, became evident early in the war. After Lexington and Concord, the militia demanded that the assembly raise money through taxes to pay and supply the independent militia companies then forming in the colony. The assembly tried to adopt a tax law, but Governor John Penn vetoed it, and the members were forced to move beyond the law. In June, 1775, they issued £35,000 in bills of credit by mere resolution—which did not require the governor's signature—to meet "present exigencies," and they authorized a tax raised "on the same persons and property, in the same proportion and in the same manner and mode as the provincial tax by the laws now in force is raised." Since this new tax had not been properly imposed by law, the assembly appealed to the principle *Salus populi suprema lex* and asked local officials to collect the tax out of regard for "the freedom, welfare and safety of their country."[57]

Throughout the summer of 1775, petitioners demanded that nonassociators—men who would not serve in the Continental army or the Pennsylvania militia and who refused to swear allegiance to the rebel government—pay special punitive taxes. The Committee of the City and Liberties of Philadelphia insisted that reason and justice taught that "all members of the community" were "equally interested in the preservation and security of our common liberties," and therefore all "should contribute to the assistance and support of those who take a more active, laborious and dangerous part," an argument that was eventually incorporated into the state constitution. Such demands brought the militia into direct conflict with the Pennsylvania Quaker community and rubbed raw an old sore spot in Pennsylvania politics. Quakers objected to a policy that left them no option but taking up arms or supporting a war through taxes in lieu of service.[58] The matter was especially delicate, explained James Smith, chairman of the York Committee of Correspondence, because forcing nonassociators to pay would open the rebel government to the very charge it had leveled at England: "taking money out of our brethren's pockets without their consent." On the other hand, Smith's militiamen had threatened to lay down their guns and go home if punitive taxation did not begin quickly. In 1777, Thomas Paine suggested that nonassociators should pay one fifth of their property in taxes annually for the duration of the war, and although the new revolutionary government refused to go that far, in December, 1777, it did double the taxes on all persons "not subject to nor performing military duty."[59]

As the war wore on and taxes and inflation soared, demands for punitive taxes grew more shrill. There were only two kinds of people in Pennsylvania, explained one Whig essayist in 1780, "unquestionable Whigs" and "all the rest." The latter "ought to be made slaves, yes slaves," and should be allowed to keep their property only until the public needed it; then it "should be taken from them." Neutrality, he insisted, was a luxury Pennsylvania could not indulge, and although many nonassociators had "done nothing" to hurt the Revolution, it was "high time they were made to do something" to help it. When a new tax law was passed late in the war that did not discriminate against nonassociators, critics denounced it as "generally disgusting to the Whigs" and warned that popular opposition might nullify the tax if the legislature did not.[60] Such warnings were more than idle threats. Pennsylvania President Joseph Reed thought that punitive taxes were all that prevented "a general opposition" to tax collections in the state, and he was painfully aware that the militiamen were willing, if provoked, to adopt revolutionary practices when dealing with their own state government. Reed himself had helped suppress a violent demonstration by Philadelphia militiamen against high prices and profiteering merchants in October, 1779, an experience that left him and other well-placed Pennsylvanians badly frightened and acutely aware of discontent among the common people of the state. "The feelings of an insulted and injured people," he explained to Robert Morris in 1781, required "some sacrifices." Discrimination against Tories and neutrals alone, he thought, "reconciled the well-affected to the weight and burthen of taxation."[61]

In November, 1775, the Pennsylvania assembly reluctantly agreed to levy an annual tax of £2 10s. on nonassociators. This was too gentle to satisfy the militiamen, who demanded that nonassociators pay not only a fixed fine, which the new tax amounted to, but a special property tax on their estates as well. Without such taxes, they complained, the burden of the war would fall "chiefly on the poor or middling sort," who already bore more than their share by serving in the army. The assembly raised the tax to £3 10s. in April, 1776, but this was still short of what the militia had in mind.[62] When in June, 1776, Pennsylvania's revolutionary convention replaced the assembly as the effective government of the colony, the assembly's failure to tax nonassociatiors heavily enough was one of the reasons offered by the convention to justify the change. And one of the convention's first acts was to levy a £1 per month tax on nonassociators and an additional tax of 4s. per pound of assessed value on their property, over and above the regular general property taxes that everyone had to pay. And in December, 1777, the state assembly doubled the property taxes on nonassociators.[63]

Quakers and other nonassociators were not the only men to come under attack. The state assembly, dominated by Constitutionalists, also moved against profiteering merchants and price gougers, although Pennsylvania never delivered its merchants as completely into the hands of popularly elected local officials as did New York. In February, 1777, the assembly condemned merchants who made greater profits out of the war "than was customary . . . or than is just and reasonable." Such men, it declared, "should contribute to the public expences accordingly." Most of the colonial revenue laws, including the excises, had been suspended between May, 1776, and February, 1777, but the Assembly ordered the excises for those months collected anyway, in order to tax merchants' profits. In March, 1779, the assembly tripled tavern license fees and raised the tax on retail liquor from 4d. to 1s. per gallon. The new fees did little to raise money, since in some counties scarcely one tavern owner in three bothered to take out a license, but by such actions the legislators showed their willingness to respond to complaints about merchants popularly thought to be levying unconscionable taxes on the people through inflated prices.[64] The assembly met demands for tax relief by adopting programs more or less common to all the states, such as granting exemptions for people who suffered enemy attack and directing collectors to accept army supply certificates for taxes "on account of the want of sufficient quantity of cash among the poorer people of this state." Various state paper emissions technically receivable only for specified taxes, were nevertheless accepted by the treasury for all kinds of taxes.[65]

The war settled once and for all the question of taxing Penn lands, but it did little to settle the old debate between Philadelphia and the western counties about the city's fair share of public taxes. Revolution made the city's position worse than it had been, since the western counties now sent to the legislature more delegates than before, and the delegates had no interest whatever in raising their own rates by lowering Philadelphia's. That the western delegates were predominantly Constitutionalists and that Philadelphia was a Republican stronghold were facts not lost on the new assemblymen either. When they assigned tax quotas to the counties in 1778, they fixed Philadelphia's share—that is, the share of the city and county of Philadelphia combined—at one third of the taxes to be raised. But in fact, the city and county paid a higher percentage of the money actually collected. They paid, for instance, over 50 percent of all taxes in Continental currency (except excices) collected between January, 1777, and October, 1781. The three eastern counties together contributed more than 75 percent. Of the supply tax of 1781, Philadelphia paid 37 percent of all specie collected by October, 1782, and 48 percent of all state currency. Out of £100,909 in excises collected by October, 1781, Philadelphia paid £74,740.[66]

Soon after the British army withdrew from Philadelphia, the city's representatives began to complain about their quotas. They tried to have the quotas lowered in March, 1779, but Constitutionalists in the assembly outvoted Philadelphia's Republican spokesmen and their allies, twenty-seven to twenty-one. The dispute continued throughout the war. When Philadelphia delegates tried again to have their taxes lowered in March, 1782, the assembly decided, thirty-one to twenty-eight, to keep the old quotas. That the Revolution had not eliminated the old colonial sectional divisions over taxes is clear from that vote. Twenty-two of the twenty-eight votes in favor of changing the quotas came from the three eastern counties and included all delegates from the city and county of Philadelphia. Only one representative from the three eastern counties was opposed.[67]

Although Pennsylvania's revolutionary government tried under both parties to avoid innovations in the revenue laws and to collect familiar taxes in familiar ways, there were some changes. In March, 1777, the assembly adopted a poll tax of ten shillings on all freemen over twenty-one not serving in the army. In October it tripled the tax and shortly thereafter doubled it again. By 1779, however, such poll taxes fell only on single freemen not in the army and not paying other taxes. Pennsylvania's poll taxes thus fell far short of the general poll taxes that raised nearly a third of New England's general revenues or that were collected in several of the southern states. In December, 1780, the assembly adopted new imposts on wines, liquors, sugar, coffee, tea, and cocoa (primarily luxuries) and a 1 percent ad valorem tax on all other foreign imports. Even earlier, the state had increased taxes on the wealthy by taxing gold and silver plate, "pleasurable carriages" but not farm wagons, and money in hand. When in March, 1782, legislators approved a £420,297 specie tax, they showed a good grasp of public relations by agreeing at the same time to tax "all offices and posts of profit" in the government.[68]

The assembly's concern for public relations was justified, for Pennsylvania's war tax system was even less efficient than its sievelike colonial system. As early as February, 1777, clerk of the assembly Timothy Matlack reported that "a considerable number" had "refused or neglected to pay their taxes." By October, 1782, collections due in Continental currency were behind £3,300,000, those due in state currency were behind £84,700, and those due in specie were behind more than £19,500. Pennsylvania collected only about one third of the £645,000 it levied between 1782 and 1783.[69] These arrears infuriated Benjamin Franklin. Men have a right, he declared in December, 1783, only to that property immediately necessary to their survival. "All property superfluous to such purposes" was "the property of the public, who by their laws, have created it." Such superfluous property might be justly seized, by taxation, "whenever the welfare of the public shall demand such disposition. He that does not like civil society on these terms, let him retire and live among the savages."[70]

There were several reasons for poor collections besides the general disruption of the war and a British invasion of eastern Pennsylvania. Some of the war tax laws, written by new legislators with more enthusiasm than skill, were unclear. Harried tax commissioners appealed to the supreme executive council and to the state treasurer for advice, but even treasurer David

Rittenhouse admitted that he was not always sure what the laws meant. President Joseph Reed agreed that many of them were vague, but officially he could offer collectors no better advice than to await action by the assembly. Unofficially he promised them "all the aid and assistance" the council could give if they would take a chance, act on their own authority and make collections anyway.[71]

Discriminatory taxes against Quakers and nonassociators may have reconciled Whigs to paying their own rates, but such levies also confused and delayed collections. Quakers often stood mute at assessment time and refused to report their taxable property. When Quaker lawyers sued collectors who tried to force payment, the collectors, ill informed about the vaguely worded laws and afraid of losing in court, sometimes stopped trying to collect. After an involved series of appeals to the council, the attorney general, and the courts, the tax might eventually be paid.[72]

Special-interest provisions created other problems. The tax act of March 12, 1778, for instance, permitted county treasurers to compensate masters with state currency for allowing their servants to serve in the army, but Lancaster's treasurer finally stopped the practice because he found his county paying out more state currency to masters than it took in in taxes. Other collectors, facing complaints from local people that they could not pay, flatly refused to force collections. The Lancaster tax commissioners put the matter bluntly. They had done everything in their power, they told President John Dickinson, to collect overdue taxes "excepting putting the laws in force."[73] Collectors ran into so much trouble that the state had difficulty getting men to take the job. "We are obstructed in every quarter," complained the Berks County tax commissioner Adam Whitman in March, 1780. "Some threaten our lives, others say they will all come in a body at the appeal, etc." Officers who tried to collect, he continued, were "abused by impudent scamps." Five of his collectors had quit, and he had little hope of replacing them. Some refused to serve because they were afraid of being attacked, but others were unwilling to enforce the laws in the face of "the poverty of the people." Seizing property and auctioning it off for taxes did little good because by 1780 many people were so strapped for cash they could not bid on it, and many who had money would not bid on their neighbors' property. Jailing delinquents did not help much either, since the expense of jailing a man often came to more than the back taxes he owed.[74] Outright fraud added to the problems. Joseph Reed knew of one man who made £10,000 through collusion with tax officials, and one collector pretended he had been robbed of his collections and then named his own brother as the thief. Such corruption naturally led to loud complaints and endless appeals for reassessments, and added to the widespread suspicion that public officials were making fortunes from the war while ruining common farmers with taxes.[75]

Not only government officials, but the wealthy in general were suspect, and by 1780 many tax complaints were couched in terms of rich versus poor. People were willing enough to pay taxes, "A Citizen of the States" argued in the *Pennsylvania Gazette* of November 8, 1780, but they had "no money in their hands" because it had all "got into the hands of a few fortunate individuals who have amassed great wealth." Such men would be "wise" to give more for the war, to prevent "that envy which is apt to attend fortunes suddenly acquired." Even Joseph Reed, who tried as president to tighten collections and who opposed several popular tax relief programs, believed the greatest tax evaders were "the rich," who bought gold and silver plate and "hoarded [it] up as too sacred to be touched for taxes."[76]

Improved collections depended in part on improved public relations, and when the state overhauled its accounting system in 1782 and appointed John Nicholson comptroller general, it hoped to increase efficiency (which did not noticeably improve) and to convince complaining taxpayers that every penny taken in was necessary and being put to good use.[77] Not even Tom Paine's skillful pen was much help. Although he wrote several essays urging people to pay, the author of *Common Sense* had more success convincing Pennsylvanians to declare their independence than he did convincing them to pay taxes to achieve it. Amid runaway inflation, it made sense for people to delay as long as they could and thus to take advantage of the inflation by paying in devalued currency. By the time the treasury actually got tax money, Joseph Reed complained, it might be worth half what it was worth when the assembly originally imposed the tax. As a result of all these things, Pennsylvania war taxes actually produced only a fraction of the money they were designed to raise.[78]

By 1780 the violence against collectors that threatened the New England governments had appeared in Pennsylvania. The currency scarcity that followed the Continental refunding plans of 1780 and 1781 was especially severe in Pennsylvania's western counties, where people already thought themselves grossly overtaxed by eastern legislators, who understood little and cared less about frontier problems. One hundred thirty-five residents of Northumberland County complained, in a typical petition, that they were "utterly unable to pay these taxes unless by the sale of our lands."[79] Western Pennsylvania also included many Virginians, who lived on land claimed by Virginia and who had little love for Pennsylvania government in general and none at all for Pennsylvania tax collectors. Disgruntled frontiersmen sometimes flatly refused to pay any taxes and assaulted collectors. William Irvine reported from Fort Pitt in 1782 that "a great majority of the people are determined not to pay in any mode," and in Westmoreland County armed crowds fired at tax assessors and drove them off.[80]

But Pennsylvanians everywhere, not just on the frontier, suffered from the currency scarcity and from the state's inability to pay the debts owed to the very citizens who owed it taxes. The economic problems were statewide, and so was the violence that grew from them. President Reed, for instance, complained that Chester and Bucks counties were among those that gave him the most trouble about taxes.[81] And in Berks County, just west of Philadelphia and Chester counties, mobs threatened collectors' lives, and officials reported "whole townships where not a man has sworn to his return." When Reed and Rittenhouse visited Berks County in 1780 to examine tax records and to encourage county officials to collect more, they found rioting against heavy taxes. One frightened commissioner from Lancaster (just south of Berks) warned President John Dickinson three years later that discontent over taxes was still so rampant that forcing payment might be "dangerous."[82]

By the end of the war, as the continuing economic crisis drove many close to ruin, newspaper essayists began to compare Pennsylvania's revolutionary war taxes with Parliament's colonial taxes. Americans made "a glorious stand" against the tea tax and "gained their point," a writer in the *Pennsylvania Packet* explained, and he saw no reason they could not do the same with unreasonable state taxes. The moment they submitted, he went on, "to one fraction of an over or unjust tax, then will they deserve that slavery which their valor has snatched from them." Thus he raised the possibility of a new revolution. "When one part of the community is to be exacted on to please and serve another, then disorder follows: to this may be imputed many of the Revolutions that has laid the world in blood; our own is a recent instance; why then will the men of influence lay a foundation for another, or is war so desirable as to induce us to contrive a continuation of it among ourselves." The people humbled George III and they should not now be awed, he concluded, by "any officers of government, either in the state or in Congress."[83]

Pennsylvania legislators thus found themselves trapped between dwindling collections and the threat of still stronger resistance if they tried to force payments. Facing this dilemma, legislators refused to insist on strict enforcement of the tax laws because, as President Reed put it, "they are afraid . . . of disobliging their constituents." Reed's complaint was echoed by governors in every one of the middle states during the Revolution: the new governments were too responsive to popular pressure; they tended, in the words of John Dickinson, to indulge "the prejudices of the uninformed," which he considered "treasonable cowardice."[84]

But what seemed like "treasonable cowardice" to Dickinson seemed like good government to many others, particularly those who supported the constitution of 1776. Many thought that lax collections and the various tax relief policies adopted during the war—such as a 1781 act permitting veterans and soldiers to pay half their specie taxes in paper—signified not a government dangerously inefficient, but precisely the reverse, a government efficiently responsive to the public will. Joseph Reed eventually agreed that the complaints of the "laboring poor" and middle-class people were truthful, that they could not pay rather than would not pay. "We have miscalculated the abilities of the country," Reed told Washington, "and entirely the disposition of the people to bear taxes in the necessary extent." For the Constitutionalists of Pennsylvania, the strength of the state lay in precisely those characteristics of government that Republicans saw as major defects: the willingness of legislators to respond to popular pressure, and the political independence that permitted them to alter and apply the revenue laws as they pleased, without Continental interference. For the Constitutionalists, the economic crisis that followed independence showed how important it was to keep control of taxes in local hands. The states individually must keep the power to tax "perfect and entire," warned "Democratus" in March, 1783, for once the Continental Congress won the power to tax, it might impose so many new and unjust taxes—even stamp and poll taxes—that people would have no recourse but "another revolution."[85] Thus the politics of revolutionary taxation helped set the course of postwar politics in Pennsylvania as in the other middle states. There were those who saw in the tax reform and relief policies of the war years evidence of strong, responsive state governments, governments whose willingness to respond to popular pressure was, in their view, both an outgrowth of the Revolution and a natural application of its principles. And there were those who, like Robert Morris and John Dickinson, saw in those same laws and policies, and in that same responsiveness, a fatal weakness.

CHAPTER SIX

The South

The southern colonies approached independence with tax laws that were on the whole more regressive and more unpopular than those of the northern and middle colonies. The New England colonies imposed high poll taxes but they also taxed land ad valorem. The middle colonies protected the landed wealthy through widespread property exemptions but they did not impose general poll taxes. In the South, however, most colonies collected general poll taxes *and* they taxed land equally by the acre (where they taxed it at all substantially) regardless of its productivity or value. In several southern colonies the equity of such taxes had been bitterly attacked before independence, but with little success. The movements for tax reform that accompanied revolution in the South, therefore, were stronger than they were elsewhere, and the changes they brought about were more pronounced. The most sweeping reforms came in the colony that had imposed the South's most regressive taxes.

The bloody suppression of the Regulators and the contempt with which North Carolina's assembly had treated backcountry demands for tax and other reforms left a legacy of discontent in the colony that Loyalists hoped to exploit.[1] Many North Carolinians had come to believe that their real enemies were sitting not in Parliament at London but in the colonial legislature at Edenton, and so the men who established the state's revolutionary government faced a serious problem when they tried to unite North Carolinians behind the Revolution. To do it, they had to make concessions to popular opinion, to deal with long-standing grievances, and to adopt reforms in government, particularly in the tax laws, that the old colonial assembly had refused to adopt time and time again.

Joseph Hewes, a delegate to the Continental Congress, was wary of delivering too much power into the hands of the common people and opposed revising the colonial constitution in any radical way. He nevertheless conceded that any new war taxes in North Carolina would have to come not from the old assembly but from a popularly elected congress, one in which representation was as full as possible so that it might legitimately claim to be acting by authority of the people. Hewes's colleague at Philadelphia, William Hooper, agreed. He too saw little hope of raising money to fight the war unless a majority of the population could be directly involved in adopting new taxes. "Every man," he explained in May, 1775, "let his property be ever so small, has still his rights to preserve, and claims a share in the public consultation, which must eventually affect him." Hooper thought a convention to which each county could send at least ten delegates "would be prudent."[2]

If North Carolina's more conservative leaders, like Hewes and Hooper, thought the old discriminatory revenue system, which raised money primarily through poll taxes, might be preserved intact merely by a provincial congress' endorsement they were soon disillusioned. An expanded congress met in August, 1775, and issued $125,000 in paper to be supported in the traditional way, through poll taxes, beginning in 1777. By May, 1776, the congress had ordered £500,000 more emitted, with taxes—again on polls rather than property—not to start until 1780. But when the congress ordered a survey of ratable polls, as a first step toward collections, the response was less than encouraging. On July 4, 1776, while the Continental Congress at Philadelphia solemnly declared American unity and independence, the provincial congress of North Carolina was still begging committees of safety around the state to complete their surveys.[3]

At the same time, many North Carolinians were becoming aware of the potential for change inherent in revolution. Not content to fight merely for independence from England, they expected a general reformation of their own internal government as well. In September, 1775, for instance, Mecklenburg County asked that county officials under the new revolutionary government be popularly elected rather than appointed, that plural officeholding be abolished, and that election to the assembly be open to "every freeman who shall be called upon to support government either in person or property." Echoing old Regulator demands, Mecklenburg residents also called for public accounts "regularly kept in proper books open to inspection of all persons whom it may concern." The following year, they instructed their delegates to the state constitutional convention to "oppose everything that leans to aristocracy or power in the hands of the rich and chief men exercised to the oppression of the poor" and to secure in particular "a General and equal land tax" to replace the poll taxes in the state, so that all would be "taxed according to their estates."[4]

The provincial congress tried to ignore such demands, just as the old colonial assembly had, when it approved new poll taxes to support the £500,000 in paper issued in May, 1776. But before that or any of the new poll taxes could be collected, the provincial congress adopted a constitution that sharply curtailed the legislative power of the easternmost counties, whose representatives had shown little interest in tax reform, and that increased the power of the interior counties, which had long demanded such reforms.[5] Conservative leaders such as Samuel Johnston condemned portions of the new constitution as dangerously democratic, part of an assault by the common sort against the wealthy and genteel. "Everyone who has the least pretensions to be a gentleman," complained Johnston, who had not been elected to the provincial congress, "is suspected and borne down *per ignobile vulgus*—a set of men without reading, experience or principle to govern them." And James Iredell, disturbed by Johnston's defeat, suspected that the majority against him included levelers out to loot the property of gentlemen and to "shift distresses" from their own shoulders to those of the well-to-do.[6]

The actions of the new government did little to calm such fears. The first legislature under the new constitution met in 1777 and quickly made clear the Revolution's influence on public finance in North Carolina. The state's first tax laws substituted ad valorem general property taxes for the all-pervasive prewar poll taxes. Levying "a tax on property by general assessment will tend to the ease of the inhabitants of this State," the new legislature explained, "and will greatly relieve the poor people thereof." The tax was one halfpenny for each "pound value of all the Lands, Lots, Houses, Slaves, Money, money at interest, Stock in trade, Horses and Cattle in this State." The sole remnant of the poll tax fell on freemen whose estates were worth less than £100 assessed value. In a tax law adopted the following November, the assembly justified the switch from poll to property taxes on the grounds that men ought to be taxed "in Proportion to the Ability of each individual" to pay.[7]

Subsequent laws varied little, although special-interest groups occasionally won some exemptions. In 1778, for instance, the assembly exempted materials that "any Trademan or Manufacturer may have on hand for carrying on such Trade or Manufacture." Legislators lowered the taxes on money at interest in 1781 and abolished them the next year. Despite these revisions and occasional exemptions, North Carolina's commitment to general property taxes and to the ability-to-pay principle remained firm as long the the war lasted.[8]

North Carolina had not been a wealthy colony, and the Revolution left it poorer still. The assembly listened to complaints about the economic crises brought on by the war and adopted tax relief policies that pleased delegates from the interior subsistence farming regions and outraged representatives from the merchant community and from the older, well-established commercial farming regions. Of all the rebelling colonies, for instance, none imposed taxes less adequate to the task of funding its debts and paper currency than North Carolina did. Between 1775 and 1780 the state issued $6,500,000 in currency exclusive

of various military supply and pay certificates, which totaled
$26,250,000 for 1781 alone. Yet state taxes, beginning in 1777,
averaged only £6,500 sterling a year during the next decade.[9]
There was political capital to be won by supporting such low
taxes, and opponents of Hewes and Johnston (both of whom
preached fiscal orthodoxy) did just that. By 1781, tax delays and
suspensions had become common legislative policy. Taxes to retire the currency emissions of 1775 and 1776, for instance, were
postponed in 1780 and again in 1781. And taxes designed to retire
a particular emission were revised to permit payment in different emissions and in state military and supply certificates as
well. The assembly met a specie scarcity in 1782 by allowing
people to pay up to three quarters of their specie taxes in tobacco notes, deerskins, hemp, or several other commodities.[10]

Despite the low taxes, suspensions, and delays, the state's collections were apparently not much more efficient than the colony's had been. Tories and other "disorderly people" often flatly
refused to pay, and tax officials sometimes refused to collect.
Those who did collect sometimes pocketed the money instead of
paying it over to the treasury. Governors and other officials complained endlessly that taxes came in "very slow" when they came
in at all and that collections always raised less than had been
expected.[11] The inefficiency aside, however, North Carolina is a
good example of a state in which the Revolution made possible
reforms that the colonial assemblies had blocked repeatedly.
When the revolutionary government replaced general poll taxes
with general property taxes, it replaced the most regressive tax
system in the thirteen colonies with one that came a great deal
closer to the ability-to-pay standard.

But such changes did not please everyone in North Carolina,
and the battle over tax policy was far from over in 1783, and the
reforms that had been won were far from secure. The assembly's
willingness to respond to popular pressure—its penchant for tax
reform, low levies, poorly funded paper emissions, tax suspensions and delays, and relief laws—helped convince conservative
men, such as Hewes, Hooper, Johnston, and Iredell, that they
and their state faced "ruin" at the hands of a legislature that

pandered to the majority, a legislature whose laws were, as a result, "the vilest collection of trash ever formed by a legislative body."[12] Their efforts to roll back some of the wartime reforms, and to return to a more conservative economic policy despite a serious postwar depression, kept tax policy and tax reform close to the center of North Carolina politics even after the peace of 1783.

In 1775 the revolutionary government of Virginia also faced the problem of raising funds without alienating supporters, and its solution, like North Carolina's, was the simultaneous emission of paper money and postponement of funding taxes. The provincial convention issued £350,000 in the summer of 1775 and £100,000 more the following spring. Funding taxes of the usual sort—poll and acreage land taxes—were not to take effect until 1777. By the fall of 1776, Virginia had a new constitution, and the new state legislature promptly pushed the starting date for tax collections back to 1778, explaining that people in many parts of the commonwealth would be "unable to pay" if collections began as scheduled in 1777. The legislators also decided to borrow or emit an additional £400,000 with taxes to sink the debt to begin in 1784. When they authorized borrowing another £1,000,000 in May, 1777, and committed the state to repayment by December, 1784, they made no specific provisions for funding beyond a promise to levy property taxes sometime in the future.[13]

Delay also permitted the legislators to sidestep the troublesome question of tax reform. Once early hopes that independence could be swiftly and cheaply won collapsed and heavy war taxes became inevitable, the clamor for reform began. "I need only tell you of one definition that I heard of Independency," wrote a worried Landon Carter to George Washington in the spring of 1776: a government "independent of the rich men." Some irresponsible candidates, he explained, were stooping so low as to seek election to the new assembly by denouncing taxes that had been passed largely, they asserted, to serve the needs of the rich. Worse yet, Carter continued, the appeal seemed to work, and such men were getting elected.[14] Others noticed the same trend, though with approval rather than alarm. The House of Burgesses in 1776, wrote Roger Atkinson in November, was "composed of men not quite so well dressed, nor so politely educated, nor so highly born as some Assemblies" he had seen. "They are the People's men," he concluded. There was no sweeping and dramatic turnover of power in the Virginia House of Burgesses as there had been in some of the other colonies, but the Revolution did significantly reduce the power of the wealthy in the house—wealthy men held half the seats before independence but only a quarter of them after the war—as well as the influence of the great landed families. Men of humble birth and more modest means sat in their places.[15]

Petitions to the new revolutionary assemblies conceded the need for effective taxation but insisted that the burden be distributed more equitably than before. Petitioners wanted a general assessment of all property, not just land and slaves, based on value. Culpeper County residents put the case for reform before the assembly in November, 1777. They wanted taxes "established on the most equitable principles," as was "not the case when a tax is laid indiscriminately on the landed property of this state, there being a very great difference in the value thereof, arising from its situation and fertility." The less valuable lands, they continued, "are generally possessed by the poor, and, untaxed, require their utmost industry and labor to acquire therefrom a bare subsistence, while the possessors of the rich lands obtain the most plentiful crops, and are thereby enabled to enjoy not only all the comforts of life but to make annual additions to their estates." Culpeper residents asked that Virginia's old system of acreage land and poll taxes be replaced by "an act passed to tax each man in proportion to his real and personal estate." Orange County complained that taxing land equally by the acre was "unjust." Taxes ought to be "in proportion to the value of the land," and other kinds of property ought to be taxed ad valorem too. Fairfax County instructed its delegates George Mason and Philip Alexander to secure taxes by "general assessment" because such taxes would be "the most equitable."[16]

The imminence of invasion made unified public support urgent, and demands for reform could not be cavalierly shunted aside as they had been before. According to Edmund Pendleton, it took "long debate" sprinkled with "much Altercation," but in January, 1778, the Virginia assembly approved a new tax law that illustrated the way revolution altered the politics of public finance in Virginia. Equal acreage land taxes, the tax haven for the larger tidewater planters that had been successfully protected even through the brief spasm of reform after the Robinson scandal of 1766, were eliminated. The assembly substituted an annual tax of ten shillings for each £100 value of all land, plate, slaves, horses, and mules and of "all salaries, and . . . the neat income of all offices of profit," Continental military officers excepted. Assessors were to rate property "as the same would in their judgement sell for in ready money, having regard to the local situation of lands and other circumstances." The law tripled the taxes of anyone who refused to swear allegiance to the revolutionary government and it abolished all quitrents in the state except for those paid to Lord Fairfax, Washington's political mentor and friend. Additional taxes on money, interest payments, and spirits and a tobacco export duty rounded out the revenue program. Reform did not extend to the elimination of the poll tax, which was set at five shillings.[17] Nevertheless, the crisis forced on the new state government by independence created the conditions under which reforms long demanded and long denied were enacted, and revolutionary Virginia's legislature committed itself to the idea that taxation should be tied more closely to the ability-to-pay standard than it had been in the past.

Problems developed. Virginia, as did every state, had its share of corrupt sheriffs and collectors, who used public funds for private investments. And occasionally some members of the legislature were embarrassed when people applied the rhetoric of the Revolution too literally and with a bit too much enthusiasm. When Richard Henry Lee's widowed sister complained that Virginia had no right to tax her land because she, being a woman, could not vote and was therefore not represented in the House of Burgesses any more than the colonists were in Parliament, the spirit of liberty had clearly spread where it was not intended. (Lee informed his sister that she would have to pay because she was virtually represented.)[18]

More serious problems soon emerged. Assessors had at first nearly complete freedom in estimating property values, and assessments varied greatly. Edmund Pendleton reported that the assessed value of similar slaves might be as low as £70 or as high as £1,950, so that one planter might pay 21s. and another more than £22 for similar property. Some assessors based their judgments on what land would sell for in specie; others, on what it would sell for in paper currency. Still others rated land on the basis of what its selling price would be if all land in a county were put on the market simultaneously, a stretched interpretation of the law aimed at reducing land taxes to a level far below that intended by the legislature. These evasions cut deeply into the expected revenues, and by the end of 1778 the assembly, reluctantly admitting that "the taxes collected . . . are not sufficient," raised them across the board.[19]

In the fall of 1778, Virginia legislators began looking for some way to make the system operate uniformly across the state while retaining ad valorem taxes. One possibility involved dividing land into several categories or classes according to location and quality, and then fixing by law the assessed value of all land within a particular class. John Tyler proposed dividing the state into two regions, one east and one west of the Appalachian Mountains, with assessed values higher for the former than for the latter. Within each region, land would be divided into three classes according to quality, and each would in turn be broken down into three smaller classes. Maximum assessed values for each class would be set by law. Tyler suggested a total of eighteen distinct categories of land. Thomas Jefferson prepared a

plan providing for only six different classes. In the end, however, the assembly chose to increase revenues by increasing taxes
rather than by restricting the power of the local assessors.[20]

But the problem of wildly varying assessments remained, and
in the spring of 1779 the assembly again considered the tax laws.
An attempt to undo all reforms and return to the preindepen-
dence system of flat-rate acreage taxes was beaten down, for not
even Pendleton, who had earlier described taxation based on
property assessments as "disgusting where it has been tried,"
was willing to return completely to the old ways. "It would be
most unjust," he now thought, for someone to pay no more for
valuable land bordering the Rappahannock River than he paid
for his "black Jack barrens." After "violent" debates that made
doubtful for a time the passage of any tax law, the assembly
adopted Jefferson's plan for dividing land into six categories.[21]

The reforms notwithstanding, the assembly at no time became, as some Virginians had feared, the docile tool of radical
reformers seeking to destroy the existing social and political
order. Although there were new men of humble origins in the
house after 1775, with their own spokesmen and leaders, such as
Patrick Henry, the great planters retained substantial power and
wielded it effectively in their own interest. In 1779, for instance,
they succeeded in having the ad valorem tax on slaves changed
to a flat-rate tax of £5 per slave.[22] They demonstrated their power and skill again in 1780, when they defeated the most radical
tax proposal made in the state during the war.

Faced with the difficult task of recruiting more men for the
Continental army, a secret committee of the assembly suggested
that the state offer each enlistee a bounty of one slave between
the ages of ten and forty years old. To do this, one slave would
be taken from each Virginian who owned twenty or more; in
fact, one would be taken for *every* twenty he owned. The owner
would receive a nontransferable interest-bearing note, payable in
specie in eight years, for the fair market value of the seized
slaves, the first payment to come five years after the slaves were
taken. It was simply, as a disgusted and angry Joseph Jones
charged, a forced loan.[23]

Large slaveholders were in a minority in the lower house by 1780, but they began a skillful and ultimately successful campaign against the plan. First, they suggested offering recruits a cash bonus rather than slaves, sweetening the change by agreeing that the taxes to raise the bounty money should fall only on those whose estates were worth at least £500 in specie. Then, having won the point and eliminated the confiscation of slaves, they began whittling down the lower limits of the tax, first to estates worth £300, then even lower. Finally, the money was raised through normal tax assessments. What had begun as a special assessment on the rich thus ended as merely another tax levied on the whole population.[24]

Throughout the war, however, the assembly adopted several tax relief plans designed to ease payments lest the burden fall "with crushing weight on great numbers of honest, industrious men." Soldiers and sailors were generally exempt, and in May, 1778, Virginia offered enlistees a lifetime exemption from the poll tax as an inducement to join. Those on parish poor lists and relief rolls also got exemptions.[25]

Similarly, tax relief was at least part of the motive behind several plans to tax in commodities rather than money. The assembly hoped that war supplies might be gotten more cheaply by taxing them in directly than by purchasing them with money taxed in, and at the same time, commodity taxes were expected to offer people some tax relief.[26] The law, however, when it passed, *demanded* payment in commodities rather than *allowing* it in lieu of cash, and the new taxes were not distributed across the population according to wealth or income. Instead, the commodity tax became a flat-rate poll tax. All men and all female slaves over sixteen had to pay (or have paid for them) one bushel of wheat, two bushels of rye, Indian corn, or barley, ten pecks of oats, fifteen pounds of hemp, or twenty-eight pounds of inspected tobacco. A disastrous harvest, so bad that Virginia in one season went from exporting to importing wheat, made the new taxes still more burdensome. Nor did the commodity tax increase the "coin" in which general taxes might be paid, thus providing some relief. By the end of the year, the assembly was flooded with complaints that the new tax worked with "great inequality" and was particularly oppressive to "the poor," as were all general poll taxes. The assembly finally resorted to the same general relief policies it adopted with regard to money taxes: extensions and postponements.[27]

In some cases, however, commodities were acceptable at the taxpayer's option as an alternative to paying in cash, and thus offered some relief, especially after 1781, when the state sharply increased its specie taxes. After 1781 the faction in the assembly led by Patrick Henry (which normally represented the interests of smaller farmers of the southside counties and those in the west) pushed, often successfully, to expand the list of commodities acceptable in lieu of money.[28]

Throughout the remainder of the war, Virginia continued to tinker with its tax laws. In November, 1781, it abandoned classing land and delivered assessments back into the hands of local officials, who proved themselves no more consistent or trustworthy than they had before. By late 1782 the assembly turned again to classing land, dividing the state into four areas—the tidewater, the piedmont, the great valley, and the tramontane regions. The new law valued land in the first at ten shillings an acre; in the piedmont, seven shillings sixpence; in the valley, five shillings sixpence; and land beyond the mountains, three shillings.[29] But all the tinkering after 1777 and all the different plans put forth to rationalize assessments were in the end merely variations on a common theme, that taxation in Virginia would henceforth be based on the value of estates and would thus be bound more closely to the ability-to-pay principle than it had been before independence.

The form of the taxes aside, the Virginia assembly still had to decide whether it could safely collect the taxes it had imposed. The assembly quickly proved itself unwilling or unable to force collections. By 1780, for example, thirty-three counties (about half those in the state) were delinquent in taxes. Sixteen had paid into the treasury no taxes at all for 1779. The legislators responded to demands for relief by postponing the collection of some levies time and time again. They delayed final collection of the commodity tax of 1779, for example, for seven months in May, 1780, for another five months in October, and for still another five months in May, 1781. When they agreed to an annual tobacco poll tax in October, 1779, to raise money "for the use of the United States," they put off the first collections until December, 1780. At the same time, the state courted public support by adopting special taxes for profiteering merchants and tradesmen[30]

By 1783, tax collection policy had become a major political issue that polarized the assembly and foreshadowed many of the chief political divisions of the postwar years. On one side stood Madison, Joseph Jones, John Tyler, and usually George Mason, men who considered immediate payment of public debts to be a matter of the highest importance, and financial support of the Confederation Congress imperative. On the other side of the question, Patrick Henry led a faction that supported tax suspensions and other relief measures designed to aid troubled small farmers and backcountry men. Henry dwelt at length in his speeches on the "suffering of the poor people," trading effectively on his reputation as the taxpayers' friend. His impassioned support for tax suspensions brought charges from his rivals that he had stooped to "courting the popular vote" and "sailing with the wind." He did not sail alone. John Tyler noted with disgust that "he who can go back from the Assembly" and tell his constituents "he has saved a penny [in taxes] secures his popularity against the next election." Such men continued to "court the freeholders by declaring against executions and taxes."[31]

There was more involved than mere self-serving political posturing. Henry spoke for many around the state who had suffered in the war, had come close to and still faced economic disaster, and had turned to their state legislature for help. Even George Mason and Edmund Pendleton, by no means advocates of the politics of popularity, occasionally supported tax suspensions on grounds of *Salus populi suprema lex*. Thomas Jefferson made Henry's point directly: taxes, he wrote, should be no higher than what "may be annually spared by the individual," and selling a man's estate for taxes was not "evidence of his ability to spare."[32]

Henry's most successful campaigns for tax relief came late in the war. Shortly before the spring session of 1782, the *Virginia Gazette* published an essay by "The Farmer," which demanded tax delays and that the treasurer accept commodities in lieu of cash. Other essayists replied, but they had little impact, for, as St. George Tucker sourly reported, the article had "caught the popular ear most astonishingly," and the Farmer had become "an oracle of the people."[33]

Henry's tax relief policies prevailed in that and the following sessions of the legislature. Many certificates of public indebtedness—IOUs, in effect, given by the state of Virginia to its own citizens—were not acceptable for taxes, Henry pointed out. Was it just, then, for the state to insist on prompt payment of taxes from men to whom the state itself owed large debts it could not pay? The issue was an explosive one. Virginia had, as an emergency measure, authorized the army to issue, for the supplies it seized, certificates promising payment by the state. As early as November, 1780, Joseph Jones became worried that soaring taxes might push Virginians into rebellion against their own government. Something had to be done, and quickly, lest taxes become "oppressive and produce clamour and discontent." The state's decision to take military supply certificates for taxes, which seriously undercut the treasury's real income, was made in part to head off the rising discontent that worried Jones.[34]

When the state refused to accept such certificates for a time in 1781, the discontent reappeared instantly. County officials reported "much murmuring" and some "violent clamours" as well. Albemarle County public creditors warned that they could not "think much longer of paying a continental tax, unless in the collection, they have credit for what is due them from the public." One Colonel W. Curle refused under the circumstances even to attempt to collect specie taxes in Hampton, Virginia. A militia colonel in Northampton County resigned rather than violate his conscience by trying to collect taxes from people who had no money with which to pay. Without some relief (such as permitting people to pay corn or oats in lieu of specie), there would, he warned, be "the most serious consequences."[35]

Henry had his way. The assembly postponed the annual specie tax, half for one month and the remainder for six. It increased the number of commodities acceptable for taxes and extended the time for paying the commodity tax of 1781. In the next session, the assembly added several kinds of military certificates to the list of those receivable in lieu of cash for taxes, and in the spring of 1783 it authorized still more tax suspensions. For the "ease and convenience of the citizens of this commonwealth in their present distressed state," the assembly decided that "no distress for any tax imposed by the . . . [revenue act of 1782] shall be made before the twentieth of November next." Henry's opponents complained that the legislature was infected with "a rage for giving ease to the people," but they were unable to shorten the delay by more than a few weeks.[36]

By comparison with legislators in Massachusetts at least, those in Virginia were indeed "attentive to the ease and convenience of their constituents."[37] Nationalist James Madison complained that his fellow assemblymen were too attentive to their constituents and not attentive enough to the needs of Congress and the Continental army. Madison and others who opposed Henry's relief plans drew conclusions from their experience similar to those Alexander Hamilton was drawing in New York, that the state legislature was simply too responsive to public pressure and was, in a word, too democratic.

The matter of whose interests ought to prevail in the Virginia assembly—those of the Continental Congress and, presumably, of the American people as a whole, or those of the people of Virginia—surfaced early in the war, when the Congress made what many Virginians thought were impossible demands for money. In November, 1777, for example, Benjamin Harrison told Robert Morris that Virginia would probably raise and send to Congress "very little indeed, and yet," he continued, "it will be full as much as the country"—meaning Virginia—"can bear."[38]

The clash of interests, state versus national, was drawn more clearly in 1780 and 1781, when Congress set forth its plan for refunding the national debt and controlling inflation. To comply, Virginia would have had to repeal its own legal tender paper laws and to impose new taxes so heavy that Jefferson thought they would be "distressing to the last degree." Henry, supported by piedmont and mountain delegates and by nearly half the tidewater delegates as well, opposed the plan, and the assembly rejected it.[39] Shortly after the critical vote, however, Henry left the legislature. His opponents introduced the plan again, and it was narrowly adopted.[40] Yet even this victory proved to be hollow. British invasion sent war costs soaring and left Joseph Jones and other supporters of the Continental plan convinced that Virginia had no choice but to issue more paper money of its own even if the Congress' plan was thereby reduced to a shambles. "Of the evils that present themselves," Jones rationalized, "we think we choose the least."[41]

Virginia's reluctance (according to Madison) or inability (according to Henry) to fill congressional requisitions for money and supplies convinced Madison that Congress must have the power to coerce the states, including the power to send the Continental army against any state that refused to comply with Congress' demands. Continental soldiers could "compel such states to fulfill their federal engagements." The army could also "make distraint on any of the effects, vessels and merchandizes of such state or states, or of any of the citizens thereof, wherever found," and "prohibit and prevent their trade and intercourse . . . with any other of the United States." Had Madison had his way, that army would also have imposed national land and national poll taxes.[42]

No state government could welcome the prospect of Continental soldiers crossing its borders to collect taxes by force any more than colonial governments had welcomed the efforts of British soldiers to do the same. But many in Virginia opposed granting coercive revenue powers to a national government for reasons more directly related to the state's experience in taxing its own people during the Revolution. Governor Benjamin Harrison feared that if the powers of taxation and coercion were given to Congress, Virginia would no longer have the ability to shape its tax policies in response to local demands for reform and relief. Virginia had fallen far behind in meeting congressional requisitions, Harrison conceded (the state owed $1,482,490 for 1781 and 1782 alone), but that resulted from necessity not intent. The legislature, he explained, had no choice but to respond to its constituents' needs when it drafted laws. As Harrison told Robert Morris, Virginia could meet congressional requisitions and place crushing new taxes on its people or it could deal with their needs first and sacrifice Congress' requests. Harrison made it clear that his "indispensable duty" as an elected Virginia official was to do the latter.[43]

Harrison's letters forecast much of the debate in Virginia over the need for a stronger national government to replace the Confederation. During the Revolution, and largely because of it, the assembly had been willing to reform tax laws and to revise tax policies, to bring both more into line with the ability-to-pay principle. The preservation of those reforms, not to mention the winning of new ones, and the continuation of Virginia's tax relief programs presumed that the state legislature had final authority over all taxes Virginians paid and that it possessed the power to act on such matters as it saw fit, without having to bow to the wishes or prohibitions of any superior legislative body, English or American. The Virginia assembly made the same point when it refused for a time to grant Congress the power to collect imposts. "The permitting any power, other than the General Assembly of this Commonwealth, to levy duties or taxes upon the citizens of this state within the same," the legislators explained, "is injurious to its sovereignty, [and] may prove destructive to the rights and liberties of the people."[44] What, after all, had the dispute with Parliament over the stamp and trade taxes been about? That the nationalist movement of the postwar years threatened the war reforms and relief laws was well understood in Virginia by future Federalists and anti-Federalists alike. To deliver the tax power into the hands of a foreign body (the Continental Congress) meant that the reforms that had taken so long to win, the reforms made possible by the Revolution, might be lost and that the taxes Virginians paid and the methods of payment would be decided by strangers to fit their own needs, not Virginia's.

South Carolina's provincial government also began the Revolution with a policy of fighting first and paying later. In June, 1775, the provincial congress issued £1,000,000 in currency but decided to proceed cautiously with taxes because, said David Ramsay, of "a fear of alarming the people." A time of "civil convulsion," explained William Henry Drayton, was no time for heavy new taxes, particularly not in a state that had, like North Carolina, a history of Regulator discontent that Tories might exploit.[45] The provincial congress emitted £120,000 more in November, 1775, and another £750,000 in March, 1776, without initiating taxes. Not until January, 1777, did South Carolina adopt a general property tax to support the war.[46]

Tax delay, however, was not followed by major tax reforms, as was the case in North Carolina and Virginia. The provincial congress, and the new state constitutions adopted in South Carolina in 1776 and 1778, did quadruple the size of the assembly and gave the backcountry parishes more representatives than they had ever had before. The new men who filled those seats seemed to South Carolina's planter-legislators to be unfit to govern. These "Back Woods men," grumbled Henry Laurens, were "unaccustomed to the formalities" of parliamentary procedure and expected to see the business of government completed "with no more words than are necessary in the bargain and sale of a cow." But despite the reapportionment, the back counties still did not receive the number of delegates to which they were entitled strictly on the basis of population, and control of the assembly remained in the hands of the low-country planters. Low-country seats not actually held by planters were often held by lawyers or well-to-do merchants, and except on matters where their interests clashed directly, such men could generally be counted on to support the planters. The new legislatures contained more men of middling fortune, and the power of the wealthy was somewhat diluted, but even after 1778, five out of eight seats were held by wealthy or well-to-do men, and the new constitution of 1778 the legislature approved included a clause that tied future representation not to population alone but to "the particular and comparative strength and taxable property" of the various parishes as well. The implications were clear: however many new delegates the western parishes and the common sort might add through population growth, the tidewater parishes and the rich would remain powerful through representation based on wealth.[47] In any case, the first reapportionment under the constitution of 1778 would not happen for seven years, so that low-country planter interests continued to prevail in the revolutionary tax laws of South Carolina. The general property tax of 1777 left the prewar tax system virtually unchanged. It imposed a land tax of ten shillings per hundred acres across the state without regard to quality, location, or value, and it established a fixed poll tax on slaves. But the kind of property owned by nonplanters—by urban artisans or the merchant community—was taxed as it had been before independence, ad valorem. Town lots, wharves, buildings in towns, merchants' stock-in-trade, income from faculties and trades—all were taxed according to value, thus continuing the usual tax discrimination against Charleston.[48]

The next general tax law, adopted in March, 1778, included a few minor changes. "Free indians in amity with this state," for instance, were excused from land taxes, a prudent gesture where the loyalty or at least the neutrality of the local tribes was desperately wanted. The law cut by half taxes on money loaned to the state and doubled the rates on property owned by absentees presumed to be Tories. It also imposed a tax on the carriages of the wealthy (but not on the "wagons" used on working farms). For the most part, however, the bulwark of the planters' pre-war tax protection, the acreage land taxes, remained unchanged. And it continued substantially unchanged throughout the war, despite attempts by Christopher Gadsden and other city and back-country representatives to alter it. Time and again, low-country delegates beat back reform drives both major and minor. In September, 1779, the house voted to assess town lots, wharves, and merchants' stock-in-trade at "the full value thereof," but the next year it crushed a move to tax slaves on the same basis. When Gadsden moved to tax the rich more heavily, by levying special rates on all cash over £10,000 in any man's possession, the house defeated him. When he tried to tax the very rich by doubling land taxes on all land beyond 20,000 acres held by one man, the house again refused to go along. In 1780 the assembly agreed to placate Alexander Gillon's raucous and riotous Charleston workers' organization by exempting artisans from faculty taxes, but that was all.[49]

South Carolina had problems collecting the taxes it did adopt, just as every other rebelling colony did. As early as March, 1778, Henry Laurens complained that little money for the war could be gotten out of the so-called patriots of South Carolina. At the same time, Rawlins Lowndes complained that the state's income barely sufficed to meet day-to-day expenses, much less to support armies to the north.[50] The problems grew worse after 1780, when British armies overran the coastal parishes. The assembly passed no general tax law in 1780, and governor John Rutledge begged Congress for a subsidy. "Taxes," he explained, "where a Country is attacked or possessed by the Enemy can't be collected to keep pace with the demands for it." Trying to collect taxes too vigorously might have been dangerous in any case. "Taxes and murmurings," sighed Henry Laurens, "more or less are inseparable companions."[51]

Although South Carolina's planter-delegates thwarted the kinds of tax reform taking place elsewhere in the South during the war, they dealt with such murmurings by adopting relief policies similar to those adopted throughout the states. Beginning in February, 1780, for example, the assembly agreed that people who supplied the army with "provisions or other necessary articles" might have the value of those articles credited against their next tax, plus interest for the time between the day the supplies were delivered and the day the taxes came due. And in 1782 the state levied an impost, trying to raise new revenues without raising the general property taxes. The imposts included a tax of three pounds sterling on each adult slave brought in from Africa and twenty pounds sterling on each imported from the West Indies. There were additional rates on liquors, wines, and billiard tables and a 2.5 percent impost on all other imports. These were expected to be primarily luxury taxes, which only those wealthy enough to afford imported goods would pay.[52]

But as the war drew to a close, the low-country planters, who had succeeded in fending off major tax reforms, began to review the nature of the revolution they had just experienced and their probable future in an independent republic. Edward Rutledge mulled over "the subject of taxes" in the summer of 1782 and concluded that "many years" would pass "before our people will be convinced of the necessity of paying [direct] taxes." The trouble, he decided, was that the "spirit of subordination" among the people at large had completely "evaporated" in the Revolution, making efficient government and effective public finance nearly impossible.[53] And by 1783 the planters had been frightened by serious rioting in Charleston against Tories and returning British merchants. But the rioters' anger might easily shift to a new target. The Revolution had already produced a great deal of newspaper rhetoric and mob action directed against South Carolina's aristocratic Whigs. "This revolution," wrote a worried David Ramsay, "has introduced so much anarchy that it will take half a century to eradicate the licentiousness of the people."[54] The planters in the assembly feared that backcountry people, who would no longer tolerate what "Democratic Gentle-Touch" called "attempts to filch the money out of their pockets to ease the rich Rice and Indigo planters," might unite with Charleston delegates and create a coalition powerful enough to challenge planter dominance. By the end of the war, the planter-delegates began to court backcountry and other delegates, to pass bills appealing to the back settlements, bills they had opposed earlier. They adopted an amended confiscation act in 1782, and in 1784 they passed into law a tax act that destroyed the prewar tax system and introduced reforms that had been demanded by Regulators and city delegates since the mid-1760s. The tax act of

1784 abolished flat-rate acreage land taxes and instituted ad valorem general property taxes. The law imposed the most comprehensive plan adopted by any state for classing land according to value. It set up twenty-four categories of land with values ranging from twenty-six dollars to twenty cents an acre. Thus those who owned the richest land, closest to shipping and producing (or capable of producing) the most, would pay the highest taxes, while those owning less valuable land would pay lower taxes. Low-country planters, David Ramsay noted, had long conceded the justice of the reforms, but they were only "very slowly convinced to adopt them."[55] The process of convincing them was not complete until after the war for independence ended, but then the kinds of changes the Revolution had worked elsewhere in the South finally came to South Carolina too.

The last royal governor of Georgia, James Wright, reported to Lord Dartmouth in January, 1775, that the Georgia provincial congress intended to levy a tax of £150,000 sterling to support opposition to England, but the members of the provincial congress itself had no such delusions. They issued £10,000 in paper as an emergency measure and bound all Georgians to contribute by an "equal and general tax" toward sinking it, but that was all. The date of collection and the method of apportioning the tax were both left comfortably vague.[56] The rebel government of Georgia managed to delay taxing longer than most of the rebelling governments, and not until 1778 was a new general tax law adopted. The law altered the pattern of taxes in the state, though hardly in the direction of greater equity. Land continued to be taxed equally by the acre, as it had been before, but for the first time, general poll taxes became an important part of the revenue system. It is doubtful, however, that much was collected under the law, since within a year British invasion reduced rebel Georgia to a couple of upland counties. Within another year the governor and a large part of his council, along with most of the state's records, departed for North Carolina, leaving only a handful of officials behind to maintain the pretense of government with the aid of rump assemblies that were chosen irregularly and met sporadically. None ever passed a tax law, and it would not have done much good if they had. For all practical purposes, the patriot government of Georgia ceased to exist from 1780 to 1782. In fact, two rival shadow governments, exclusive of the royal government that was reinstated in areas under British control, emerged for a time, one headed by conservative John Wereat and the other by the more radical George Walton. Both spent much of their time charging each other with fraud and lobbying with Congress' agents, who were trying to decide which government should receive the Continental subsidy payments sent to the state to enable it to continue fighting.[57]

Georgia supported itself during the Revolution largely as it had in the late colonial period, by issuing paper currency and by accepting subsidies from a superior government. The Continental Congress pumped over $2,500,000 in currency into Georgia by the end of 1780, and more subsidies followed. Not until January, 1782, did an effective American legislature reconvene in the state, and conditions were so chaotic that it did not even consider adopting new taxes, though it did issue more currency.[58] Finally, in July, 1783, the assembly passed the state's first tax act since 1778. The house slashed by half the taxes the governor requested, drawing the usual complaints that members were pandering shamelessly to their constituents, and then imposed taxes that differed markedly from those approved in 1778. The revenue act of 1783 retained the acreage land taxes (twenty-five cents on each one hundred acres of land, and on each slave and every town lot), but it eliminated the general poll taxes except for free blacks, who had to pay one dollar, and for white men over twenty-one who did not farm at least five acres of land or otherwise follow "some lawful profession or mechanical trade." They had to pay two dollars. The new law was, however, a temporary measure, for the assembly also ordered a complete survey of taxable property in the state so that "a future legislature" could "lay an equitable tax on the inhabitants." The members intended to replace the acreage land tax with an ad valorem general property tax—including levies on money at interest, cattle, and some luxury items, such as carriages—and thus bring the state's tax laws closer to the ability-to-pay standard. At the same time, the legislators made clear their intention to reimpose poll taxes.[59] Georgia emerged from the revolutionary war, then, with an ambiguous record on tax reform.

There was no ambiguity at all about the impact of the Revolution on Maryland taxation. As elsewhere, Maryland's early provincial congresses made do with interim measures, such as issuing paper currency funded by distant taxes and asking for voluntary contributions. Disgruntled Tories complained that the collections were anything but voluntary and that when it came to the forced collection of arbitrary taxes, Marylanders were in no position to criticize Britons.[60] Permanent reform had, as elsewhere, to await the completion of a new state constitution.

In August, 1776, "A Watchman," writing in the *Maryland Gazette*, applied the principles of the Revolution as he saw them to Maryland's internal government and demanded that the state establish taxpayer suffrage. "Every poor man has a life," the Watchman reasoned, "a personal liberty and a right to his earnings, and is in danger of being injured by government in a variety of ways; therefore it is necessary that these people should enjoy the right of voting for representatives, to be the protectors of their lives, personal liberty and property, which though small is yet on the whole a very great object to them." With notions like that gaining currency, leaders of Maryland's patriot party (for the most part, leaders of the old antiproprietary or country party) found themselves forced to make important concessions to popular feeling, concessions that fundamentally altered Maryland's tax system.[61] Reforms that country party leaders had championed earlier, safe in the knowledge that the proprietor would never permit them, now had to be implemented. The overthrow of the proprietary government had removed all excuse for not doing so. Thus Anne Arundel County instructed its delegates to the constitutional convention in 1776 to insist that "all monies to be raised on the people be by fair and equal assessment in proportion to every person's estate; and that the unjust mode of taxation by the poll, heretofore used, be abolished." These and other demands for fundamental reforms in Maryland's government filled some of the old country party leaders with deep misgivings. Charles Carroll of Carrollton feared a plot to "introduce a levelling scheme" under the "cloak of providing great privileges for the people." Although he and those who agreed with him succeeded in staving off many reforms (such as the elimination of property qualifications for voting), they were nevertheless forced by fear of a popular rebellion against their own leadership to make some concessions.[62]

The Maryland convention dealt with taxation by abolishing poll taxes and by adopting taxation based on wealth, and therefore on ability to pay. These reforms were not left to mere statute. The new principles were embedded in the state bill of rights, which declared that "the levying taxes by the poll is grievous and oppressive, and ought to be abolished; that paupers ought not to be assessed for the support of government, but every other person in the state ought to contribute his proportion of public taxes for the support of the government according to his actual worth in real or personal property within the state."[63] Two tax laws that passed in the spring of 1777 and one passed in October, 1778, established the state's first independent tax system in accord with the constitutional mandate. All property, real and personal, would be taxed according to value. Assessors were to rate the property—except public property and "provisions necessary for the use and consumption of the Family for the year, and wearing Apparel"—"as the same would in his judgement sell for in ready money." The laws later directed that the best land in the state should be valued at four pounds per acre and the worst at five shillings per acre and that all other land be assessed between those extremes. Buildings and other improvements would be assessed separately and their value added to the worth of the land on which they stood. Slaves too would be taxed ad valorem, as would silver plate and the income of lawyers, doctors, factors, and tradesmen. Subsequent laws refined the definition of taxable property somewhat, but did not materially weaken the basic reforms incorporated into the bill of rights. Carroll thought the new policies unjust, unwise, and certain to be costly to Maryland's wealthiest men, himself included. But, he explained to his father, who was similarly outraged, no matter how heavily the taxes bore on the wealthy, it would be fruitless, even hazardous, to oppose them too strongly. "There is a time," he wrote later, "when it is wisdom to yield to . . . popular heresies and delusions," particularly when such "unjust proceedings are popular."[64]

With the Calvert family and the proprietorship gone, other prewar country party commitments on taxes had to be honored as well. Clauses requiring landlords to pay the property taxes on the land their tenants occupied, and allowing debtors to pay taxes with money deducted from the interest they owed their creditors, had been confidently inserted in colonial bills that were never expected to take effect. In 1777, these measures became law. The new acts required owners of leased land to pay all taxes on their lands, regardless of any prior agreements that may have been included in their tenants' leases. Debtors were allowed to deduct ten shillings from the interest payments on each £100 they owed and to use the money to pay taxes. Creditors had to absorb the loss, regardless of the terms of their contracts. After 1780, debtors could withhold one sixth of their interest payments in order to pay taxes.[65]

Revolution substantially altered the composition of Maryland's lower house by sharply reducing the strength of the wealthy in general and of the great planters in particular, and increasing representation for farmers and the middling sort. But in the senate, Maryland's great planters and merchants, who were outraged by the new revenue arrangements, remained powerful. In May, 1779, the senate complained that such taxes discriminated against the "monied interest" by forcing creditors in effect to subsidize debtors. In 1781, opponents of the new laws made a determined effort at repeal, but the house crushed the attempt by better than a two-to-one margin. Representatives of the merchant community, such as James McHenry, and of the wealthy planter aristocracy, such as Charles Carroll, continued to object and enter protests on the senate journals, but they accomplished little, so popular were the new laws.[66]

Concern among Maryland's great planters that the new assembly was playing dangerously fast and loose with the sanctity of private property grew when the lower house called for the confiscation of Tories' property. In December, 1779, the house insisted that Maryland could not possibly tax in all the money the Continental Congress demanded, without confiscating and selling Tories' property. Any attempt to collect heavy new taxes another way, the assembly warned, would produce "universal discontent." Led by representatives of the colony's old planter aristocracy, the senate refused to concur, after which the house appealed to the public for support. Petitions demanding confiscation began to come in. Newspaper writers praised the plan as a tax relief measure and attacked all who dared oppose it. "Good God," asked "A Sentry" in 1780, "what is this state come to," that it refuse to "take the property of our enemies to pay our taxes." "I have borne a firelock," he added dramatically, "and I can say it is damned Toryism." In the face of such pressures, the senate relented, and Maryland adopted a confiscation act in 1781.[67]

Despite the reforms, Maryland taxes were not efficiently collected. On the Eastern Shore, Tories were plentiful, organized, and opposed to collections, and throughout the state, rampant inflation made delay in paying worthwhile for nearly everyone, Tory and Whig alike. Opposition to collections occasionally came to violence as the economic crisis brought on by the war worsened after 1780.[68] "There is sundry people in this country," reported Joseph Dashiell from Worcester County in February, 1781, "that seem determined to give all the opposition they can, to the collection of the taxes." One man had "tried all in his power to kill the sheriff," after which the sheriff resigned "for fear of losing his life."[69] People complained, with some justice, of corrupt officials who twisted the laws for their own profit. They occasionally delivered to the treasury military supply certificates, which they had bought cheaply, in place of the hard cash they had collected from the people. Others bought up most of the unconsigned tobacco in a locality and then sold it to poor people, who needed it to pay their tobacco taxes, at prices "greatly exceeding the current market price." This had the effect of artificially raising taxes on exactly those people who could least afford to pay them. Elsewhere, assessors collaborated with taxpayers to lower rates far below what the assembly intended. Several tax laws, for instance, exempted the "working tools of mechanics and manufacturers" from the general property tax, but some assessors did not tax gristmills, forges, furnaces, stills and fulling mills on the pretext that they were "tools." That was plainly not what the legislature meant.[70]

The Maryland assembly, furthermore, applied various tax relief policies in response to popular demand during the war. The council of state granted exemptions or remissions to those who suffered in enemy raids. And the state permitted payment of several taxes in commodities rather than currency or specie.[71] And taxes were kept far lower than Maryland nationalists thought prudent. "The legislature," charged "Rusticus" in the *Maryland Gazette* of August 9, 1781, "have been more tender of laying taxes than our affairs or good policy required." Between the first tax law of February, 1777, and October, 1780, Maryland passed eleven tax acts. If inflation is taken into account, the total taxes levied on property in that period probably came to less than 2£ 2s. sterling for each £100 value of assessed property, and even that figure is inflated, since Maryland consistently undervalued land for tax purposes and overvalued commodities accepted in payment. The state did not reintroduce full specie value assessments on land until 1783, when assessors were directed to determine the current specie value of land, having regard to "all circumstances, and advantages of the land from situation and convenience to market, and what the same is capable of producing by the acre in grain, tobacco or hay, and the average annual price of the produce in coin."[72] Overvaluing commodities gave at least some people the chance to pay taxes in produce at favorable rates. Occasional tax delays and suspensions, and a willingness to accept quartermaster's and other supply certificates in payment, completed the assembly's tax relief policy.[73]

In few states did the legislature's bowing to popular pressure and demands bring about greater changes than in Maryland. In keeping taxes low and adopting tax relief laws, the assembly placed the needs of Maryland's citizens before those of the national government. Continental financier Robert Morris disgustedly pointed out that from the national government's point of view, it made little difference whether Maryland assemblymen sought to relieve their constituents by voting against heavy taxes or by merely failing to provide "competent means to compel" payment of the taxes they did approve. The result was the same: little revenue delivered to the Continental Congress on time.[74]

Maryland's relief policies, however, were far less significant than the changes won at the state constitutional convention in 1776. By eliminating poll taxes in the state, and by embedding the idea that taxes should be based on ability to pay in the state constitution, Maryland joined North Carolina, Virginia, and, to a lesser extent, South Carolina as an example of the way the Revolution provided the opportunity to reform regressive tax systems. But the revolutionary government's ability to act rested on its autonomy in matters of internal taxation, an autonomy that was well protected by the Articles of Confederation. Any attempt to establish a government superior to the Maryland legislature and armed with coercive powers of taxation, however, necessarily implied a challenge to the assembly's ability to respond to popular demands for tax relief and reform. To those, like Charles Carroll, who viewed war finance in Maryland as an unpleasant and personally expensive experiment in popular politics, the legislative immunity from public pressure that a powerful national government might provide was something to be desired, but to others who approved of the changes the Revolution brought to Maryland's taxes, that was a danger to be fought.

Long before independence, the idea that taxes ought to be proportional to wealth or income was current in the southern colonies among those whose interest were not effectively represented in the legislatures. The idea underlay many of the reforms such people demanded unsuccessfully before the Revolution and many of the calls for reform that followed independence. Not all the resulting attempts at reform succeeded, and of those that did, not all were permanent. But in the contest between those who fought against reform of the South's colonial tax systems and those who fought for it, victory lay wholly with the former before independence but substantially with the latter after it. By the end of the war or shortly thereafter, four of the five southern states had taken long steps in the direction of fundamental tax reform, steps that brought their respective revenue systems more in line with the ability-to-pay ideal than they had ever been before.

Epilogue

In 1783, Americans from New Hampshire to Georgia celebrated the success of their revolution and looked forward to the long years of prosperity and progress they were certain lay ahead, now that independence was secure and the guns were silent.[1] It was commonly expected that Americans would now enjoy the benefits of their victory, each man able to rest at noon beneath his own fruit trees, enjoying wine and bread of his own making, surveying fields planted by his hands, without being molested by kings, nobles, parliaments, or meddlesome governments of any kind. Yet for many, the war was not completely over in 1783, for it continued to affect their lives for at least the next decade. "As there has been a time which 'tried men's souls' in one respect, so there is a time approaching which will try them in another," predicted the *Virginia Gazette* in May, 1783, and the prophecy proved accurate.[2] The states spent vast sums to win the war, and the national government was deeply in debt to creditors at home and abroad. Although the fighting had stopped, the war still had to be paid for through taxes. To a man about to lose his land at a tax sale for a fraction of its real worth, there was little comfort in being told by newspaper essayists and his creditors that in the long run independence had been cheaply bought, that the benefits to the nation outweighed the momentary inconvenience to those who failed to pay their taxes.[3]

The large war debts, efforts of British creditors to collect debts owed them in America, as well as American creditors' efforts, delayed during the war, to collect debts from their countrymen, and a postwar depression all combined to make state postwar economic policy a matter of overriding concern to most Americans. The wartime debates over tax reform and tax relief lost none of their importance and little of their vehemence after 1783, and the matter remained at or near the center of postwar politics in every region, but especially in those states where poll taxes survived the war.

Critics in Connecticut during the 1780s kept up a constant drumfire of complaints against poll taxes, which in 1787 still provided more than a third of the state's public revenues, a situation many thought "an affront to common sense."[4] Similarly, in Rhode Island the burden of taxes and their incidence became important campaign issues during the years from 1783 to 1788, and were closely connected with the central issue of Rhode Island politics during the Confederation years: paper money policy.[5]

In Massachusetts, taxation was important in fomenting Shays's Rebellion, though the discontent was by no means limited to taxation or confined to the rebelling western counties. Newspaper articles, town meetings, and county conventions around the state criticized not only the size of postwar taxes but also the fact that poll tax reform had failed in Massachusetts as it had in Connecticut.[6] In the spring of 1787 a Boston essayist explained that

> The worm at the root of the tree, which robs us of the fruits of liberty, of peace of contentment, is the shocking mode of taxation; which cramps industry by oppressing the poor, and which in every other country should produce the same effects. All human nature revolts at the idea of a sixth part being wrested from the wretched individual for the sake of his political protection; and the poll tax of this state has been nearly, if not quite equal to this enormous burden. . . . It is in vain that the reasons of state are disclosed, and that the understanding of the sufferers is enlightened by labored addresses; the people soon feel but they seldom reason abstractly on points of political necessity; and if it were not for their feelings, all the arts of the incendiaries in the world would not excite in them the frenzy of rebellion. . . . Capita-

tion taxes, in all countries, have done the same mischief, when pressed beyond a certain point.[7]

Another Boston writer made the point more succinctly:

—By equal laws, and equal sway,
Teach *landed wealth* an equal tax to pay;
Not on the *laboring* arm, the burden rest;
Nor *crush* the man, who ever are depressed.[8]

Massachusetts' commercial community and representatives of the coastal trading areas that dominated legislative policy tried after 1786 to tar all tax reformers with the brush of Shaysism and sedition, much as their counterparts during the Revolution had tried to brand tax reformers as secret Tories bent on destroying American unity.[9] Such charges made little sense when even staid Braintree, bailiwick of John Adams, issued instructions to its representatives in the General Court that would not have been out of place at a Shaysite convention. And Massachusetts was not alone in facing the threat of violence over questions of economic policy in general and over taxes in particular. Connecticut and New Hampshire both had brief eruptions of Shaysite violence, and their leaders recognized the possibility of a wider uprising.[10]

In Pennsylvania, tax policy became a central political issue in the battles between the Constitutionalist party and the developing Republican (or nationalist) party, with the latter favoring the strict collection of heavy new national taxes to pay the national debt at full face value. "Centinel" warned in the *Pennsyvlania Gazette* in February, 1785, that new taxes levied to pay the full face value of the public debt held by speculators would lead to violence. "If you persist," he warned the legislature, "to cram this law down our throats, I forewarn you that it will be resisted. We are not to be dragooned by men, whom we have appointed to make just and equal laws for the benefit of the people, and not for their own and their friends' emolument."[11] The threat was not an idle one. Pennsylvanians organized after the war to oppose tax collections in various ways. They often refused to bid on their neighbors' property at tax sales.[12] In the western counties, particularly those recently claimed by Virginia, collectors met intimidation and violence that occasionally drove them to resign in terror. Collector Philip Jenkins of Fayette County described being beaten and robbed by three men armed with pistols and clubs in June, 1784:

> Then all three stood before me and demanded of me if ever I would have any more to do with tax gathering, I said I did not think I should, you damn son of a bitch, says they, if you do go collecting any more and distressing for the tax you will be a dead man and we will burn all you have, god Damn you, says they, we have great mind now to smash you to the earth and lift up their clubs, but only one beat me and he not on my head but on my side, saying, the first man that is concerned with tax gathering is or shall be a dead man.[13]

As Shaysism in Massachusetts was not limited to counties in the Berkshires, so tax protests and riots were not limited to Pennsylvania's far western counties. When a collector in York County gave up trying to hold tax sales in his own township because residents refused to bid, he carried some property he had seized to a neighboring town to try to sell it there. Michael Hahn wrote to John Nicholson, describing what happened next. "On the day of sale, a number as I supposed of about 200 men, inhabitants of the adjacent townships, came into town, some armed with guns, others with clubs, the appearance of which threatened something hostile; they took post before the house in which the goods seized were lodged." The sale was finally held, but not until the mob took some of the property and not until local people who wanted to bid on the goods joined the sheriff and his deputies to drive off the mob. Worried civil officials later wrote the council of state, urging that the rioters' trials be moved out of the county because local justices could not be counted on "in the punishment of their neighbors." Others organized "a select corps of light infantry," composed of "some firm and good citizens" of the town, and asked the council of state to provide weapons.[14]

In New York, postwar tax politics continued where the prewar debates had left off: New York City fought attempts by the rural counties to increase its taxes. The city's representatives had not been very successful before the war, and the fact that many city residents spent most of the war under British rule reduced their influence even more. In the spring of 1784 the legislature agreed to levy a £100,000 punitive tax on the "southern District" to compensate the rest of the state for the taxes southern residents had not paid while under British occupation.[15]

Alexander Hamilton, representing the city, tried to have the city's quota lowered, but he also continued his unsuccessful campaign to have New York State's tax laws completely revised. The system of local control over assessments that had caused the Livingstons and other manor lords such pain meant, said Hamilton in 1787, that taxation was "a business of *honest guessing* or interested calculations of county convenience, in which each member would endeavor to transfer the burden from his county to another." "*Arbitrary,*" he argued, is "indeed another word for *assessment,* where all is left to the discretion of the assessors." For Hamilton, the cause of such ill-considered laws was in 1787 what it had been in 1783: a government too responsive to public will and popular pressure, too interested in serving up "dishes that suit the public palate" rather than laws designed to nourish the public treasury.[16] John Jay drew similar conclusions and condemned the "manufacturers of laws" who "more generally consult the prevailing fashions and predilections of the day than the utility of their goods to those who are to wear them." He saw in New York all the makings of an incipient Shaysism: "a reluctance to taxes, an impatience of government, a rage for property and little regard to the means of acquiring it, together with a desire of equality in all things." The state's tax policies, paper money policies, and less than urgent desire to assist the national government in paying off its debts led Jay to pessimistic conclusions about the ability of Americans in general to govern themselves. "The mass of men," he wrote, "are neither wise nor good, and the virtue like the other resources of a country, can only be drawn to a point and exerted by strong circumstances ably managed, or a strong government ably administered."[17]

In the South, Virginia's postwar economic policies taught James Madison a similar lesson. His battles with Patrick Henry over tax policy continued unabated after the peace, and Madison continued to lose regularly as the assembly adopted tax delays, remissions, and schemes for allowing payment in commodities. "There is no maxim," Madison concluded in 1786, "in my opinion, which is more liable to be misapplied and which therefore more needs elucidation, than the current one, that the interest of the majority is the political standard of right and wrong. Taking the word 'interest' . . . in the popular sense, as referring to immediate augmentation of property and wealth, nothing can be more false."[18]

The South, like New England and the middle states, also had to contend with violence over taxes. Virginia had as much difficulty as Pennsylvania had recruiting tax collectors, and Virginia farmers banded together to prevent tax sales or to refuse to bid on their neighbors' property. Occasionally sheriffs were threatened with death.[19] In 1785, settlers in Washington and Montgomery counties went to the brink of open rebellion over taxes and land and monetary policy. "Don't you let or suffer any sheriff whatever to take your property and sell it, but rather apply to your muskets for redress," Arthur Campbell advised frontier Virginians in 1785. He swore that "before he would submit to the laws for enforcing of taxes, he would rather take up his musket and fight till he lost the last drop of his blood." And he found other Virginians who agreed with him.[20] Campbell's were not the only attempts to organize violence in the state. James McClurg told Madison in the summer of 1787 that three hundred men in Greenbrier County had "signed an Association to oppose the payment of the certificate tax, and in general of all debts; and it is apprehended there that they will attempt forcibly to stop the proceedings of the next court."[21] In response to these problems, and to waves of petitions arriving at Richmond, the legislature consistently followed a policy of tax relief, trying to remain "in the happy medium between that rigor which borders on oppression of the people and a negligence which tends to injure the public revenue."[22]

In North Carolina, peacetime brought taxes back to center stage in the legislature, and in April, 1784, virtually all wartime tax reforms were rolled back. Heavy poll taxes again became important in the revenue system, and acreage land taxes replaced ad valorem rates. The change set off a three-year struggle to win back at least some of the reforms. In 1787, though poll taxes remained, land taxes returned to a modified ad valorem assessment system. The return to prewar practices extended beyond mere legislation, and the 1780s in North Carolina were marked by scandals, embezzlements, and fraud involving high public officers, including the state treasurer. As in other southern states, frontier settlers protested their taxes and threatened violence.[23]

Peace brought defeat for North Carolina reformers but marked, for a time, victory for those in South Carolina when in 1784 that state adopted ad valorem land taxes for the first time. At the same time, the legislature raised luxury taxes and the taxes on merchants' stock-in-trade and on professional incomes. Perhaps these reforms were instrumental in reducing tax protests in South Carolina to a level far below those in the rest of the South.[24]

Postwar relief policies varied from state to state, extending from continued paper emissions in Rhode Island to tax suspensions in Virginia and tax reforms in South Carolina, but most of the new states adopted some legislative programs in response to public complaints and threats of violence. The organization of the new nation under the Articles of Confederation assured state legislatures independence where finance was concerned, thus guaranteeing their ability to tailor tax and monetary policy to the needs or wishes of their own constituencies rather than to policies formulated at Philadelphia or New York City. Both their fiscal autonomy and the responsiveness it made possible were challenged directly by the federal constitution proposed at the Philadelphia convention in the summer of 1787, and anti-Federalist essayists returned constantly to that point during the subsequent debate over ratification.

Deliver the taxing power into the hands of some government other than your own, warned George Clinton, and regressive taxes unknown to New York, such as the general poll tax, would follow inevitably. New Yorkers knew or should have known from their own experience, he continued, that "great landholders" always try to protect themselves by imposing poll taxes rather than property taxes. That would be no different, he warned, in the proposed new national congress. "A Poll tax is at all times oppressive to the poor, and their greatest misfortune will consist in having more prolific wives than the rich." Depend upon it, he concluded, ratification would mean poll taxes in New York.[25]

Essayists in the other middle states, also largely free from general poll taxes, made the same point. "The power of direct taxation," warned the minority at the Pennsylvania ratifying convention, "applies to every individual, as Congress under this government is expressly vested with the authority of laying a capitation or poll tax upon every person in any amount. This is a tax that, however oppressive in its nature, and unequal in its operation, is certain, as to its produce and simple in its collection. . . . This tax is so congenial to the nature of despotism that it has ever been a favorite under such governments."[26]

From whatever region the protests came, the central argument was the same: only *state* legislators were familiar enough with local problems and conditions to draw up equitable tax laws. No one but Virginians, insisted Patrick Henry, could devise laws that would permit Virginians to "pay our money in the most easy manner for our people." So fundamentally did the states differ that any attempt to create a national basis for taxation would inevitably be burdensome and unjust to some. A fair and equitable tax in Delaware might be neither in Virginia. "The taxes cannot be uniform throughout the states without being oppressive to some," warned Virginia's William Grayson.[27] Such dangerous uniformity might well cause the loss of tax reforms long battled for and only recently won in many states. Were North Carolinians ready to abandon ad valorem general land taxes and return to equal acreage assessments? asked one opponent of the Constitution there. Ratification, he predicted, would lead to a national land tax, which would mean that a rich New Englander would pay no more per acre than the poorest North Carolinian. "A common poor man here will have much more to pay [in taxes] for poor land than the rich man there for land of the best quality."[28] Such arguments, of course, did not prevent ratification. No single issue can account for passage or rejection of the Constitution in all the states. Nevertheless, the thirteen states' experience with internal taxation from 1763 to 1783 and beyond helped shape both Federalist and anti-Federalist thought.

In many of the colonies in 1763, tax policy was formulated in such a way as to benefit groups dominant in the various legislatures. Sometimes the manipulation was blatantly political, as in Rhode Island, where tax burdens shifted north to south, depending on which political faction had won the last election. Occasionally, discrimination was more related to economic than political factors, as in New York, where landed property remained protected no matter which faction, Livingston or De Lancey, controlled the assembly. Almost everywhere outside the middle colonies, poll taxes aided large landowners by shifting significant portions of the taxes off real property. Elsewhere, particularly in the South, the propertied men who dominated the assemblies insisted on taxing land, when they taxed it at all, on the basis of acreage rather than value. None of these policies existed without protest and opposition, but virtually all were successfully maintained until the war for independence began in 1775.

Although internal taxes were not an important factor in precipitating the Revolution, independence did provide an opportunity to reform the colonies' internal governments, as many colonists had long demanded. The elimination of proprietary governments in Maryland and Pennsylvania, for instance, also eliminated many of the land tax havens of the Penn and Calvert families. The war created the potential for reform in other ways too. Discontented groups could no longer be cavalierly ignored; the rebellious assemblies needed popular support in order to conduct the war, and consequently more consideration was given to petitions for tax reform and relief than they had received before. Maryland's constitutional convention, which raised a prohibition against poll taxes to the level of constitutional principle, is a good example of this trend, as are North Carolina's wartime abandonment of poll taxes, the shift from acreage taxes to ad valorem rates in Virginia, the elimination of equal county quotas in Delaware, and the addition of unimproved land to the tax rolls in New York. Legislative reforms that ended or at least reduced the overrepresentation of eastern areas also aided reformers in several states. They soon discovered that as a result of the Revolution, they had more legislative muscle to back their demands. The elimination of the royal charters, the adoption of new constitutions, and the need to rewrite many laws, all the while maintaining public support, provided countless opportunities for legislators so disposed to reform tax laws in accord with popular demands and later to institute tax relief policies that their constituents demanded. Commodity payments in lieu of money, accepting numerous paper issues and certificates of state debt, tax delays, suspensions, and on occasion outright remissions all came under this heading.

As the old colonial taxes had not been maintained without opposition, so the new order in many states and the new responsiveness to public pressure did not go unopposed. Conservative-minded men in every region viewed such responsiveness as a fatal defect of the new state constitutions and of the Articles of Confederation. They saw its results in the tax reform laws, in state paper money and legal tender laws, in laws suspending the collection of debts, and in state refusals to meet congressional requisitions, to tax heavily enough, or to collect the taxes that were passed. And they reasoned that if state autonomy under the Articles of Confederation was what allowed such irresponsibility to flourish, then the imposition of a superior government beyond the reach of the state legislatures (and thus farther from the reach of state voters as well) might be the cure.[29]

Although internal taxes were far from being a cause of the American Revolution, the changes that came about after 1775 were clearly a result of the Revolution, and the pattern of those changes in American taxation lends support to the thesis J. Franklin Jameson advanced a half century ago: that "the stream of revolution once started could not be confined within narrow banks"; that "many economic desires, many social aspirations were set free" by the Revolution; and that colonial society was "profoundly altered by the forces thus set loose."[30]

Appendix

TABLE 1
Boston City Taxes, 1763–1774

YEAR	AMOUNT (£)	YEAR	AMOUNT (£)
1763	4,600	1769	8,000
1764	7,000	1770	4,000
1765	5,000	1771	8,000
1766	5,000	1772	6,500
1767	5,500	1773	7,000
1768	6,000	1774	8,000

SOURCES: *Boston Town Records, 1758–1769*, pp. 93, 118, 145, 185, 214, 247, 293; *Boston Town Records, 1770–1777*, pp. 26, 60, 86, 135, 180.

TABLE 2
Assessed Value per Poll for Rhode Island Towns, 1767

NEWPORT COUNTY	VALUE PER POLL (£)	KINGS COUNTY	VALUE PER POLL (£)
Newport	295	Westerly	158
Portsmouth	419	Charlestown	236
New Shoreham	259	Richmond	178
Jamestown	421	North Kingstown	207
Middletown	430	South Kingstown	459
Tiverton	292	Hopkinton	166
Little Compton	289	Exeter	156
PROVIDENCE COUNTY		KENT COUNTY	
Providence	277	Warwick	283
Smithfield	224	East Greenwich	193
Scituate	135	West Greenwich	143
Gloucester	133	Coventry	145
Cumberland	132		
Cranston	223	BRISTOL COUNTY	
Johnston	190	Bristol	319
North Providence	203	Warren	188

SOURCE: General estimate for 1767, in Bartlett (ed.), *Rhode Island Colonial Records*, VI, 576.

TABLE 3
Rhode Island General Taxes, 1763–1774

YEAR	TAX (£)	YEAR	TAX (£)
1763	12,000	1769	6,000 LM
			93,687 OT
1764	12,000	1770	12,000
1765	12,468	1771	12,000
1766	6,000 LM	1772	12,000
	75,000 OT		
1767	(no tax)	1773	4,000
1768	(no tax)	1774	4,000

SOURCE: *Rhode Island Acts and Resolves,* August, 1763, pp. 65–67, September, 1764, pp. 43–44, October, 1765, pp. 67–69, December, 1766, pp. 56–59, February, 1769, pp. 90–93, September, 1770, pp. 62–65, August, 1771, pp. 64–67, August, 1772, pp. 41–45, August, 1773, pp. 67–70, October, 1774, pp. 118–21. LM is lawful money, OT is old tenor money.

TABLE 4
Connecticut General Taxes,
1763–1775

YEAR	AUTHORIZED RATE (PER POUND OF ASSESSED VALUE)	ACTUAL RATE
1763	15d.	6d.
1764	15d.	8d.
1765	7d.	1d.
1766	8d.	(no tax)
1767	(no tax)	(no tax)
1768	(no tax)	(no tax)
1769	(no tax)	(no tax)
1770	2d.	2d.
1771	(no tax)	(no tax)
1772	2½d.	2½d.
1773	1½d.	1½d.
1774	2d.	2d.
1775	½d.	½d.

SOURCE: Gipson, *Connecticut Taxation*, 9, 18–20, 31–37. NOTE: A tax of one penny per pound raised about £5,000 in the mid-1760s. See Hoadly (ed.), *Public Records of Connecticut Colony*, XII, 339.

TABLE 5
New Hampshire General Taxes,
1767–1774

YEAR	AMOUNT (£)
1767	2,200
1768	2,200
1769	3,000
1770	2,000
1771	2,500
1772	2,000
1773	2,000
1774	1,000

SOURCE: Metcalf *et al.* (eds.), *Laws of New Hampshire*, III, 408–409, 509–10, 530, 536, 556, 580, 602, 627.

TABLE 6
Massachusetts General Taxes, 1762–1774

YEAR	TOTAL TAX (£)	POLL TAX
1762	78,447	10s.
1763	50,000	6s. 8d.
1764	50,000	6s. 8d.
1765	50,000	6s. 8d.
1766	40,000	5s. 4d.
1767	40,000	5s. 4d.
1768	(no tax)	(no tax)
1769	30,000	4s.
1770	25,000	3s. 4d.
1771	27,300	3s. 4d.
1772	27,500	3s. 4d.
1773	20,625	2s. 2d.
1774	10,312	1s. 1d.

SOURCE: The tax laws on which the table is based are in *Massachusetts Acts and Resolves,* IV, 583–98, 645–60, 708–19, 812–32, 883–99, 959–73, 1024–27, V, 5–20, 89–106, 107–109, 305–21, 395–409.

TABLE 7
Outstanding Taxes Due from Massachusetts Towns, 1763–1773

DATE OF REPORT	AMOUNT DUE (£)	DATE OF REPORT	AMOUNT DUE (£)
June 9, 1763	95,375	July 4, 1769	51,232
Oct. 23, 1764	101,954	Oct. 27, 1770	65,219
June 11, 1765	79,549	June 19, 1771	61,750
June 17, 1766	85,139	July 14, 1772	67,118
June 23, 1767	82,542	June 29, 1773	61,723
June 23, 1768	87,305		

SOURCES: Massachusetts House Journals for the dates given.

TABLE 8
Income from Pennsylvania Property Tax, 1763–1775

DATE OF AUDITORS' REPORT	AMOUNT (£)	DATE OF AUDITORS' REPORT	AMOUNT (£)
Sept. 30, 1763	21,235	Sept. 25, 1770	24,800
Sept. 22, 1764	18,419	Sept. 24, 1771	24,491
Sept. 21, 1765	23,032	Sept. 19, 1772	24,014
Sept. 18, 1766	22,225	Sept. 27, 1773	22,869
Sept. 22, 1767	28,097	Sept. 27, 1774	24,000
Sept. 20, 1768	26,317	Sept. 29, 1775	22,750
Sept. 21, 1769	22,365		

SOURCES: Hazard *et al.* (eds.), *Pennsylvania Archives*, 8th Ser., Vol. VI, 5463–73; Vol. VII, 5647–54, 5781–88, 5906–29, 6042–53, 6245–68, 6403–31, 6540–66; Vol. VIII, 6689–713, 6860–90, 6987–7018, 7105–40, 7263–95.

TABLE 9
Income from Pennsylvania Excise Taxes, 1763–1775

DATE OF AUDITORS' REPORT	AMOUNT (£)	DATE OF AUDITORS' REPORT	AMOUNT (£)
Sept. 30, 1763	4,022	Sept. 25, 1770	4,705
Sept. 22, 1764	3,916	Sept. 24, 1771	4,791
Sept. 21, 1765	3,698	Sept. 19, 1772	6,607
Sept. 18, 1766	3,241	Sept. 27, 1773	9,360
Sept. 22, 1767	4,465	Sept. 27, 1774	9,156
Sept. 20, 1768	5,162	Sept. 29, 1775	8,239
Sept. 21, 1769	5,187		

SOURCES: Same as in table 8.

TABLE 10
Income from New York Imposts, 1760–1774

YEAR	AMOUNT (£)
1760	10,346
1761	10,319
1762	7,109
1763	8,574
1764	7,597
1765	4,920
1766	7,271
1768	4,895
1769	4,678
1770	4,814
1771	3,615
1772	3,875
1773	5,078
1774	5,200

SOURCE: O'Callaghan (ed.), *Documentary History of New York*, I, 479–80; New York House Journal, November 25, 1766, November 17, 1768, December 8, 1769, January 8, 1771, January 28, 1772, January 27, 1773, February 3, 1774, February 9, 1775.

TABLE 11
Percentage of Colony Excise and Property Taxes
Paid by Philadelphia, 1763–1775

DATE OF AUDITORS' REPORT	PHILA. % OF EXCISE	PHILA. % OF PROP. TAX
Sept. 30, 1763	53	44
Sept. 22, 1764	55	42
Sept. 21, 1765	49	42
Sept. 18, 1766	53	42
Sept. 22, 1767	49	52
Sept. 20, 1768	55	37
Sept. 21, 1769	51	42
Sept. 25, 1770	53	42
Sept. 24, 1771	51	48
Sept. 19, 1772	57	40
Sept. 27, 1773	59	42
Sept. 27, 1774	58	41
Sept. 29, 1775	64	41

SOURCES: Same as in table 8.

TABLE 12
Comparison of New Jersey Tax Quotas, 1768 and 1771

COUNTY	1768 TAX[a] (£)	% OF TOTAL TAX	1771 TAX[b] (£)	% OF TOTAL TAX	CHANGE (£)
Middlesex	1,133	9	1,090	9	− 43
Monmouth	1,643	13	1,336	11	−307
Essex	973	8	900	7	− 73
Somerset	1,395	11	1,130	9	−265
Bergen	823	7	830	7	+ 7
Burlington	1,563	13	1,339	11	−224
Gloucester	977	8	953	8	− 24
Salem	873	7	849	7	− 24
Cape May	209	2	208	2	− 1
Hunterdon	1,772	14	1,704	14	− 68
Morris } Sussex }	695	6	1,645	13	+950
Cumberland	443	4	481	4	+ 38

SOURCES: Tax acts of October, 1757, and March, 1760, and "An Act to Settle the Quotas of the Several Counties in This Colony for the Levying of Taxes," October, 1769, all in New Jersey Session Laws, Early State Records; "A Table of Rateables in New Jersey," in New Jersey House Journal, November 10, 1769.

[a]The amounts are each county's portion of the total property tax to be raised (to retire the colony debt) in 1768, i.e., before the reapportionment of 1769.

[b]The amounts are each county's portion of the total property tax to be raised (to retire the colony debt) in 1771, i.e., after the reapportionment of 1769.

NOTE: Percentages have been rounded off and thus do not total precisely 100.

TABLE 13
Some Arrears in Pennsylvania Property Taxes, 1769–1773

COUNTY	1769	1770	1771	1772	1773
Philadelphia	£3,628	£3,897	£2,608	£4,045	£4,885
Bucks	539	346	700	804	502
Chester	1,030		2,656	2,651	1,897
Lancaster	1,202	320	510	883	1,304
York	1,583	2,164	1,608	1,635	1,541
Cumberland	2,748	2,251	2,680	2,184	2,506
Berks		14	101	81	101

SOURCES: Hazard *et al.* (eds.), *Pennsylvania Archives*, 8th Ser., Vol. VII, 6403–31, 6540–66; Vol. VIII, 6689–713, 6860–90, 6987–7018.

TABLE 14
North Carolina Colony Poll Taxes, 1763–1773

YEAR	COLONY POLL TAX	AMOUNT DELIVERED TO TREASURY (£)
1763	7s. 6d.	3,733
1764	7s. 2d.	8,117
1765	6s.	8,215
1766	4s. 4d.	8,762
1767	7s.	9,334
1768	6s. 6d.	2,336
1769	5s. 10d.	2,573
1770	3s. 10d.	(none)
1771–1773	(5s. to 7s. 6d.)	(none)

SOURCE: W. K. Boyd (ed.,) *Tracts Concerning North Carolina*, 413–17; Saunders *et al.* (eds.), *State Records of North Carolina*, XXIII, 781–83, 840–41, 850–51.

NOTE: The laws suggest the poll taxes from 1771 to 1773 were at least five shillings but were probably closer to seven shillings sixpence. In any case, it is well to recall that North Carolina tax laws often bore only a casual relation to what was actually collected.

TABLE 15
Virginia Land and Poll Taxes for the Sinking Fund, 1763–1769

	POLL TAX		LAND TAX	
YEAR DUE	AUTHORIZED	COLLECTED	AUTHORIZED	COLLECTED
1763	4s.	4s.	2s.	2s.
1764	5s.	5s.	2s.	2s.
1765	5s.	4s.	2s.	2s.
1766	5s.	4s.	2s.	2s.
1767	5s.	4s.	2s.	2s.
1768	5s.	(none)	2s.	(none)
1769	4s.	(none)	2s.	(none)

SOURCES: The authorized amounts are from Hening (ed.), *Statutes of Virginia*, VII, 69–87, 163–70, 171–79, 255–65, 347–53, 357–63, 495–502. Subsidies from Parliament allowed the reduction in poll taxes beginning in 1765, and land and poll taxes for 1768 and 1769 were canceled before collection. *Ibid.*, VIII, 295–98, and Edmund Pendleton to James Madison, April 17, 1765, in W.C. Ford (ed.), "Unpublished Letters of Pendleton," 108–109.

TABLE 16
Yield from Major South Carolina Imposts,
1763–1769

PERIOD	GENERAL DUTY ACT (£)	SLAVE IMPORT TAX (£)	SPECIAL LEVY ON RUM, WINE, FLOUR, AND BISCUIT (£)
Sept., 1763– Sept., 1764	35,841	19,500	17,000
Sept., 1764– Sept., 1765	31,990	51,000	16,000
Sept., 1765– Sept., 1766	31,597	50,000	12,000
Sept., 1766– Sept., 1767	36,070	26,500	6,000
Dec., 1768– Dec., 1769	32,157	44,000	16,500

SOURCES: All figures are compiled from treasurers' reports, 1763–1769, in Early State Records, South Carolina, D24, Reel 1.

NOTE: Figures in the last two columns are rounded off and are approximate. All figures are in South Carolina currency.

TABLE 17
Yield from South Carolina Import and Export Taxes, 1764–1772

PERIOD	AMOUNT (£)
Mar., 1764–Mar., 1765	77,681
Mar., 1765–Mar., 1766	111,425
Mar., 1766–Mar., 1767	50,979
Mar., 1767–Mar., 1768	187,984
Mar., 1768–Dec., 1768	41,543
Dec., 1768–Dec., 1769	95,604
Dec., 1769–Dec., 1770	68,525
1772	98,000

SOURCES: All figures except the last are compiled from treasurers' reports, 1764–1779; in Early State Records, South Carolina, D24, Reel 1. The 1772 figure is from Whitney, *Government of South Carolina*, 99–101.

NOTE: All figures are in South Carolina currency.

TABLE 18
South Carolina General Tax Acts, 1761–1769

DATE PASSED	TO BE RAISED	FOR YEAR'S EXPENSES	YEAR COLLECTED
1761	284,758	1760	1761
May, 1762	162,000	1761	1762
Oct., 1764	220,307	1762, 1763	1764
Apr., 1765	102,927	1764	1765
July, 1766	35,529	1765	1766
May, 1767	85,950	1766	1767
Apr., 1768	105,733	1767	1768
Aug., 1769	73,326	1768	1769

SOURCE: Cooper and McCord (eds.), *Statutes of South Carolina*, IV, 155, 179, 189–206, 214–28, 238–54, 268–83, 306, 315.

NOTE: All figures are in South Carolina currency.

TABLE 19
Georgia Taxes, 1763–1773

Year	Per Slave and Land (per 100 acres)	Town Lots (per £100 value)	Buildings on Town Lots (per £100 value)	Per Free Negro over 16	Imported Stock-in-Trade (per £100 value)	Money at Interest by Choice (per £100 value)	Total to Be Raised (£)
1763	3s. 9d.	11s. 3d.	7s. 6d.	15s.	11s. 3d	18s.	1,934
1764	2s. 6d.	7s. 6d.	5s.	15s.	7s. 6d.	12s.	2,117
1765	2s. 6d.	7s. 6d.	5s.	15s.	7s. 6d.	12s.	1,599
1766	2s. 6d.	7s. 6d.	5s.	15s.	7s. 6d.	12s.	1,925
1767	2s.	6s.	4s.	12s. 6d.	6s.	10s.	1,843
1768	2s. 6d.	7s. 6d.	5s.	15s.	7s. 6d.	12s. 6d.	3,375
1769	2s.	6s.	4s.	15s.	6s.	(10s. ?)	3,047
1770	1s. 6d.	4s. 6d.	3s.	12s. 6d.	4s. 6d.	7s. 6d.	3,355
1771				(no tax laws passed)			
1772							
1773	2s. 6d.	7s. 6d.	5s.	20s.	5s.	12s. 6d.	5,172

SOURCES: For 1763 through 1768, the tax acts are in Georgia Session Laws, Early State Records. For 1779 and 1773, they are in Chandler (ed.), *Colonial Records of Georgia*, XIX, 161–98, 449–505.

TABLE 20

Charleston's Share of South Carolina's General Tax Revenues, 1760–1765

YEAR	TOTAL TAX REVENUE (£)	CITY'S SHARE (£)
1760	163,710	43,027
1761	284,758	60,681
1762	162,121	40,645
1764	220,307	60,566
1765	102,928	29,191

SOURCE: South Carolina House Journal, April, 16, 1767.
NOTE: All figures are in South Carolina currency.

TABLE 21

Proportion of Connecticut General Property Taxes Raised on Various Taxable Items, 1778–1779

	% IN 1778	% IN 1779
Polls	33.7	31.8
Plowlands and Swine	8.4	9.1
Grassland and Other Livestock	50.7	49.6
Woodlands	(not taxed)	1.9
Houses	2.4	4.0
Money on Loan, at Hand, and Livestock on Shares	1.2	1.0
Clocks, Watches, Carriages, Gold and Silver Plate	0.2	0.5
Shipping and All Faculties	3.4	3.0

SOURCE: *Connecticut Gazette*, September 7, 1781.

Notes

PART ONE

INTRODUCTION

1. John Adams to Thomas Jefferson, August 24, 1815, in Charles Francis Adams (ed.), *The Works of John Adams* (10 vols.; Boston, 1850–56), X, 172; J. Franklin Jameson, *The American Revolution Considered as a Social Movement* (Princeton, N.J., 1926).
2. See, for example, H. Trevor Colburn, *The Lamp of Experience: Whig History and the Intellectual Origins of the American Revolution* (Chapel Hill, 1965); Bernard Bailyn, *The Ideological Origins of the American Revolution* (Cambridge, Mass., 1967); Gordon S. Wood, *The Creation of the American Republic, 1776–1787* (Chapel Hill, 1969).
3. See, for example, Percy S. Flippin, *The Financial Administration of the Colony of Virginia*, Johns Hopkins University Studies in History and Political Science, Vol. XXXIII, No. 2 (Baltimore, 1915); Frederick R. Jones, *History of Taxation in Connecticut, 1639–1776*, Johns Hopkins University Studies in History and Political Science, Vol. XIV, No. 8 (Baltimore, 1896).

CHAPTER ONE

1. Henry H. Metcalf *et al.* (eds.), *Laws of New Hampshire* (10 vols.; Manchester, N.H., 1904–22), III, 533–34, 585–87; [State of Massachusetts], *The Acts and Resolves, Public and Private, of the Province of Massachusetts Bay* (21 vols.; Boston, 1869–1922), V, 156–59, 182; [Colony of Rhode Island], [*Acts and Resolves*] *at the General Assembly of the Governor and Company of the English Colony of Rhode Island and Providence Plantations, in New England, in America* [*1755–1783*] (Newport, 1755–84), June, 1761, pp. 33–39, February, 1762, pp. 78–80.
2. *Rhode Island Acts and Resolves*, June, 1767, pp. 21–26; Metcalf *et al.* (eds.), *Laws of New Hampshire*, III, 533–34, 585–87; Charles J. Hoadly (ed.), *The Public Records of the Colony of Connecticut* (15 vols.; Hartford, 1850–90), VIII, 129–34; Massachusetts House Journal, January 14, February 23, June 3, 1768, June 7, July 2, 1771, July 14, 1772. This and other legislative journals, unless otherwise noted, are found in William S. Jenkins (ed.), *Records of the States of the United States: A Microfilm Compilation Prepared by the Library of Congress in Association with the University of North Carolina* (Washington, D.C., 1949–).
3. *Massachusetts Acts and Resolves*, V, 156–59; Metcalf *et al.* (eds.), *Laws of New Hampshire*, III, 533–34.
4. Jackson T. Main, *Political Parties Before the Constitution* (Chapel Hill, 1973), 93; Paul S. Boyer, "Borrowed Rhetoric: The Massachusetts Excise Controversy of 1754," *William and Mary Quarterly*, XXI (1964), 328–51.

5. Davis R. Dewey, "Finance and Paper Money (1692–1775)," in Albert B. Hart (ed.), *The Commonwealth History of Massachusetts, Colony, Province and State* (5 vols.; New York, 1927–30), II, 215–16; Jackson T. Main, "The Distribution of Property in Colonial Connecticut," in James K. Martin (ed.), *The Human Dimensions of Nation Making: Essays on Colonial and Revolutionary America* (Madison, Wis., 1976), 101–102; Lawrence H. Gipson, *Connecticut Taxation, 1750–1775* (New Haven, 1933), 7–8; H. H. Burbank, "The General Property Tax in Massachusetts, 1775–1792" (Ph.D. dissertation, Harvard University, 1915), 154; Albert S. Batchellor *et al.* (eds.), *Provincial [and State] Papers of New Hampshire* (40 vols.; Concord, 1867–1943), VII, 37; F. R. Jones, *Taxation in Connecticut*, 356–57.

6. *Massachusetts Acts and Resolves*, IV, 583–98, V, 156–59, 395–409; Hoadly (ed.), *Public Records of Connecticut Colony*, XIII, 513–14; Metcalf *et al.* (ed.), *Laws of New Hampshire*, III, 533–34.

7. Sources cited in note 6 above; Hoadly (ed.), *Public Record Connecticut Colony*, XI, 14; *Massachusetts Acts and Resolves*, V, 305–21; F. R. Jones, *Taxation in Connecticut*, 363–64.

8. Massachusetts House Journal, January 3, 5, 20, 1764, February 18, 1767, June 1–2, 1768; Boston town meeting, May 23, 1768, in [Boston, Massachusetts], *A Report of the Record Commissioners of the City of Boston, Containing the Boston Town Records, 1758–1769* (Boston, 1886), 252; *Massachusetts Acts and Resolves*, IV, 680; Boyer, "Borrowed Rhetoric," 328–51.

9. *Boston Town Records, 1758–1769*, pp. 90–92, 182, 218; [Boston, Massachusetts], *A Report of the Record Commissioners of the City of Boston, Containing the Boston Town Records, 1770–1777* (Boston, 1887), 26, 56, 87, 135.

10. *Massachusetts Acts and Resolves*, IV, 583–98.

11. Massachusetts House Journal, June 2, 1763, February 27, 1765; [Boston, Massachusetts], *Boston Town Records, 1758–1769*, pp. 90–95, 143, 202; *A Report of the Record Commissioners of the City of Boston, Containing the Selectmen's Minutes From 1764 Through 1768* (Boston, 1889), 22–23.

12. John Adams to Abigail Smith, February 14, 1763, in Lyman H. Butterfield (ed.), *Adams Family Correspondence* (2 vols.; Cambridge, Mass., 1963–65), I, 3; Lyman H. Butterfield (ed.), *The Diary and Autobiography of John Adams* (4 vols.; Cambridge, Mass., 1961), I, 212–15; Massachusetts House Journal, April 26, 1771; Dewey, "Finance and Paper Money," 215.

13. Hoadly (ed.), *Public Records of Connecticut Colony*, VIII, 129–34, XIII, 72–74, 365, 513–14; Metcalf *et al.* (ed.), *Laws of New Hampshire*, III, 533–34; Gaspare J. Saladino, "The Economic Revolution in Late Eighteenth-Century Connecticut" (Ph.D. dissertation, University of Wisconsin, 1964), 13–14.

14. *Massachusetts Gazette* (Boston), July 11, 1765; Boston *Gazette*, July 22, 1765; Gipson, *Connecticut Taxation*, 1–8; Clifford K. Shipton, "The New England Frontier," *New England Quarterly*, X (1937), 25–36; Charles

S. Grant, *Democracy in the Connecticut Frontier Town of Kent* (New York, 1961), 115–16; William H. Fry, *New Hampshire as a Royal Province*, Columbia University Studies in History, Vol. XXIX, No. 2 (New York, 1908), 155–56.

15. Ipswich petition, October 22, 1762, and proprietors' reply, April 25, 1763, in Batchellor *et al.* (ed.), *New Hampshire State Papers*, XII, 731–33; Jeremy Belknap, *The History of New Hampshire* (3 vols.; Boston, 1791–92), II, 342; *Massachusetts Acts and Resolves*, IV, 583–98, XVIII, 495; Joseph E. A. Smith, *The History of Pittsfield Massachusetts from the Year 1734 to the Year 1800* (Boston, 1869), 147–49; Shipton, "New England Frontier," 25–36; Grant, *Democracy in Kent*, 25–27; Roy H. Akagi, *The Town Proprietors of the New England Colonies* (Philadelphia, 1924).

16. *Rhode Island Acts and Resolves*, May, 1769, p. 14; Rhode Island Council Journal, May 6, 1769; Hoadly (ed.), *Public Records of Connecticut Colony*, VIII, 129–34; Metcalf *et al.* (ed.), *Laws of New Hampshire*, III, 533–34, 585–87; *Massachusetts Acts and Resolves*, V, 156–59. Ministers were normally excused from the poll taxes, and Connecticut excused as well all members of the council and the faculty and students of Yale.

17. These figures are approximate. For Rhode Island, they are based on the poll tax and general estimate of 1769 in *Rhode Island Acts and Resolves*, May, 1769, pp. 14–19, and John R. Bartlett (ed.), *Records of the Colony of Rhode Island and Providence Plantations, in New England* (10 vols.; Providence, 1856–65), VI, 576. For Massachusetts, they are based on census figures in Joseph B. Felt (ed.), *Statistics of Taxation in Massachusetts*, Collections of the American Statistical Association, Vol. I, Pt. 3 (Boston, 1847), 148–57, and on the property tax act of 1765 in *Massachusetts Acts and Resolves*, IV, 812–32. For Connecticut, I used the census of 1774, which reported 38,807 white men between the ages of twenty and seventy but did not identify them as ratable polls, and the general assessment for 1774, which set the worth of the colony at £1,957,208. If ratable polls included men from sixteen to twenty, the yield would have been still higher. Hoadly (ed.), *Public Records of Connecticut Colony*, XIV, 384–86, 491; F. R. Jones, *Taxation in Connecticut*, 362.

18. William Williams' letters are in J. E. A. Smith, *History of Pittsfield*, 145–47.

19. Rufus R. Wilson (ed.), *Burnaby's Travels Through North America* (New York, 1904), 125–29.

20. *Ibid.*

21. David S. Lovejoy, *Rhode Island Politics and the American Revolution, 1760–1776* (Providence, 1958), Chap. 1.

22. *Ibid.*, Chaps. 1–5; William E. Foster, *Stephen Hopkins, a Rhode Island Statesman*, Rhode Island Historical Tracts, 1st Ser., No. 19 (2 vols.; Providence, 1884), II 1–3, 6–11.

23. Open letter by Stephen Hopkins, March 31, 1757, and Samuel Ward to Hopkins, April 12, 1757, in *Narragansett Historical Register*, III (1884–85), 258–63, IV (1885–86), 40–45.

24. F. B. Wiener, "Rhode Island Merchants and the Sugar Act," *New*

England Quarterly, III (1930), 464–500; Arthur M. Schlesinger, *The Colonial Merchants and the American Revolution, 1763–1776*, Columbia University Studies in History, Economics, and Public Law, Vol. LXXVIII, No. 182 (New York, 1918), 42–49.

25. *Rhode Island Acts and Resolves*, June, 1761, pp. 33–37, February, 1762, pp. 79–80, September, 1762, pp. 200–203; Bartlett (ed.), *Rhode Island Colonial Records*, VI, 367–68. There was more involved here than just factional politics; there was a dispute between merchant and agrarian interests as well. The protesters complained that the new estimate "laid too large a proportion upon the country towns" and too small a one on merchants. Although the estimate was recognizably pro-Hopkins, no delegates from the port towns of Newport and Portsmouth signed the protest.

26. *Rhode Island Acts and Resolves*, August, 1763, pp. 65–67, September, 1764, pp. 43–44, October, 1765, pp. 67–69. June, 1766, p. 20; Bartlett (ed.), *Rhode Island Colonial Records*, VI, 494–95; Lovejoy, *Rhode Island Politics*, 85–90.

27. Rhode Island House Journal, December 4, 1766.

28. *Rhode Island Acts and Resolves*, December, 1766, pp. 56–59.

29. Carl Becker, *The Eve of the Revolution* (New Haven, 1920), 131–33.

30. Rhode Island Council Journal, February 26, 1767.

31. *Rhode Island Acts and Resolves*, May, 1767, pp. 6–7.

32. *Ibid.*, June, 1767, p. 25; general estimate for 1767, in Bartlett (ed.), *Rhode Island Colonial Records*, VI, 576.

33. *Rhode Island Acts and Resolves*, February, 1769, p. 82, 90–93; Lovejoy, *Rhode Island Politics*, 135–41.

34. *Rhode Island Acts and Resolves*, May, 1769, pp. 14–19, September, 1770, pp. 63–65, August, 1771, pp. 64–67, August, 1772, pp. 41–44, August, 1773, pp. 67–70; Lovejoy, *Rhode Island Politics*, 85–90, 135–37, 151–53.

35. *Rhode Island Acts and Resolves*, February, 1762, pp. 79–80, June 1767, p. 25.

36. *Ibid.*, May, 1768, p. 7, October, 1768, pp. 58–59; Rhode Island House Journal, June 16–18, September 15, October 28, 1768; Providence *Gazette*, May 28, 1768.

37. Gipson, *Connecticut Taxation*, 31–37; Oscar Zeichner, *Connecticut's Years of Controversy, 1750–1776* (Chapel Hill, 1949), 46–48, 59.

38. Benjamin Gale to Jared Ingersoll, December 13, 1765, in *New Haven Colony Historical Society Papers* (9 vols.; New Haven, 1865–1918), IX, 372–73; *Connecticut Courant* (Hartford), February 23, March 9, 1767; Zeichner, *Connecticut's Years of Controversy*, 24–34, 70–75; Lawrence H. Gipson, *Jared Ingersoll: A Study of American Loyalism in Relation to British Colonial Government* (New Haven, 1920), 90–91.

39. Gipson, *Connecticut Taxation*, 31–37.

40. *Connecticut Journal* (New Haven), August 3, 1770.

41. Benjamin Gale, "Letter to J.W.," July 25, 1769, in Julian P. Boyd and Robert J. Taylor (eds.), *The Susquehannah Company Papers* (11 vols.; Ithaca, N.Y., 1962–71), III, 230–39; Benjamin Gale, "The State of the

Lands," *ibid.*, 346–59; Eliphalet Dyer, "Remarks on Dr. Gale's Letter to J.W.," December, 1769, *ibid.*, 247–48; *Connecticut Courant,* May 21, 1770; *Conncticut Journal,* August 31, 1770; [Ezra Stiles] "To the Candid Public," New Haven, March, 1774, in Clifford K. Shipton (ed.), *Early American Imprints, 1639–1800: A Microprint Compilation by the American Antiquarian Society,* (Worcester, Mass., 1955–), No. 42708; Hoadly (ed.), *Public Records of Connecticut Colony,* XIII, 187.

42. "Plaind Facts," "Justice," and "Candor," in *Connecticut Courant,* January 12, March 9, 23, 1767.

43. "Plain Truth," "A.Z.," and "Thomas Moderation," *ibid.*, February 23, March 2, 23, 1767; *Connecticut Gazette* (New London), February 20, 1767.

44. Thomas Hutchinson, *The History of the Colony and Province of Massachusetts Bay* (3 vols.; London, 1760–1828), III, 195–98; Massachusetts House Journal, June 6–7, 1770; *Massachusetts Acts and Resolves,* IV, 1024–27.

45. Massachusetts House Journal, June 7, 12, 15–25, July 25–August 3, September 5–October 10, 1770, July 4, 1771; *Massachusetts Acts and Resolves,* V, 53–55, 89–106, 142–43, 167–69, 209–11, 305–21, 363–64; Hutchinson, *History of Massachusetts,* III, 344–45.

46. Massachusetts House Journal, May 26, 1763.

47. On currency scarcities, see E. James Ferguson, "Currency Finance: An Interpretation of Colonial Monetary Practice," *William and Mary Quarterly,* X (1953), 153–80; Joseph A. Ernst, *Money and Politics in America, 1755–1775: A Study in the Currency Act of 1764 and the Political Economy of Revolution* (Chapel Hill, 1973).

48. Lawrence H. Gipson, *The Coming of the Revolution, 1763–1775* (New York, 1962), 55–58, 128–29; Stephen Dowell, *A History of Taxation and Taxes in England, from the Earliest Times to the Present Day* (4 vols.; New York, 1965), II, 128–29.

49. The per capita figures are approximate. The Rhode Island figure is based on *Rhode Island Acts and Resolves,* June, 1774, p. 54, and population estimates in Kurt B. Mayer, *Economic Development and Population Growth in Rhode Island* (Providence, 1953), 11. I estimated the colony's 1765 population at 50,000. The Connecticut figure is based on the census of 1774 in Hoadly (ed.), *Public Records of Connecticut Colony,* XIV, 491, and on Gipson, *Connecticut Taxation,* 8–9. The New Hampshire figures are derived from New Hampshire House Journal, April 16, 1770, and Metcalf *et al.* (ed.), *Laws of New Hampshire,* III, 536, 556, 580, 602, 627.

50. *Massachusetts Acts and Resolves,* IV, 708–19, 1024–27, V, 395–409; Massachusetts House Journal, June 28, 1768; Felt (ed.), *Statistics of Taxation,* 148–57; Evarts B. Greene and Virginia D. Harrington, *American Population Before the Federal Census of 1790* (New York, 1932), 17.

51. William Samuel Johnson to William Pitkin, February 13, 1768, in *The Trumbull Papers,* Collections of the Massachusetts Historical Society,

NOTES TO PAGES 35–40

IX–X (Boston, 1885–88), IX, 162; Pitkin to Lord Hillsborough, November, 1768, in *Pitkin Papers: Correspondence and Documents During William Pitkin's Governorship of the Colony of Connecticut, 1766–1769,* Collections of the Connecticut Historical Society, XIX (Hartford, 1921), 152–53.

52. Johnson to Joseph Trumbull, April 15, 1769, in *Trumbull Papers,* IX, 330–34; Silas Deane to Trumbull, August 16, 1774, in *The Deane Papers,* Collections of the New-York Historical Society, XIX–XXIII (New York, 1887–91), XIX, 2–3.

53. Bartlett (ed.), *Rhode Island Colonial Records,* VI, 480–81, 546; Hillsborough to the governor, January 23, 1768, and Josias Lyndon to Hillsborough, June 17, 1768, *ibid.,* 539–40, 547.

54. Metcalf *et al.* (eds.), *Laws of New Hampshire,* III, 499–501, 536; *Concord [New Hampshire] Town Records, 1732–1820* (Concord, 1894), 123–24; H. D. Foster *et al.* (eds.), *The Records of the Town of Hanover, New Hampshire, 1761–1818* (Hanover, 1905), 16; *Massachusetts Acts and Resolves,* V, 8; Brookline town meetings, March 5, May 25, 1770, in *Muddy River and Brookline Town Records, 1634–1838* (Boston, 1875).

55. *Massachusetts Acts and Resolves,* IV, 421, 427, 458–59; Gipson, *Connecticut Taxation,* 31–37; Metcalf *et al.* (eds.), *Laws of New Hampshire,* III, 234–37, 322–23, 574; New Hampshire House Journal, January 8, 1765, January 25, 1770, December 14, 1771.

56. Bartlett (ed.), *Rhode Island Colonial Records,* VI, 299–300; New Hampshire House Journal, January 16, December 15, 1770, January 4, March 21, 26, 1771; "Heads of Inquiry Relative to the Present State and Condition of His Majesty's Colony of Connecticut," [New London, 1775], in Hoadly (ed.), *Public Records of Connecticut Colony,* XIV, 500.

57. Charles Carroll, *Rhode Island: Three Centuries of Democracy* (4 vols.; New York, 1932), I, 195–96; Lovejoy, *Rhode Island Politics,* 65–68; Hoadly (ed.), *Public Records of Connecticut Colony,* XIV, 493–507; Butterfield (ed.), *Diary of John Adams,* II, 108; *Massachusetts Acts and Resolves,* IV, 812–13, 882, 956, 1014–15, V, 305–21; Massachusetts House Journal, June 1, 1764.

58. New Hampshire House Journal, June 9, 1768, April 22, 1769, January 11, April 16, December 13, 24, 1770, January 6, May 27, 1773.

59. Butterfield (ed.), *Diary of John Adams,* I, 301; *Massachusetts Acts and Resolves,* IV, 995; Massachusetts House Journal, June 12, 1767.

60. New Hampshire House Journal, June 12, 1765, July 10, 1766, October 20, 1768, January 19, 1770, May 13, 1774.

61. Ingersoll to Richard Jackson, November 3, 1765, in *New Haven Colony Historical Society Papers,* IX, 359; Hoadly (ed.), *Public Records of Connecticut Colony,* XIII, 94–95, 128–29; Gipson, *Connecticut Taxation,* 10–13, 40–41.

62. *Rhode Island Acts and Resolves,* May, 1767, p. 10.

63. New Hampshire House Journal, April 8, 1774; Richard F. Upton, *Revolutionary New Hampshire: An Account of the Social and Political Forces Underlying the Transition from Royal Province to American*

Commonwealth (Hanover, N.H., 1936), 133; Hutchinson, *History of Massachusetts,* III, 349–50; Johnson to Joseph Trumbull, April 15, 1769, in *Trumbull Papers,* IX, 330–34.

64. Instructions to delegates at the Albany Congress, May, 1754, in *Fitch Papers: Correspondence and Documents During Thomas Fitch's Governorship of the Colony of Connecticut, 1754–1766,* Collections of the Connecticut Historical Society, XVII–XIX (Hartford, 1918–21), XVII, 15–16.

CHAPTER TWO

1. [State of New York], *The Colonial Laws of New York, from 1664 to the Revolution* (5 vols.; Albany, 1894), IV, 398–418, 721–24, 827, 1110–11, V, 677–80; Irving Mark, *Agrarian Conflicts in Colonial New York, 1711–1775,* Columbia University Studies in History, No. 469 (New York, 1940), 68–69; Beverly McAnear, "Mr. Robert R. Livingston's Reasons Against a Land Tax," *Journal of Political Economy,* XLVIII (1940), 65–66.

2. *New York Colonial Laws,* V, 858–62; John Watts to James Napier, June 1, 1765, in *Letterbook of John Watts, Merchant and Councillor of New York,* Collections of the New-York Historical Society, LXI (New York, 1928), 354–55.

3. *New York Colonial Laws,* IV, 801–804; William Tryon to Lord Dartmouth, June, 1774, in E. B. O'Callaghan (ed.), *Documents Relative to the Colonial History of the State of New York* (15 vols.; Albany, 1853–87), VIII, 452–54.

4. Governor William Franklin to the house, April 23, 1771, in William A. Whitehead *et al.* (eds.), *The Archives of the State of New Jersey* (36 vols.; Newark, 1880–1941), X, 243–51; New Jersey Session Laws, February 12, 1752, October, 1769, in Early State Records.

5. The Franklin-assembly exchange is in Whitehead *et al.* (eds.), *New Jersey Archives,* X, 238–68.

6. New Jersey Session Laws, October, 1769, in Early State Records; Franklin to the house, April 29, 1771, in Whitehead *et al.* (eds.), *New Jersey Archives,* X, 265–68.

7. Pennsylvania House Journal, January 25–27, 1764; James T. Mitchell and Henry Flanders (eds.), *The Statutes at Large of Pennsylvania from 1682 to 1801* (17 vols.; Harrisburg, 1896–1915), VI, 344–67, VIII, 378–82.

8. Samuel Hazard *et al.* (eds.), *Pennsylvania Archives* (138 vols.; Harrisburg and Philadelphia, 1852–1935), 3rd Ser., Vol. XVII, 32–36.

9. Mitchell and Flanders (eds.), *Statutes of Pennsylvania,* VIII, 378–82.

10. [State of Delaware], *Laws of the State of Delaware [1770–1797]* (2 vols.; Newcastle, 1797), I, 257–67, 396–401, 429–35; Richard S. Rodney, *Colonial Finances in Delaware* (Wilmington, Del., 1928), 30–40; John Penn to Thomas Penn, May 5, 1764, in John Penn Manuscripts, Historical Society of Pennsylvania, Philadelphia.

11. Mitchell and Flanders (eds.), *Statutes of Pennsylvania,* VII, 100–107, 204–11, VIII, 15–22, 204–20, 447–55; Hazard *et al.* (eds.), *Pennsylvania*

Archives, 3rd Ser., Vol. IV, 633–34; "Heads of Inquiry Relating to New Jersey and the Governor's Answer Thereto," March 28, 1774, *ibid.*, X, 447; Edgar J. Fisher, *New Jersey as a Royal Province, 1738 to 1776,* Columbia University Studies in History, Vol. XLI, No. 107 (New York, 1911), 303.

12. Pennsylvania House Journal, September 22, 1764, September 27, 1774, September 29, 1775; "A General State of the Public Funds in the Province of New York and the Uses to Which They Are Applied, 1767," in E. B. O'Callaghan (ed.), *The Documentary History of the State of New York* (4 vols.; Albany, 1850–51), I, 479–81; Tryon to Dartmouth, June, 1774, in O'Callaghan (ed.), *Documents Relative to New York,* VIII, 452–53; Virginia D. Harrington, *The New York Merchants on the Eve of the Revolution,* Columbia University Studies in History, No. 404 (New York, 1935), 277.

13. For De Peyster's indiscretions, see *New York Colonial Laws,* V, 75–76, 212–17; for the imposts and civil list, see *Letterbook of John Watts,* 355, and Harrington, *New York Merchants,* Chap. 7. The civil list cost £4,663 in 1763 but dropped to £3,120 by 1773. New York House Journal, November 24, 1763; Tryon to Dartmouth, June, 1774, in O'Callaghan (ed.), *Documents Relative to New York,* VIII, 453–57.

14. New York House Journal, November 24, 1763, September 19, 1764; Watts to Moses Franks, June 9, 1764, and to General Robert Monckton, June 30, 1764, in *Letterbook of John Watts,* 263, 270; *New York Colonial Laws,* V, 149–70; Tryon to Dartmouth, June, 1774, in O'Callaghan (ed.), *Documents Relative to New York,* VIII, 452–53.

15. Pennsylvania House Journal, September 13, 1768; Delaware Session Laws, October, 1774, in Early State Records; Rodney, *Finances in Delaware,* 30–40.

16. "Account of Governor Franklin," December 28, 1766, in Whitehead *et al.* (eds.), *New Jersey Archives,* IV, 579–81; Franklin to Hillsborough, August 24, 1768, *ibid.*, X, 48–50; "Heads of Inquiry," March 28, 1774, and Franklin to Hillsborough, June 13, 1774, *ibid.*, X, 447–48, 461–63; New Jersey Session Laws, November, 1773, in Early State Records.

17. "To the Freeholders and Electors of the Province of Pennsylvania" [1765], in Miscellaneous Broadsides, Historical Society of Pennsylvania, Philadelphia.

18. On malapportionment, see Charles H. Lincoln, *The Revolutionary Movement in Pennsylvania, 1760–1776* (Philadelphia, 1901), 47–50.

19. Thomas F. Gordon, *The History of Pennsylvania from Its Discovery by Europeans to the Declaration of Independence in 1776* (Philadelphia, 1829), 336; Leonard W. Labaree and William B. Willcox (eds.), *The Papers of Benjamin Franklin* (20 vols.; New Haven, 1959–76), VI, 129–30. Labaree's discussion of the Penn lands and the tax dispute is by far the best extant, and I relied on it for my summary of events from 1755 to 1763.

20. The dispute can be followed in the notes and documents in Labaree and Willcox (eds.), *Franklin Papers,* VI, 129–30, 504–506, VII, 49–50*n*, 106–109, 116–33, 136–52, 248–52, 255–63, 281–84, 370–73, VIII, 54–57,

101–105, 178–86, 302–305, 326–28; Mitchell and Flanders (eds.), *Statutes of Pennsylvania*, V, 379–96.

21. Order-in-council, September 2, 1760, in Labaree and Willcox (eds.), *Franklin Papers*, IX, 203–208; Thomas Penn to Richard Peters, July 5, 1758, in Thomas Penn Letterbooks, Historical Society of Pennsylvania, Philadelphia.

22. Mitchell and Flanders (eds.), *Statutes of Pennsylvania*, VI, 7–22; Theodore G. Thayer, *Pennsylvania Politics and the Growth of Democracy* (Harrisburg, 1953), 73–74; Labaree and Willcox (eds.), *Franklin Papers*, IX, 43–44*n;* Thomas Penn to Governor James Hamilton, July 10, October 8, 1762, in Thomas Penn Letterbooks; Pennsylvania House Journal, January 18, 1763.

23. Thomas Penn to John Penn, March 9, June 8, 1764, in Thomas Penn Letterbooks; Cecil Calvert to Lord Calvert, June 1, 1764, in *Maryland Historical Society Fund Publications*, Vol. XXXIV, No. 2 (1894), 223.

24. Pennsylvania House Journal, February 24, March 8, 10, 14, 19–20, 1764.

25. *Ibid.*, March 20–21, 1764.

26. *Ibid.*, March 23–24, 1764; Thomas Penn to John Penn, November 10, 1764, and to Benjamin Chew, December 17, 1764, in Thomas Penn Letterbooks.

27. Pennsylvania House Journal, May 17–30, 1764.

28. Benjamin Franklin, "Explanatory Remarks on the Assembly's Resolves Published in the *Pennsylvania Gazette*, No. 1840" [1764], in Shipton (ed.), *Early American Imprints*, No. 9656; "To the Freeholders and Other Electors for the City and County of Philadelphia and Counties of Chester and Bucks" [1764], in *ibid.*, No. 9854; Labaree and Willcox (eds.), *Franklin Papers*, XI, 206–208; Merrill Jensen, *The Founding of a Nation* (New York, 1968), 88.

29. Thomas Penn to John Penn, June 1, 8, and to Chew, June 8, and to Hamilton, June 13, 1764, all in Thomas Penn Letterbooks.

30. Thomas Penn to John Penn, June 8, July 13, 1764, and to Chew, July 20, 1765, *ibid.*; Hazard *et al.* (eds.), *Pennsylvania Archives*, 8th Ser., Vol. VI, 5216, 5220–21.

31. Carl Bridenbaugh, *Cities in Revolt: Urban Life in America, 1743–1776* (New York, 1955), 221; C. H. Lincoln, *Revolutionary Movement in Pennsylvania*, 47–50; Pennsylvania House Journal, February 17, September 13, 1768, January 25, 1773; Mitchell and Flanders (eds.), *Statutes of Pennsylvania*, VII, 9–17.

32. Pennsylvania House Journal, January 17, 21, February 16, 1764, January 25, 1773; Thomas Penn to John Penn, October 13, 1764, in Thomas Penn Letterbooks; Isaac Norris to Benjamin Franklin, June 15, 1758, in Labaree and Willcox (eds.), *Franklin Papers*, VIII, 101–105, and Labaree's comment, 103*n*.

33. Petitions of York and Lancaster counties, in Pennsylvania House Journal, October 17, 1765, September 9, 1766; John Penn to Thomas Penn, November 22, 1764, in John Penn Manuscripts; Mitchell and Flanders (eds.), *Statutes of Pennsylvania*, VII, 55–56; receiver general to John Penn,

May 24, 1764, in *Colonial Records: Minutes of the Provincial Council of Pennsylvania from the Organization to the Termination of the Proprietary Government* (16 vols.; Harrisburg, 1852–53), IX, 178–89; Thomas Penn to Richard Hockley and Edmund Physick, October 12, 1764, in Thomas Penn Letterbooks.

34. Pennsylvania House Journal, September 23, 1773.

35. *Ibid.*, February 17, September 18, 1770, January 10–11, 1771; E. R. Gould, "Local Self-Government in Pennsylvania," *Pennsylvania Magazine of History and Biography*, VI (1882), 156–58.

36. Mitchell and Flanders (eds.), *Statutes of Pennsylvania*, VIII, 378–82; Pennsylvania House Journal, December 16, 24, 1773, January 4, 1774.

37. C. H. Lincoln, *Revolutionary Movement in Pennsylvania*, 49–50; Westmoreland County commissioners to Governor Penn, April 8, 1774, in Hazard *et al.* (eds.), *Pennsylvania Archives*, 1st Ser., Vol. IV, 487; petition of Westmoreland County commissioners, in Pennsylvania House Journal, February 21, 1775.

38. Pennsylvania House Journal, January 19, February 6, 1770; Mitchell and Flanders (eds.), *Statutes of Pennsylvania*, VII, 100–107; "Publicus" to "The Good People of Pennsylvania," January 5, 1773, in Shipton (ed.), *Early American Imprints*, No. 12697.

39. "AF" to "The Freemen of Pennsylvania," 1772, in Miscellaneous Broadsides, Historical Society of Pennsylvania; "Publicus," January 5, 1773, in Shipton (ed.), *Early American Imprints*, No. 12697.

40. "Civis," February, 1772, in Shipton (ed.), *Early American Imprints*, No. 12353.

41. Pennsylvania House Journal, February 26, 1772.

42. Carl Becker, *The History of Political Parties in the Province of New York, 1760–1776* (Madison, Wis., 1909), Chap. 1; Alfred F. Young, *The Democratic Republicans of New York: The Origins, 1763–1797* (Chapel Hill, 1967), 6–16.

43. Jackson T. Main, "Social Origins of a Political Elite: The Upper House in the Revolutionary Era," *Huntington Library Quarterly*, XXVII (1964), 155; Jackson T. Main, "Government by the People: The American Revolution and the Democratization of the Legislatures," *William and Mary Quarterly*, XXIII (1966), 394.

44. George Dangerfield, *Chancellor Robert R. Livingston of New York, 1746–1813* (New York, 1960), 21–23, 39–41; McAnear, "Robert R. Livingston," 67–69, 76, 82.

45. McAnear, "Robert R. Livingston," 82–90.

46. New York *Gazette Revived in the Weekly Post-Boy*, November 11, 1751.

47. "A Few Observations on the Conduct of the General Assembly of New York, for Some Years Past," February 9, 1768, in Shipton (ed.), *Early American Imprints*, No. 11039.

48. Peter Livingston to Robert R. Livingston, 1770, quoted in McAnear, "Robert R. Livingston," 72–73.

49. [New York City, Chamber of Commerce], *Colonial Records of the*

New York Chamber of Commerce, 1768–1784 (New York, 1867); Cadwallader Colden to the Board of Trade, September 20, 1764, in *The Colden Letterbooks,* Collections of the New-York Historical Society, IX–X (New York, 1877–78), IX, 361–64; Harrington, *New York Merchants,* 133–45.

50. Robert R. Livingston, Sr., to R. R. Livingston, April 10, 1765, in Dangerfield, *Robert R. Livingston,* 33, 455n; New York House Journal, March 31, 1775; *New York Colonial Laws,* V, 367–68; McAnear, "Robert R. Livingston," 69–82.

51. Colden to the Board of Trade, September 20, 1764, in *Colden Letterbooks,* IX, 361–64; Cadwallader Colden, "The Second Part of the Interest of the Country in Laying Duties," in *Letters and Papers of Cadwallader Colden,* Collections of the New-York Historical Society, L–LVI, LXVII–LXVIII (New York, 1918–37), LXVIII, 267–69; Joseph Dorfman, *The Economic Mind in American Civilization* (5 vols.; New York, 1946–59), I, 130–31.

52. Gideon D. Schull (ed.), *Journals of Captain John Montressor, 1757–1775,* Collections of the New-York Historical Society, XIV (New York, 1882), 366, 375–76, 384; Mark, *Agrarian Conflicts in New York,* 140–43; Governor Henry Moore to Henry Conway, April 30, 1766, in O'Callaghan (ed.), *Documents Relative to New York,* VII, 825–26.

53. Charles W. Spencer, "Sectional Aspects of New York Provincial Politics," *Political Science Quarterly,* XXX (1915), 396–424; Bridenbaugh, *Cities in Revolt,* 11–12; Mark, *Agrarian Conflicts in New York,* 98; Watts to Napier, June 1, 1765, in *Letterbook of John Watts,* 354–55; council meetings, January 10, 1796, in [New York City], *Minutes of the Common Council of the City of New York, 1665–1766* (8 vols.; New York, 1905), VII, 142; *New York Colonial Laws,* IV, 1044–46.

54. *New York Colonial Laws,* IV, 699–706, 779–86, 852–59, 916–23, 984–99; "An Address to the Freeholders of Dutchess County," 1769, in Shipton (ed.), *Early American Imprints,* No. 11135.

55. *New York Colonial Laws,* IV, 1028–36, V, 1–8, 134–42, 272–80, 500–510.

56. "Aristedes" to "John Cruger, James Jauncy, James De Lancey and Jacob Walton, Esqrs.," February, 1774, broadside, in New-York Historical Society, New York City; Colden to Archibald Kennedy, November 17, 1756, in *Letters and Papers of Colden,* LXVIII, 165–67.

57. Becker, *Political Parties,* Chap. 1.

58. Thomas Penn to James Hamilton, February 11, 1763, in Thomas Penn Letterbooks; Edmund S. Morgan and Helen Morgan, *The Stamp Act Crisis: Prologue to Revolution* (New York, 1963), 198, 206–207, 224, 256, 259; New Jersey House Journal for March, 1770, when a special session met to deal with the rioting.

59. James Parker to Cortland Skinner, 1765, in Donald L. Kemmerer, "A History of Paper Money in Colonial New Jersey, 1668–1775," *Proceedings of the New Jersey Historical Society,* LXXIV (1956), 137–38; Richard T. Hoober, "Finances of Colonial New Jersey," *Numismatist,* LXIII (1950), 212–13.

60. New Jersey House Journal, May 22, 1765, June 16, 1766, June 12, 1767; Edmund Halsey *et al., History of Morris County, New Jersey* (New York, 1882), 143; James P. Snell, *History of Sussex and Warren Counties, New Jersey* (Philadelphia, 1881), 162–63; John Barber and Henry Howe (eds.), *Historical Collections of the State of New Jersey* (New York, 1844), 463.

61. Fisher, *New Jersey*, 143–54; D. L. Kemmerer, "Paper Money," 124–25; Edwin W. Kemmerer, *Path to Freedom: The Struggle for Self-Government in Colonial New Jersey, 1703–1776* (Princeton, N.J., 1940), Chaps. 11–13.

62. New Jersey House Journal, April 15, May 5–6, 1768, October 13, 18, November 10, 22, 27, 1769; New Jersey Session Laws, April, 1768, October, 1769, in Early State Records.

63. New Jersey House Journal, February 4, 12, 16, 1774.

64. The figures are based on population estimates from Greene and Harrington, American *Population*, 115–16.

65. New Jersey Session Laws, October, 1769, in Early State Records; "Heads of Inquiry," March 28, 1774, in Whitehead *et al.* (eds.), *New Jersey Archives*, X, 447–48; D. L. Kemmerer, "Paper Money," 136–37; Ernst, *Money and Politics*, 367. The colony issued at least £347,000 in paper during the war and at least £275,000 remained oustanding in 1764.

66. "Account of Governor Franklin," December 28, 1766, in Whitehead *et al.* (eds.), *New Jersey Archives*, IX, 579–81; "Heads of Inquiry," March 28, 1774, *ibid.*, X, 434–54; Fisher, *New Jersey*, 284–85; New Jersey House Journal, November 6, 1769. I used Governor Franklin's estimate of 120,000 inhabitants.

67. "JW" [John Wetherill?], "Address to the Freeholders of New Jersey," March 16, 1763, in Shipton (ed.), *Early American Imprints, No. 9532;* William Franklin to the house, April 23, 1771, and house to Franklin, April 25, 1771, in Whitehead *et al.* (eds.), *New Jersey Archives*, X, 243–56.

68. Ernst, *Money and Politics*, 365.

69. Watts to Monckton, April 14, May 24, 1764, and to Franks, June 9, 1764, in *Letterbook of John Watts*, 242–43, 257–58, 261–64; Ernst, *Money and Politics*, 265–66. I estimated population in 1765 at 140,000.

70. New Jersey House Journal, November 6, 1769, December 18, 1771; D. L. Kemmerer, "Paper Money," 133–34; New York House Journal, October 4, 1764, November 29, 1766, June 2, 1767; Rodney, *Finances in Delaware*, 40–44, 64; *Delaware Laws*, I, 396–401.

71. Pennsylvania House Journal, September 28, 29, 1763, September 18, 1766, September 13, 1768; Mitchell and Flanders (eds.), *Statutes of Pennsylvania*, VI, 226, 311–19; Edward Shippen to James Burd, October 3, 1761, in Thomas Balch (ed.), *Letters and Papers Relating Chiefly to the Provincial History of Pennsylvania* (Philadelphia, 1855), 189.

72. Thomas Penn to James Hamilton, August 10, 1763, in Thomas Penn Letterbooks. Franklin's problems with the parliamentary grant can be followed in Labaree and Willcox (eds.), *Franklin Papers*, IX–X.

73. New York House Journal, January 8, 1771, February 19, 21, November 1, 1772, February 3, 1774, January 25, 1775; *New York Colonial Laws*, IV, 666, 1103–1104, V, 83–85, 568–70.

74. New Jersey House Journal, September 8, 1772; William Franklin to the Board of Trade, October 21, 1771, in Whitehead et al. (eds.), New Jersey Archives, X, 315–17; D. L. Kemmerer, "Paper Money," 141.

75. Pennsylvania House Journal, September 18, 1766, September 25, 1767, September 19, 1772; Mitchell and Flanders (eds.), Statutes of Pennsylvania, VIII, 179–83.

CHAPTER THREE

1. Lewis C. Gray, "The Market Surplus Problems of Colonial Tobacco," Agricultural History, II (1928), 19–21.

2. On the domination of southern legislatures by men of landed wealth, see Jack P. Greene, "Foundations of Political Power in the Virginia House of Burgesses, 1720–1776," William and Mary Quarterly, XIV (1959), 485–506; Charles A. Barker, The Background of the Revolution in Maryland (New Haven, 1940), 180–83; William A. Schaper, "Sectionalism and Representation in South Carolina," Annual Report of the American Historical Association, I (1900), 345–54; Jack P. Greene, The Quest For Power: The Lower Houses of Assembly in the Southern Royal Colonies, 1689–1776 (Chapel Hill, 1963), Chap. 2.

3. Marvin L. Kay, "The Payment of Provincial and Local Taxes in North Carolina, 1748–1771," William and Mary Quarterly, XXVI (1969), 222–25; Marvin L. Kay, "Provincial Taxes in North Carolina During the Administrations of Dobbs and Tryon," North Carolina Historical Review, XLII (1965), 440–41; "A Table of North Carolina Taxes, 1748–1770," in William K. Boyd (ed.), Some Eighteenth-Century Tracts Concerning North Carolina (Raleigh, N.C., 1927), 413–16. In 1760, ratable polls included "all Persons of Mixt Blood to the Fourth Generation, of the Age of Twelve Years and upwards, and all white Persons intermarrying with any Negro, Mulatto, Mustee, or other Person of Mixt Blood, while so intermarried." William L. Saunders et al., (eds.), The State Records of North Carolina (26 vols.; Goldsboro, N.C., 1886–1907), XXIII, 526–31.

4. Saunders et al. (eds.), State Records of North Carolina, XXIII, 664–65, 781–83, 850–51; W. K. Boyd (ed.), Tracts Concerning North Carolina, 413–16; Kay, "Local Taxes," 223–25.

5. Saunders et al. (eds.), State Records of North Carolina, XXIII, 526–31, 970; Julian P. Boyd, "The Sheriff in Colonial North Carolina," North Carolina Historical Review, V (1928), 164–65.

6. William R. Smith, South Carolina as a Royal Province, 1719–1776 (New York, 1903), 283; Thomas Cooper and D. J. McCord (eds.), The Statutes at Large of South Carolina (10 vols.; Columbia, S.C., 1836–41), IV, 189–206, 238–54; Georgia tax acts, 1763–1769, are available in Early State Records; Allen D. Chandler (ed.), The Colonial Records of the State of Georgia (26 vols.; Atlanta, 1904–16), XIX, 161–98, 449–505, contains the 1770 and 1773 acts.

7. William Z. Ripley, The Financial History of Virginia, 1609–1776, Columbia University Studies in History, Vol. IV, No. 1 (New York, 1893),

32–41; Flippin, *Financial Administration of Virginia*, 79–80; William W. Hening (ed.), *The Statutes at Large: Being a Collection of All the Laws of Virginia* (13 vols.; Richmond, 1809–23), VI, 435–38, 522–30, VII, 69–87, 163–70, 171–79, 255–65, 347–53, 357–63, 495–502. Unlike the laws of most northern colonies, Virginia's did not always clearly distinguish between cultivated and wild lands or between surveyed and unsurveyed land. But as in North Carolina, slaves were ratable polls, and to that extent poll taxes were property taxes on slave owners.

8. Virginia House Journal, May 24, 1763; Hening (ed.), *Statutes of Virginia*, VIII, 38–41, 273–75, 340–42, 533–34.

9. Hening (ed.), *Statutes of Virginia*, VIII, 38, 190, 335–36, 529–30; Ripley, *Financial History of Virginia*, 104, and Chap. 3; Flippin, *Financial Administration of Virginia*, 79.

10. Governor Horatio Sharpe to Lord Shelburne, May 14, 1767, in Colonial Office Papers, Public Record Office, London; William H. Browne *et al.* (eds.), *Archives of Maryland* (72 vols.; Baltimore, 1883–1972), LXI, 264–75, 505–13, LXII, 156–59, LXIV, 254–56. Although the legislature determined the religious tax rate, the tax was collected, administered, and spent locally and thus was not a colony rate.

11. Maryland Council Journal, April 24, 1762, November 23, 1763; Maryland House Journal, October 14, 1763; Sharpe to Shelburne, May 14, 1767, in Colonial Office Papers.

12. Cooper and McCord (eds.), *Statutes of South Carolina*, IV, 150–51, 128–44; W. R. Smith, *South Carolina*, 283.

13. Cooper and McCord (eds.), *Statutes of South Carolina*, III, 739–53, IV, 150–51, 257–61; Edson L. Whitney, *Government of the Colony of South Carolina*, John Hopkins University Studies in History and Political Science, Vol. XIII, No. 1–2 (Baltimore, 1895), 99–101; South Carolina treasurers' reports, 1763–1766, in Early State Records, South Carolina, D24, Reel 1.

14. Cooper and McCord (eds.), *Statutes of South Carolina*, IV, 128–44, 189–206; M. E. Sirmans, *Colonial South Carolina: A Political History, 1663–1763* (Chapel Hill, 1966), 243–44.

15. Chandler (ed.), *Colonial Records of Georgia*, XVIII, 691–703, XIX, 449–505; Georgia Session Laws, February, 1764, March, 1767, in Early State Records.

16. Main, "Government by the People," 396; Charles Sydnor, *American Revolutionaries in the Making* (New York, 1962), Chap. 5; Richard L. Morton, *Colonial Virginia* (2 vols.; Chapel Hill, 1960), II, 749; Lyon G. Tyler, *The Letters and Times of the Tylers* (3 vols.; Richmond and Williamsburg, 1884–96), I, 71*n*.

17. Sydnor, *Revolutionaries*, Chap. 8.

18. James Maury to John Fontaine, June 15, 1756, in Ann Maury (ed.), *Memoirs of a Huguenot Family* (New York, 1853), 400–408.

19. Maury to [?], January 10, 1755, and to John Fontaine, June 15, 1756, and to Philip Ludwell [1755], all *ibid.*, 400–408, 431–42.

20. Peter Fontaine to John Fontaine, July 8, 1765, *ibid.*, 373–76.

21. George F. Willison, *Patrick Henry and His World* (Garden City, N.Y., 1969), Chap. 3; Maury to John Camm, December 12, 1763, in A. Maury (ed.), *Memoirs*, 418–24.

22. Virginia House Journal, November 14, 1764, May 24, 1765; Jefferson to William Wirt, April 12, 1812, in Paul L. Ford (ed.), *The Writings of Thomas Jefferson* (10 vols.; New York, 1892–99), IX, 238–39. The details of the burgesses' plan are from Virginia House Journal, May 24, 1765. On the Robinson scandal, see David J. Mays, *Edmund Pendleton, 1721–1803: A Biography* (2 vols.; Cambridge, Mass., 1952), I, Chaps. 11–13; Joseph A. Ernst, "The Robinson Scandal Redivivus: Money, Debts and Politics in Revolutionary Virginia," *Virginia Magazine of History and Biography*, LXXVII (1969), 146–73.

23. Virginia House Journal, November 2, 1764.

24. Jefferson to Wirt, April 14, 1814, in P. L. Ford (ed.), *Writings of Jefferson*, IX, 466; Willison, *Henry*, Chap. 11; Virginia Council Journal, May 28, 1765.

25. Jefferson to Wirt, April 12, 1812, in P. L. Ford (ed.), *Writings of Jefferson*, IX, 339; Richard Corbin is quoted in Ernst, "Robinson Scandal," 155.

26. Hening (ed.), *Statutes of Virginia*, VIII, 177–82; Virginia House Journal, December 12, 1766; Burton J. Hendrick, *The Lees of Virginia* (Boston, 1935), 105–10.

27. Robert Carter Nicholas to the printer, *Virginia Gazette* (Williamsburg; Purdie and Dixon), June 27, 1766; "Consideratus," *ibid.*, July 11, 1766.

28. "A Planter," in *Virginia Gazette* (Rind), August 8, 1766; Hening (ed.), *Statutes of Virginia*, VIII, 211–14; Virginia House Journal, April 11, 1767, March 21, April 7, 1768; Virginia Council Journal, April 13, 1768. This action was justified by the committee's report that £170,420 of the treasury notes issued between 1754 and 1762 were still circulating. Counting as assets the £109,335 the Robinson estate owed the public (plus about £55,000 in various tax arrears), the committee concluded that the tobacco and carriage taxes and license fees would be more than sufficient to redeem the rest within two years. The purpose and result of the measure were to keep the old treasury notes circulating still longer. In 1772 over £88,000 worth were still out. Virginia House Journal, April 17, 1768, March 6, 1772.

29. Virginia House Journal, November 8, 9, 1769, July 11, 12, 16, 18–20, 1771; Hening (ed.), *Statutes of Virginia*, VIII, 343, 381–85, 493–503, 515–16.

30. Governor Fauquier to secretary of State, April 27, 1767, in Colonial Office Papers; Maury to Camm, December 12, 1763 in A. Maury (ed.), *Memoirs*, 418–24; Ernst, "Robinson Scandal," 165–67.

31. Governor Horatio Sharpe to Cecilus Calvert, May 8, 1764, and to John Sharpe, May 27, 1756, in Browne *et al.* (eds.), *Archives of Maryland*, XIV, 156–58, VI, 424–28.

32. Barker, *Maryland*, 138–51; Calvert to Governor Sharpe, March 17, 1761, in Browne *et al.* (eds.), *Archives of Maryland*, XIV, 1–13.

33. Main, "Government by the People," 395–96; Barker, *Maryland*, 22–24,

180–95; Ronald Hoffman, *A Spirit of Dissension: Economics, Politics and the Revolution in Maryland* (Baltimore, 1973), 44–47. Barker examined the estates of 125 members from 1740 to 1771 and found only 16 that totaled less than 500 acres.

34. Browne *et al.* (eds.), *Archives of Maryland*, LVIII, 525–71; Daniel Dulany to Calvert, September 10, 1764, in *The Calvert Papers*, Publications of the Maryland Historical Society, XXXIV (Baltimore, 1894), 231–33.

35. Browne *et al.* (eds.), *Archives of Maryland*, LVIII, 545–50; "Remarks upon a Message Sent by the Upper to the Lower House of Assembly of Maryland," April 24, 1762 [broadside], *ibid.*, LIX, 372–408.

36. *Ibid.*, LVIII, 549, 551–52.

37. Council to Governor Sharpe, April 24, 1762, *ibid.*, LVIII, 45; Sharpe to Calvert, February 15, 1762, *ibid.*, *XIV*, 24; Dulany to Calvert, September 10, 1764, in *Calvert Papers*, 231–33.

38. Maryland House Journal, April 15, 1762.

39. "Remarks upon a Message," April 24, 1762, in *Archives of Maryland*, LIX, 386–88; Governor Sharpe to Shelburne, May 14, 1767, in Colonial Office Papers; Maryland House Journal, November 25, 1763; Maryland Council Journal, April 24, 1762, November 26, 1763.

40. Governor Sharpe to Calvert, November 9, 1757, June 4, 1763, in Browne *et al.* (eds.), *Archives of Maryland*, XI, 99–101, XIV, 92–93.

41. *Ibid.*, LII, 480–521; Governor Sharpe to John Sharpe, May 27, 1756, *ibid.*, VI, 424–28; Edward Channing, *A History of the United States* (6 vols.; New York, 1905–25), III, 33*n*.

42. Browne *et al.* (eds.), *Archives of Maryland*, LXI, 264–75.

43. See Hoffman, *Dissension*, Chap. 5; Barker, *Maryland*, Chap. 10; Jean H. Vivian, "The Poll Tax Controversy in Maryland, 1700–1776: A Case of Taxation *with* Representation," *Maryland Historical Magazine*, LXXI (1976), 151–76.

44. Hugh T. Lefler and William S. Powell, *Colonial North Carolina* (New York, 1973), 17–22.

45. "The Request of the Inhabitants of the West Side of *Haw-River*, to the Assembly-men and Vestry-men of *Orange* County," March 22, 1768, in W. K. Boyd (ed.), *Tracts Concerning North Carolina*, 264–65; Orange County instructions to representatives, December, 1773, in William L. Saunders (ed.), *The Colonial Records of North Carolina* (10 vols.; Raleigh, N.C., 1886–90), IX, 699–706; Tryon to Shelburne, 1767, in Gipson, *Revolution*, 144; J. P. Boyd, "The Sheriff," 161–72.

46. Governor Arthur Dobbs to the Board of Trade, undated, 1761, and February 23, 1761, in Saunders (ed.), *Colonial Records of North Carolina*, VI, 613–14, 967; Tryon to Shelburne, July 4, 1767, *ibid.*, VII, 497; J. P. Boyd, "The Sheriff," 161–72.

47. Herman Husband, "An Impartial Relation of the First Rise and Cause of the Recent Differences, in Public Affairs, in the Province of North Carolina," in W. K. Boyd (ed.), *Tracts Concerning North Carolina*, 260–62; George Sims, "An Address to the People of Granville County," June 6, 1765, *ibid.*, 182–92; John A. Caruso, *The Appalachian Frontier* (Indianapolis, 1959), 85–86.

48. Saunders (ed.), *Colonial Records of North Carolina*, VII, 801–806; Jack P. Greene, "The North Carolina Lower House and the Power to Appoint Public Treasurers, 1711–1775," *North Carolina Historical Review*, XL (1963), 37–53.

49. Governor Josiah Martin to Dartmouth, September 1, 1774, in Saunders (ed.), *Colonial Records of North Carolina*, IX, 1053–54; Amos A. Dill *Governor Tryon and His Palace* (Chapel Hill, 1955), 132–33, 241.

50. Saunders (ed.), *Colonial Records of North Carolina*, VIII, 459–60; Saunders *et al.* (eds.), *State Records of North Carolina*, XXIII, 723–52, 970; Kay, "Provincial Taxes," 449–52.

51. Saunders (ed.), *Colonial Records of North Carolina*, VII, 772–73; Husband, "Impartial Relation," in W. K. Boyd (ed.), *Tracts Concerning North Carolina*, 262–63.

52. "A Letter from Mecklenburg in North Carolina," Boston *Chronicle*, November 7, 14, 1768, in William S. Powell *et al.* (eds.), *The Regulators in North Carolina: A Documentary History, 1759–1776* (Raleigh, N.C., 1971), 195–96; Petition of Citizens of Rowan and Orange Counties," October 4, 1768, *ibid.*, 187–88.

53. "The Petition of the Inhabitants of Anson County," October 9, 1769, in Saunders (ed.), *Colonial Records of North Carolina*, VIII, 75–80; Husband, "Impartial Relation," in W. K. Boyd (ed.), *Tracts Concerning North Carolina*, 318; Orange County instructions, December, 1773, in Saunders (ed.), *Colonial Records of North Carolina*, IX, 701.

54. Saunders *et al.* (eds.), *State Records of North Carolina*, XXIII, 781–83; Governor Martin to Hillsborough, January 30, 1772, and to Dartmouth, April 2, 1774, in Saunders (ed.), *Colonial Records of North Carolina*, IX, 230–35, 958–67; North Carolina House Journal, December 5, 1768; Dill, *Tryon*, 142–43; Robert M. Weir, "North Carolina's Reaction to the Currency Act of 1764," *North Carolina Historical Review*, XL (1963), 190–97.

55. Husband, "Impartial Relation," in W. K. Boyd (ed.), *Tracts Concerning North Carolina*, 264–66, 318. For an example of arguments commonly used by colonial legislators against England being put to internal use, see *ibid.*, 264–66.

56. Main, "Government by the People," 396; Schaper, "Sectionalism," 345–54.

57. South Carolina House Journal, November 5, 1767, July 4, 1768; Alexander Gregg, *History of Old Cheraws* (New York, 1867), Chap. 7.

58. Peter Timothy to Benjamin Franklin, September 3, 1768, in Hennig Cohen (ed.), "Four Letters from Peter Timothy, 1755, 1768, 1771," *South Carolina Historical Magazine*, LV (1954), 161–64; Henry Middleton to Arthur Middleton, September 22, 1768, in Joseph W. Barnwell (ed.), "Correspondence of Hon. Arthur Middleton, Signer of the Declaration of Independence," *South Carolina Historical and Genealogical Magazine*, XXVII (1926), 108–12; Presentment of the Charleston Grand Jury, October, 1765, in *South Carolina Gazette* (Charleston), June 2, 1766; South Carolina House Journal, November 11, 1767, November 17, 1768, June 27–30, July 22–29, 1769; Gregg, *Cheraws*, 153–55.

59. South Carolina House Journal, July 4, 1768, July 5, 11, November 25, 1769.

60. Peter Timothy to Benjamin Franklin, September 3, 1768, in Cohen (ed.), "Four Letters," 161–64; South Carolina House Journal, February 26, 1767; Cooper and McCord (eds.), *Statutes of South Carolina*, IV, 257–61.

61. South Carolina House Journal, November 25, 1766, April 6, 1767.

62. *Ibid.*, February 22, 1770; Presentment of the Charleston Grand Jury, January 21, 1771, in *South Carolina Gazette*, February 7, 1771; Presentment of the Charleston Grand Jury, January 15, 1770, in *South Carolina Gazette and Country Journal* (Charleston), January 23, 1770.

63. South Carolina House Journal, March 4, 12, 13, April 6, 8, 1767.

64. *Ibid.*, April 8, 1767, February 22, 1770; Cooper and McCord (eds.), *Statutes of South Carolina*, VII, 90–92; *South Carolina Gazette and Country Journal*, January 23, 1770; *South Carolina Gazette*, February 7, 1771.

65. South Carolina House Journal, April 16, 1767, February 27, 1770.

66. *Ibid.*, April 16, 1767, February 22, 27, 1770. Even if the petition exaggerated the undervaluation of rural lands by 100 percent, the non-Charleston tax would still have been only £14.

67. *Ibid.*, and March 2, 15, 1770.

68. James Habersham to Hillsborough, April 30, 1772, and to William Wright, July 16, December 4, 1772, in *The Letters of the Hon. James Habersham, 1756–1775*, Collections of the Georgia Historical Society, VI (Savannah, 1904), 174–80, 190–92, 215–17.

69. Habersham to William Knox, November 24, 1763, April 4, 1765, in *Letters of Habersham*, 13–14, 28–30; Chandler (ed.), *Colonial Records of Georgia*, XVIII, 691–703, XIX, 415–18.

70. Georgia House Journal, November 16, 1769; *Georgia Gazette* (Savannah), February 28, 1769, March 21, 1770; Habersham to Benjamin Franklin, May 23, 1770, in *Letters of Habersham*, 79–81; Kenneth Coleman, *The American Revolution in Georgia, 1763–1789* (Athens, Ga., 1958), 33; Charles C. Jones, *The History of Georgia* (2 vols.; Boston, 1883), II, 115–19.

71. Hillsborough to Wright, July 31, 1770, in C. C. Jones, *History of Georgia*, II, 115–19; Coleman, *Revolution in Georgia*, 34.

72. Habersham to Benjamin Franklin, May 19, 1768, in *Letters of Habersham*, 71–73; merchants' petition to the house, February 5, 1767, in C. C. Jones, *History of Georgia*, II, 100–101; *Georgia Gazette*, February 28, March 21, 1770; Chandler (ed.), *Colonial Records of Georgia*, XIX, 161–98; Ernst, *Money and Politics*, 373.

73. Wright to Dartmouth, September 20, 1773, in *Collections of the Georgia Historical Society*, III (Savannah, 1873), 158–79; Coleman, *Revolution in Georgia*, 35–37.

74. Per capita rates are based on Governor Fauquier's estimate of 170,000 whites and an equal number of blacks in the colony in 1763, and on the Burgesses' estimate of 120,000 tithables in the colony in 1764. Virginia

House Journal, May 24, 1763; Hening (ed.), *Statutes of Virginia*, VII, 385, VIII, 38–41, 273–75, 340–42, 533–34; Greene and Harrington, *American Population*, 141–42.

75. Hening (ed.), *Statutes of Virginia*, VIII, 342–48, 493–503, 647–51; Gipson, *Revolution*, 142n. The tobacco export tax raised about £7,000 in 1770. Ripley, *Financial History of Virginia*, 104.

76. Governor Sharpe to Shelburne, May 14, 1767, in Colonial Office Papers. I estimated 139,000 whites in 1770. Greene and Harrington, *American Population*, 126–27.

77. Cooper and McCord (eds.), *Statutes of South Carolina*, IV, 189–206. The population estimate is 110,000. Greene and Harrington, *American Population*, 175–77; W. R. Smith, *South Carolina*, 274.

78. David Ramsay, *The History of South Carolina from Its First Settlement in 1670 to the Year 1808* (2 vols.; Charleston, 1858), II, 66, 69; South Carolina House Journal, November 19, 1766; Peter Timothy to Benjamin Franklin, September 3, 1768, in Cohen (ed.), "Four Letters," 161–64; Lewis C. Gray, *History of Agriculture in the Southern United States to 1860* (2 vols.; Washington, D.C., 1933), II, 574; Gipson, *Revolution*, 149–50.

79. Wright to Shelburne, May 15, 1767, in Colonial Office Papers; Chandler (ed.), *Colonial Records of Georgia*, XIX, 449–505. The population estimate is 17,500. Greene and Harrington, *American Population*, 181–82.

80. Gipson, *Revolution*, 144–45.

81. Watts to Monckton, April 14, 1764, in *Letterbook of John Watts*, 242–43; Gipson, *Revolution*, 138–39; George L. Beer, *British Colonial Policy, 1754–1765* (New York, 1933), Chap. 4, and pp. 54–60. 67n; Hening (ed.), *Statutes of Virginia*, VII, 372–73; Saunders (ed.), *Colonial Records of North Carolina*, VI, 1146–47.

82. Sirmans, *South Carolina*, 348–49; *The Annual Register* (1767), 218, (1773), 227, (1777), 268; Wright to Shelburne, May 15, 1767, in Colonial Office Papers.

83. Hening (ed.), *Statutes of Virginia*, VII, 331–37, 369–75, 381–83, 495–502; Edmund Pendleton to Madison, April 17, 1765, in Worthington C. Ford (ed.), "Unpublished Letters of Edmund Pendleton," *Proceedings of the Massachusetts Historical Society*, 2nd Ser., Vol. XIX (1906), 108–109.

84. Habersham to Knox, November 24, 1763, April 4, 1765, and to Governor Wright, April 17, 1765, in *Letters of Habersham*, 13–14, 28–30, 190–92.

85. Hening (ed.), *Statutes of Virginia*, VII, 539–45. Arrears declined steadily as tobacco taxes fell. Eight counties owed 57,900 pounds in 1769, but only two owed 8,000 pounds by 1772. *Ibid.*, VIII, 340–42, 533–34.

86. *Virginia Gazette*, July 4, 1766; Virginia House Journal, December 12, 1766, April 7, 1768, November 23, 1769, March 6, 1772.

87. Kay, "Local Taxes," 223–25; Martin to Hillsborough, January 30, 1772, in Saunders (ed.), *Colonial Records of North Carolina*, IX, 235.

88. South Carolina House Journal, July 31, 1764. Seven parishes owed money for 1760, sixteen for 1761, and twenty-one for 1762. *Ibid.*, April 2, 1765.

89. *South Carolina Gazette*, October 13, 1766; South Carolina House Journal, April 16, 1767, August 8, September 9, 1773, March 3, 10, 1774.

90. Maryland House Journal, April 24, 1762, November 25, 1763.

91. William Bull to Dartmouth, July 31, 1774, quoted in Jerome J. Nadelhaft's history of the Revolution in South Carolina (typescript in Nadelhaft's possession), Chap. 1.

92. Peter Timothy to Benjamin Franklin, September 3, 1768, in Cohen (ed.), "Four Letters," 161–64.

93. Maryland House Journal, December 10, 11, 14, 1765; John T. Scharf, *History of Maryland from the Earliest Period to the Present Day* (3 vols.; Baltimore, 1879), I, 549; Governor Sharpe to Calvert, December 21, 1765, in Browne *et al.* (eds.), *Archives of Maryland*, XIV, 253.

94. Bull quoted in Richard Walsh, "Christopher Gadsden: Radical or Conservative Revolutionary?," *South Carolina Historical Magazine*, LXIII (1962), 203.

95. Jameson, *American Revolution*, 9.

PART TWO

Chapter Four

1. In my discussion of Massachusetts' revolutionary finances, I have relied on Van Beck Hall's *Politics Without Parties: Massachusetts, 1780–1791* (Pittsburgh, 1972).

2. Massachusetts Provincial Congress Journal, August 31, October 14, 1774; the proceedings of the various conventions are in William Lincoln (ed.), *The Journals of Each Provincial Congress of Massachusetts in 1774 and 1775 and of the Committee of Safety* (Boston, 1838), 601–605, 620, 624, 627–32, 647, 656–59.

3. Massachusetts Provincial Congress Journal, October 14, 28, 1774, May 20, July 7, 1775; Hall, *Politics*, Chap. 4; Robert A. East, "The Massachusetts Conservatives in the Critical Period," in Richard B. Morris (ed.), *The Era of the American Revolution* (New York, 1939), 349–55; Whitney K. Bates, "The State Finances of Massachusetts, 1780–1789" (M.A. thesis, University of Wisconsin, 1948), 43–44.

4. Oscar Handlin and Mary Handlin, "Revolutionary Economic Policy in Massachusetts," *William and Mary Quarterly*, IV (1947), 7.

5. *Ibid.*; Abner L. Braley, "Provisional Government of Massachusetts," in Hart (ed.), *Commonwealth History*, III, 82; *Massachusetts Acts and Resolves*, V, 442, 547, 559, 589, 606, 610; Bates, "State Finances," 154–55.

6. *Massachusetts Acts and Resolves*, V, 423, 1079–113; Massachusetts

House Journal, August 21, 24, 1775; the house to Governor John Hancock, November 7, 1780, in Edwin M. Bacon (ed.), *Supplement to the Acts and Resolves of Massachusetts* (Boston, 1896), 26–31; *Massachusetts Spy* (Worcester), May 18, 1776, November 29, 1781; Hall, *Politics*, 94–113; Robert J. Taylor, *Western Massachusetts in the Revolution* (Providence, 1954), 109–10; Main, *Political Parties*, 84–90.

7. *Massachusetts Acts and Resolves*, V, 564–83, 742–58, 782–95, 1079–113; John Adams to his wife, February 7, 1777, and to James Warren, August 18, 1777, and to Elbridge Gerry, December 6, 1777, in Edmund C. Burnett (ed.), *Letters of Members of the Continental Congress* (8 vols.; Washington, D.C., 1921–36), II, 237, 455, and in C. F. Adams (ed.), *Works of John Adams*, IX, 469–70; Handlin and Handlin, "Economic Policy," 19–21; Davis R. Dewey, "Economic and Commercial Conditions," in Hart (ed.), *Commonwealth History*, III, 341–45.

8. The tax act of May, 1781, authorized a poll tax of £1 5s. The act of June, 1773, authorized a 2s. 6d. poll tax and that of June, 1774, a 1s. 1d. tax. For more comparisons, see Hall, *Politics*, 97. For local tax increases, see Handlin and Handlin, "Economic Policy," 10.

9. Northampton Return [May, 1780], in Oscar Handlin and Mary Handlin (eds.), *The Popular Sources of Political Authority: Documents on the Massachusetts Constitution of 1780* (Cambridge, Mass., 1966), 572–75.

10. Dorchester Return, 1780, in Samuel E. Morison, "The Struggle over the Adoption of the Constitution of Massachusetts, 1780," *Proceedings of the Massachusetts Historical Society*, 3rd Ser., Vol. L (1917), 391; Pittsfield petition, December 26, 1775, in Robert J. Taylor (ed.), *Massachusetts, Colony to Commonwealth: Documents on the Formation of its Constitution, 1775–1780* (Chapel Hill, 1961), 19.

11. Sutton Return, May 18, 1778, in R. J. Taylor (ed.), *Colony to Commonwealth*, 65; Theophilus Parsons, "Essex Result," May 12, 1778, *ibid.*, 79.

12. "An Address of the Constitutional Convention to Their Constituents," 1780, *ibid.*, 125; the constitution of 1780, *ibid.*, 127–46; East, "Massachusetts Conservatives," 353.

13. Bates, "State Finances," 84–93; Handlin and Handlin, "Economic Policy," 24-25; Hall, *Politics*, 104–14; Elisha P. Douglass, *Rebels and Democrats: The Struggle for Equal Political Rights and Majority Rule During the American Revolution* (Chapel Hill, 1955), Chap. 11; Main, *Political Parties*, 89.

14. *Massachusetts Acts and Resolves*, V, 933–56; Burbank, "Property Tax," 94–99; Hall, *Politics*, 99.

15. Burbank, "Property Tax," 155–60, 164–73; *Massachusetts Acts and Resolves*, V, 799–803.

16. Hardwick town meeting, January 8, 1782, in Lucius R. Paige, *History of Hardwick, Massachusetts* (Boston, 1883), 121; Joseph Hawley to Ephraim Wright, April 16, 1782, in *American Historical Review*, XXXVI (1931), 776–77; Ralph V. Harlow, "Economic Conditions in

Massachusetts During the American Revolution," *Publications of the Colonial Society of Massachusetts*, XX (1920), 182.

17. Robert Treat Paine to Gerry, 1777, in James T. Adams, *New England in the Republic, 1776–1850* (Boston, 1926), 44; Timothy Dwight to General Samuel H. Parsons, spring, 1779, in Charles E. Cunningham, *Timothy Dwight, 1752–1817* (New York, 1942), 93; Alexander Hamilton to Robert Morris, April 30, 1781, in Harold C. Syrett (ed.), *The Papers of Alexander Hamilton* (25 vols.; New York, 1961–77), II, 612.

18. Hancock to the house, February 3, 1783, in Bacon (ed.), *Supplement*, 23–26; Hall, *Politics*, 111–12.

19. Hancock to the house, June 17, 1782, October 31, 1780, in Bacon (ed.), *Supplement*, 141, 148; *Massachusetts Spy*, April 18, May 23, 1782; Seth Padleford to R. T. Paine, July 23, 1782, in Thomas Treat Paine Papers, Massachusetts Historical Society, Boston; "At a Meeting of Thirty-four Members from Twenty-six Towns in the County of Worcester, on Tuesday, the 9th of April [1782]," in Shipton (ed.), *Early American Imprints*, No. 19447; Paige, *History of Hardwick*, 121; William Lincoln, *History of Worcester, Massachusetts, from Its Earliest Settlement to September, 1836* (Worcester, 1862), 116–23; R. J. Taylor, *Western Massachusetts*, 110–23.

20. Samuel E. Morison, "Remarks on Economic Conditions in Massachusetts, 1775–1783," *Publications of the Colonial Society of Massachusetts*, XX (1920), 191–92; Joseph Hawley to [?], 1782, and to Josiah Strong, June 7, 24, 1782, in Robert E. Moody, "Samuel Ely: Forerunner to Shays," *New England Quarterly*, V (1932), 110–11, 111–13, 142; Charles Martyn, *The Life of Artemas Ward* (New York, 1921), 265–67.

21. Hawley to Ephraim Wright, April 16, 1782, in *American Historical Review*, XXXVI (1931), 776–77.

22. Batchellor *et al.* (eds.), *New Hampshire State Papers*, VII, 399–401, 477, 481; Upton, *Revolutionary New Hampshire*, 67–69.

23. "Junius," in *New Hampshire Gazette* (Portsmouth), January 9, 1776; Portsmouth petition, January 10, 1776, in Batchellor *et al.* (eds.), *New Hampshire State Papers*, VIII, 16–17.

24. See, for example, petitions from Hanover, Lyme, Acworth, Marlow, Alstead, Surry, Chesterfield, Haverhill, Lyman, Bath, Gunthwait, Landaff, and Morristown, November and December, 1776, in Batchellor *et al.* (eds.), *New Hampshire State Papers*, VIII, 421–26; Main, *Political Parties*, 298. On the constitutional struggle, see Jere R. Daniell, *Experiment in Republicanism: New Hampshire Politics and the American Revolution, 1741–1794* (Cambridge, Mass., 1970), Chap. 6.

25. New Hampshire House Journal, January 26, July 3, 1776; Metcalf *et al.* (eds.), *Laws of New Hampshire*, IV, 11–16; Upton, *Revolutionary New Hampshire*, 135.

26. Metcalf *et al.* (eds.), *Laws of New Hampshire*, IV, 14–15, 113–15, 118–25 (but *cf.* III, 585–87); Maurice H. Robinson, "A History of Taxation in New Hampshire," *Publications of the American Economic Association*, 3rd Ser., Vol. III (1902), 733, 757.

27. Report of a committee on a new proportion for taxes, September 18, 1777, in Batchellor *et al.* (eds.), *New Hampshire State Papers*, VIII, 685–87; Metcalf *et al.* (eds.), *Laws of New Hampshire*, IV, 131–32; Robinson, "Taxation in New Hampshire," 690–92; Daniell, *Experiment*, 131.

28. Metcalf *et al.* (eds.), *Laws of New Hampshire*, IV, 265–68.

29. *Ibid.*, 163–64, 202–203, 259–61, 265–68, 421–23, 494–95, 505–506; petition of Barrington nonresident owners, June, 1781, in Batchellor *et al.* (eds.), *New Hampshire State Papers*, XI, 156; Daniell, *Experiment*, 133–34; Robinson, "Taxation in New Hampshire," 776.

30. Jonathan Smith, *Peterborough, New Hampshire, in the American Revolution* (Peterborough, 1913), 421–22; Daniell, *Experiment*, 133; Metcalf *et al.* (eds.), *Laws of New Hampshire*, IV, 386–87.

31. Batchellor *et al.* (eds.), *New Hampshire State Papers*, XI, 167, 184, 413–14.

32. Petition of Alexandria, *ibid.*, 10–11; J. Crosby (ed.), "Annals of Charlestown, in the County of Sullivan, New Hampshire," Collections of the New Hampshire Historical Society, IV (1834), 131; "Spectator Independens," in *New Hampshire Gazette*, November 17, 1781.

33. Daniell, *Experiment*, 131, 136, 164–70.

34. *Ibid.*, 130–34; Metcalf *et al.* (eds.), *Laws of New Hampshire*, IV, 290–91, 357–59, 414–15, 437–41, 453–54.

35. See, for example, Chester instructions, September 30, 1783, in Batchellor *et al.* (eds.), *New Hampshire State Papers*, XI, 317–18.

36. Daniell, *Experiment*, Chap. 7.

37. *Rhode Island Acts and Resolves*, June, 1782, p. 5; Mayer, *Economic Development*, 22–23; Irwin R. Polishook, *Rhode Island and the Union, 1774–1795* (Evanston, Ill., 1969), 46–48; Lovejoy, *Rhode Island Politics*, 193–94.

38. See Bartlett (ed.), *Rhode Island Colonial Records*, VII, 320–21.

39. *Rhode Island Acts and Resolves*, September, 1776, p. 178, October, 1776, p. 30, December, 1776, 1st sess., p. 8, December, 1776, 2nd sess., p. 8, February, 1777, pp. 6–7.

40. For examples, see *ibid.*, the sessions of February, 1778, May, 1779, July, September, November, 1780, March, May, 1781, January, 1782.

41. *Rhode Island Acts and Resolves*, March, 1777, pp. 10–12, August, 1777, pp. 19–21, December, 1777, pp. 25–31, February, 1778, pp. 29–33.

42. *Ibid.*, December, 1777, pp. 26–27; Providence petition, January 30, 1778, in William R. Staples (ed.), *Annals of the Town of Providence, from Its First Settlement to the Organization of the City Government* (Providence, 1843), 277–92.

43. *Rhode Island Acts and Resolves*, November, 1780, p. 19, January, 1782, p. 37; Polishook, *Rhode Island*, 44–47; Patrick T. Conley, "Revolution's Impact on Rhode Island," *Rhode Island History*, XXXIV (1975), 123–25.

44. Samuel Blowers to Mr. Bliss, November 24, 1778, in Admiralty Office Papers, Public Record Office, London; Governor Greene to Ellery, Marchant, and Collins, June 3, 1779, and to Marchant and Collins,

September 3, 1779, in *Revolutionary Correspondence from 1775 to 1782, Comprising Letters Written by Governors Nicholas Cooke, William Greene, John Collins, Jonathan Trumbull* . . . [*and Others*], Collections of the Rhode Island Historcial Society, VI (Providence, 1867), 235–36, 241–43.

45. *Rhode Island Acts and Resolves*, February, 1782, p. 29, November, 1782, p. 26; Jackson T. Main, *The Sovereign States* (New York, 1973), 251.

46. Conley, "Revolution's Impact," 124–25; Polishook, *Rhode Island*, 44–45.

47. *Rhode Island Acts and Resolves*, February, 1777, p. 21, June, 1779, pp. 19–23.

48. *Ibid.*, May, 1781, 2nd sess., pp. 30–31, 61, January, 1782, p. 9, June 1782, pp. 27–28, October, 1782 pp. 14–15; Carroll, *Three Centuries*, I, 348.

49. Conley, "Revolution's Impact," 125–26; Polishook, *Rhodes Island*, 44–45.

50. Conley, "Revolution's Impact," 126; Governor Greene to Governor Hancock, February 28, 1783, in Bartlett (ed.), *Rhode Island Colonial Records*, IX, 685.

51. "Proceedings of the General Assembly in the State of Rhode Island," February, 1783, in Bartlett (ed.), *Rhode Island Colonial Records*, IX, 636.

52. *Ibid.;* Greene to Hancock, February 28, 1783, *ibid.*, 685.

53. Nathanael Greene to Ward, December 31, 1775, in Bernard Knollenberg (ed.), *Correspondence of Governor Samuel Ward, May 1775–March 1776* (Providence, 1952), 152–57.

54. *Rhode Island Acts and Resolves*, February, 1780, p. 13, May, 1780, pp. 24–26, November, 1780, pp. 30–33, 43–47, May, 1781, 2nd sess., pp. 37–40, 54–57, February, 1782, pp. 21–23, June, 1783, pp. 18–21.

55. *Ibid.*, February, 1778, pp. 29–33, June, 1778, pp. 18–22, December, 1779, p. 8, and the citations in note 54 above.

56. *Ibid.*, June, 1783, pp. 18–22, October, 1783, pp. 18–19, February, 1784, p. 17, May, 1784, pp. 34–35, June, 1784, pp. 10–11, August, 1784, p. 21.

57. *Ibid.*, November, 1782, pp. 29–30, February, 1783, pp. 45–53, June, 1783, p. 25.

58. Conley, "Revolution's Impact," 126–27. Conley's analysis is based in large part on Joel A. Cohen, "Rhode Island and the American Revolution: A Selected Socio-Political Analysis" (Ph.D. dissertation, University of Connecticut, 1967).

59. Extract of a letter from Rhode Island, February 1, 1783, in *Pennsylvania Packet* (Philadelphia), March 11, 1783. On the struggle over the Continental impost in the state, see Polishook, *Rhode Island*, Chap. 3.

60. Polishook, *Rhode Island*, 48; Carroll, *Three Centuries*, I, 337. For Rhode Island politics in the Confederation period, see Polishook, *Rhode Island;* John P. Kaminski, "Democracy Run Rampant: Rhode Island in the Confederation," in Martin (ed), *Human Dimensions*, 243–69.

61. Zeichner, *Connecticut's Years of Controversy*, 9, 16–19, 219; Allan Nevins, *The American States During and After the Revolution, 1775–1789* (New York, 1924), 209; James K. Martin, *Men in Rebellion: Higher*

Governmental Leaders and the Coming of the American Revolution
(New Brunswick, N.J., 1973), 44–47.

62. For the conversion to a war footing, see Jonathan Trumbull,
Jonathan Trumbull: Governor of Connecticut, 1769–1784 (Boston, 1919),
243–44; assembly proceedings, April–October, 1775, in Hoadly (ed.), *Public
Records of Connecticut Colony*, XIV, 413–40, XV, 1–175.

63. Hoadly (ed.), *Public Records of Connecticut Colony*, XIV, 432–33,
XV, 13–14, 101–102, 306–307, 440–41.

64. *Connecticut Journal*, December 3, 1777; Rupert C. Loucks,
"Connecticut in the American Revolution" (M.A. thesis, University of
Wisconsin, 1959), 214–15; Charles J. Hoadly and Leonard W. Labaree
(eds.), *The Public Records of the State of Connecticut* (9 vols.; Hartford,
1894–1953), III, 236–37, IV, 24–25.

65. Hoadly (ed.), *Public Records of Connecticut Colony*, XV, 226, 313;
Hoadly and Labaree (eds.), *Public Records of Connecticut*, I, 139, IV,
43, 48–49, 178–79, V, 26, 126–27, 130, 209; Jonathan Trumbull to Treasurer
John Laurence, March 10, 1776, in Treasurer's Letterbook, Early State
Records; assembly proceedings, May, 1776.

66. *Connecticut Journal*, December 10, 1777, April 8, May 6, 1778.

67. Saladino, "Economic Revolution," Chap. 4, discusses the rise of the
merchant community in Connecticut politics.

68. Hoadly and Labaree (eds.), *Public Records of Connecticut*, I, 365–66.

69. *Ibid.*, III, 45, 147–48; Norwich town meeting, December 29, 1777,
in *Connecticut Gazette*, January 9, 1778; *Connecticut Journal*, September
16, 1778; Norwich town meeting, October 1, 1778, in Francis M. Caulkins,
*History of Norwich, Connecticut, from Its Possession by the Indians,
to the Year 1866* (Hartford, 1866), 395.

70. Hoadly and Labaree (eds.), *Public Records of Connecticut*, II, 172–73.

71. "At an Adjourned Town Meeting Holden at Norwich, in Connecticut, on the 29th Day of March, 1779" in Shipton (ed.), *Early American
Imprints*, No. 16420.

72. "E. W." [Erastus Wolcott?], in *Connecticut Gazette*, September 7,
1781.

73. Hoadly and Labaree (eds.), *Public Records of Connecticut*, II,
256–63; Loucks, "Connecticut," 217.

74. Hoadly and Labaree (eds.), *Public Records of Connecticut*, III, 11;
Saladino, "Economic Revolution," Chap. 4; *Connecticut Gazette*,
September 7, 21, 28, October 5, 1781, April 12, May 10, June 7, 1782.

75. *Connecticut Gazette*, April 5, 1782.

76. "A Lover of Order," in *Connecticut Gazette*, April 19, 1782; "Good
Order," *ibid.*, May 24, 1782.

77. "A Lover of Justice," *ibid.*, May 3, 1782.

78. Hoadly and Labaree (eds.), *Public Records of Connecticut*, IV,
154–56, V, 15–19. In September, 1783, a merchants' convention met at
Middletown and petitioned for repeal of these taxes. See *Freeman's
Journal* (Philadelphia), September 17, 1783.

CHAPTER FIVE

1 Young, Democratic Republicans, 16; A. C. Flick, *Loyalism in New York During the American Revolution* (New York, 1901), 113.

2. New York provincial congress to delegates at the Continental Congress, May 26, July 28, 1775, and to the committee of safety, September 20, 1775, in *Journals of the Provincial Congress, Provincial Convention, Committee of Safety of the State of New York, 1775–1777* (2 vols.; Albany, 1842), I, 14, 92, II, 17–18; New York Provincial Congress Journal, May 30, 1775; New York State, Department of Archives, *The American Revolution in New York: Its Political, Social and Economic Significance* (Albany, 1926), 108–109.

3. New York Provincial Congress Journal, August 30, 1775; Abraham Ten Broeck and Robert Yates to the Albany Committee of Correspondence, August, 1775, in James Sullivan (ed.), *Minutes of the Albany Committee of Correspondence, 1775–1778* (2 vols.; Albany), 1923–25, I, 195–96; New York Department of Archives, *Revolution*, 113.
British imports at New York fell from £437,937 to £1,228 in 1775.

4. New York Provincial Congress Journal, August 30, September 2, December 9, 16, 1775, January 6, 1776.

5. John Jay to Alexander McDougall, December 23, 1775, in Henry P. Johnston (ed.), *The Correspondence and Public Papers of John Jay* (4 vols.; New York, 1890–93), I, 40; Jay to McDougall, March 27, 1776, in Bernard Mason, *The Road to Independence: The Revolutionary Movement in New York* (Lexington, Ky., 1966), 195–96; New York Provincial Congress Journal, February 21, 27, March 5, 1776.

6. McDougall to Jay, April 16, 1776, in Mason, *Road to Independence*, 195–96; New York Provincial Congress Journal, August 13, 1776.

7. Walter Livingston to J. Carter, August 11, 1777, in Robert R. Livingston Papers, New-York Historical Society, New York City; Frank Monaghan, *John Jay* (New York, 1935), 97–99; Thomas Cochran, *New York in the Confederation: An Economic Study* (Philadelphia, 1932), 14–15, 18; Young, *Democratic Republicans*, 24, 27.

8. John Holt (ed.), *Laws of the State of New York, Commencing with the First Session of the Senate and Assembly, After the Declaration of Independence, and the Organization of the New Government of the States, Anno 1777* (Poughkeepsie, 1782), 19–22; lease issued to Joel Chamberlin by R. R. Livingston, February 24, 1779, in Livingston-Redmond Papers, Franklin Delano Roosevelt Library, New Hyde Park, New York.

9. J. Holt (ed.), *Laws of New York*, 19–22, 51–54; Cochran, *New York in the Confederation*, 4, 45, 51–54, 85–91.

10. R. R. Livingston to Gouverneur Morris, April 7, 1778, in Robert R. Livingston Papers; veto message, March 25, 1778, in Alfred B. Street (ed.), *The Council of Revision of the State of New York* (Albany, 1859), 212–13; Monaghan, *Jay*, 103–104.

11. Veto message, November 5, 1778, in Street (ed.), *Council of Revision*, 214–15.

12. J. Holt (ed.), *Laws of New York*, 93–96.

13. Thomas R. Tillotson to R. R. Livingston, December 13, 1779, and R. R. Livingston to Governor George Clinton, May 21, 1780, and Ezra L'Hommedieu to Clinton, June 17, 1780, and Philip Schuyler to Clinton, February 23, 1782, and Margaret Beekman Livingston to Clinton, July 16, 1782, all in Robert R. Livingston Papers; T. Van Vecten to R. R. Livingston, September 4, 1781, in Livingston-Redmond Papers; John Meyers to James Duane, February 14, 22, 1780, in James Duane Papers, New-York Historical Society, New York City; Alexander Hamilton to Robert Morris, August, 1782, in Syrett (ed.), *Hamilton Papers*, III, 135–37; Young, *Democratic Republicans*, 30; Edwin B. Livingston, *The Livingstons of Livingston Manor* (New York, 1910), 271–72.

14. R. R. Livingston to Peter V. B. Livingston, April 4, 1780, in E. B. Livingston, *Livingstons*, 271–72; Margaret B. Livingston to R. R. Livingston, December 30, 1779, in Robert R. Livingston Papers.

15. Cochran, *New York in the Confederation*, 50; "A Real Farmer," quoted in Main, *Political Parties*, 127; "WD," in *New York Packet* (Fishkill), August 12, 1779; "A Poor Whig," in *New York Packet*, April 20, 1780; J. Holt (ed.), *Laws of New York*, 167–71.

16. Gerald Bancker, "A State of the Taxes Paid into the Treasury of the State of New York, Since the Declaration of Independence," in Hugh Hastings (ed.), *The Public Papers of George Clinton, First Governor of New York, 1777–1795, 1801–1804* (10 vols.; New York and Albany, 1899–1914), VII, 366–67. On the continuing rural-urban divisions, see New York House Journal, September 14, 16, 23, October 6, 21, 25, 1779, January 30, February 4, 9, 15, 16, 22, June 13, 1780; analysis of the votes, in Main, *Political Parties*, 155.

17. The proceedings of the Livingston Manor meeting, January 6, 1781, are in *New York Packet*, January 18, 1781. For attacks on refugee members, see *ibid.*, April 13, 20, May 6, 18, 1780, September 5, 1782; Walter Livingston to Gouverneur Morris, September 12, 1778, in Walter Livingston Letterbook, New-York Historical Society, New York City; Staughton Lynd, *Class Conflict, Slavery, and the United States Constitution* (Indianapolis, 1968), 98–99; Staughton Lynd, *Antifederalism in Dutchess County, New York: A Study of Democracy and Class Conflict in the Revolutionary Era* (Chicago, 1962), 55–56, 64–73.

18. R. R. Livingston to Gouverneur Morris, January 18, 1781, and to George Washington, January 8, 1781, and Tillotson to R. R Livingston, June 17, 1782, all in Robert R. Livingston Papers; Clinton to congressional delegates, March 28, 1781, in Duane Papers; J. Holt (ed.), *Laws of New York*, 167–71.

19. Hamilton to Robert Morris, July 30, August 13, 1782, and Morris to Hamilton, October 5, 1782, in Syrett (ed.), *Hamilton Papers*, III, 115, 135–37, 178–79.

20. Robert Morris to Hamilton, August 28, 1782, Hamilton to Morris, October 5, 1782, and to Clinton, February 24, 1783, all *ibid.*, 154, 181, 268; [?] to Morris, July 30, 1782, and Morris to Clinton, July 30, 1782, in Hastings (ed.), *Clinton Papers*, VIII, 19–20.

21. Hamilton to Robert Morris, August 2, 1782, and Morris to Hamilton, August 28, 1782, in Syrett (ed.), *Hamilton Papers*, III, 135, 141–42, 155.

22. Clinton to collectors and assessors, August 18, 1788, in Hastings (ed.), *Clinton Papers*, III, 662; R. R. Livingston to Gouverneur Morris, April 3, 1781, in Robert R. Livingston Papers; Cochran, *New York in the Confederation*, 54–55. In the postwar years, farmers held about 40 percent of the seats in the assembly, but during the war it was virtually "an assembly of working farmers." See Young, *Democratic Republicans*, 27; Main, *Political Parties*, 123.

23. Wolvert Ecker to Clinton, April 24, 1781, in Hastings (ed.), *Clinton Papers*, VI, 794; Hamilton to Robert Morris, August 13, 1782, in Syrett (ed.), *Hamilton Papers*, III, 137–38.

24. Clinton to Robert Morris, August 2, 1782, in Hastings (ed.), *Clinton Papers*, VIII, 21–22; Clinton to the assembly, in New York House Journal, January 27, 1783; Hamilton to Morris, August 13, October 5, 1782, in Syrett (ed.), *Hamilton Papers*, III, 135–37, 181; Clinton to R. R. Livingston, January 7, 1780, in Robert R. Livingston Papers; E. Wilder Spaulding, *His Excellency George Clinton, Critic of the Constitution* (New York, 1938), 114–15; Cochran, *New York in the Confederation*, 125–26.

25. Hamilton to Robert Morris, July 22, September 28, October 5, 1782, in Syrett (ed.), *Hamilton Papers*, III, 115, 170, 181; J. Holt (ed.), *Laws of New York*, 264–67, 290–94; New York House Journal, February 5, 14, 1783.

26. Hamilton to Robert Morris, August 2, 13, 1782, in Syrett (ed.), *Hamilton Papers*, III, 135, 141–42. For Hamilton's plans for extensive Continental tax powers, see, for example, his "The Continentalist," Nos. 4, 6, first published in *New York Packet*, July 4, August 30, 1782, and his "Notes on a Plan for Providing for the Debt of the United States," in Syrett (ed.), *Hamilton Papers*, III, 248–49.

27. New Jersey Provincial Congress Journal, June, August 5, 12, October 24, 1775.

28. On sectional divisions in New Jersey, see Leonard Lundin, *The Cockpit of the Revolution: The War for Independence in New Jersey* (Princeton, N.J., 1940); Richard P. McCormick, *Experiment in Independence: New Jersey in the Critical Period, 1781–89* (New Brunswick, N.J., 1950), Chapter 1 and pp. 100–101; Main, *Political Parties*, Chap. 6.

29. William Franklin to Dartmouth, September 5, November 1, 1775, in Whitehead *et al.* (eds.), *New Jersey Archives*, X, 556–60, 669–71; New Jersey Provincial Congress Journal, October 12, 14, 24, 27, 28, 1775; New Jersey Committee of Safety, January 12, 1776, in [State of New Jersey], *Minutes of the Provincial Congress and the Council of Safety of the State of New Jersey, 1775–1776* (Trenton, 1879), 333–34; Samuel Tucker to the president of Congress, July 9, 1776, in Peter Force (ed.), *American Archives: A Documentary History of the Origin and Progress of the North American Colonies* (9 vols.; Washington, D.C., 1837–53), I, 138–39.

30. "To the Dis-United Inhabitants of the Dis-United States (So Called)

of America," July, 1779, in Shipton (ed.), *Early American Imprints,*
No. 16545; "Creon," in *New Jersey Gazette* (Trenton), April 27, 1780.

31. New Jersey Provincial Congress Journal, October 6, 19, 1775; Main,
Political Parties, 156–61.

32. New Jersey Provincial Congress Journal, October 9, 11, 12, 14, 24–28,
1775, January 31, February 3, 7, 13, 16, 1776.

33. *Ibid.,* February 1, 6–7, 9, 13, 21, 1776; Larry Gerlach, *Prologue to
Independence: New Jersey in the Coming of the American Revolution*
(New Brunswick, N.J., 1976), 317.

34. The ordinance is in *Minutes of Provincial Congress of New Jersey,*
413–27. It ordered money at interest assessed at 5 percent of the
principal; developed land, at 5 percent of the "intrinsic value thereof";
and undeveloped land, at 2.5 percent of its value.

35. E. A. Fuhlebruegge, "New Jersey Finances During the American
Revolution," *Proceedings of the New Jersey Historical Society,* LV
(1937), 169–72.

36. "T.W.," in *New Jersey Gazette,* February 25, 1778; "A.B.," *ibid.,*
March 18, 1778.

37. "A True Patriot," *ibid.,* September 2, 9, 1778, March 17, May 12, 1779.

38. "A Farmer," *ibid.,* November 17, 1778; "Equal Taxer," *ibid.,* March
18, 1778.

39. The March, 1778, law is in New Jersey Session Laws, Early State
Records. On changes in the assembly, see Main, "Government by the
People," 401.

40. See, for example, *New Jersey Gazette,* November 17, 1779.

41. William Houston to William Livingston, November 12, 1779, in
*Selections from the Correspondence of the Executive of New Jersey, from
1776 to 1786* (Newark, 1848), 200–204.

42. New Jersey Session Laws, June 8, 1779, in Early State Records.

43. *Ibid.,* December 5, 1778, June 8, December 18, 1779; New Jersey
House Journal, May 27, 1783; William Livingston to Nathaniel Scuder,
December 9, 14, 1778, in William Livingston Papers, Massachusetts
Historical Society, Boston; "Agricola," in *New Jersey Journal* (Chatham),
April 20, May 4, 1779.

44. New Jersey Session Laws, June 13, 1780, January 9, June 21, 1781, in
Early State Records.

45. By November, 1784, New Jersey had collected $645,776 of the
$706,664 in paper that had come due since September, 1781, and $730,888
of the $815,816 in specie. McCormick, *Experiment in Independence,* 170–71;
David L. Cowen, "Revolutionary New Jersey, 1763–87," *Proceedings of
the New Jersey Historical Society,* LXXI (1953), 17. On tax evasion, see J.
Stevens' draft of a message [1782], in John Stevens Papers, New
Jersey Historical Society, Newark.

46. *Delaware Laws,* II, 571–76, 608–18.

47. George Read to Washington, January 19, 1778, in William T. Read,
Life and Correspondence of George Read (Philadelphia, 1870), 290–92;

Caesar Rodney to Read, October 25, 1776, *ibid.*, 206–207; John Collins to Rodney, August 22, 1780, in G. H. Ryden (ed.), *Letters to and from Caesar Rodney, 1756–1784* (Philadelphia, 1933), 367–68; testimony of Levey Messick and Levin Vinson, 1780, quoted in Harold B. Hancock, *The Loyalists of Revolutionary Delaware* (Newark, Del., 1977), 91–92.

48. Read to Thomas McKean, March 4, 1778, in W. T. Read, *Life of George Read*, 303–306.

49. *Ibid.;* McKean to Read, February 12, 1778, *ibid.*, 298–300; Hancock, *Delaware Loyalists*, 20–23.

50. Read to McKean, March 4, 1778, and to Washington, January 19, 1778, in W. T. Read, *Life of George Read*, 303–306, 290–92.

51. *Delaware Laws*, II, 627–33, 647–55.

52. *Ibid.*, 670–77.

53. *Ibid.*, 670–77, 719–38, 741–47, 751–62, 776–82; Delaware House Journal, December 18, 1779.

54. In the late colonial period, the three eastern counties had a majority of the seats in the assembly, but in the convention of 1776 they had only twenty-four seats. The remaining counties had sixty-four. Douglass, *Rebels and Democrats*, 259–60.

55. For the realignment in Pennsylvania politics after independence, I relied on J. Paul Selsam, *The Pennsylvania Constitution of 1776: A Study in Revolutionary Democracy* (Philadelphia, 1936), and on Robert L. Brunhouse, *The Counterrevolution in Pennsylvania* (Harrisburg, 1942). Main, *Political Parties*, Chap. 7, concentrates on the postwar years but does include some analysis of political alignments before 1784.

56. Edward Burd to Jasper Yeates, June 10, 1775, in Lewis B. Walker (ed.), *The Burd Papers: Selections from Letters Written by Edward Burd, 1763–1828* (Pottsville, Pa., 1899), 75; John Penn to Dartmouth, June 30, 1775, in Hazard *et al.* (eds.), *Pennsylvania Archives*, 1st Ser., Vol. IV, 598–99; Mitchell and Flanders (eds.), *Statutes of Pennsylvania*, IX, 451–68; Brunhouse, *Counterrevolution*, 94; Arthur St. Clair to Joseph Shippen, Jr., May 18, 25, 1775, in Hazard *et al.* (eds.), *Pennsylvania Archives*, 1st Ser. Vol. IV, 624, 628–29.

57. Pennsylvania House Journal, May 4, June 21–30, 1775, February 23, June 30, November 8, 1776; Mitchell and Flanders (eds.), *Statutes of Pennsylvania*, VIII, 488–90.

58. Pennsylvania House Journal, June 23, October 27, 1775; Selsam, *Pennsylvania Constitution*, 74–90; Francis N. Thorpe (ed.), *The Federal and State Constitutions, Colonial Charters, and Other Organic Laws of the States, Territories and Colonies Now or Heretofore Forming the United States of America* (7 vols.; Washington, D.C., 1909), V, 3083; William Duane (ed.), *Extracts from the Diary of Christopher Marshall, Kept in Philadelphia and Lancaster, During the American Revolution, 1774–1781* (Albany, 1877), 49–50.

59. James Smith to Pennsylvania delegates, August 1, 1775, in Hazard *et al.* (eds.), *Pennsylvania Archives*, 1st Ser., Vol. V, 640–41; Thomas Paine, "The American Crisis," No. 3, April 19, 1777, in Philip S. Foner (ed.),

The Complete Writings of Thomas Paine (2 vols.; New York, 1945), I, 99; Mitchell and Flanders (eds.), *Statutes of Pennsylvania*, IX, 49–55, 124–28, 167–69.

60. "Milton," in *Pennsylvania Packet*, November 4, 1780; *Pennsylvania Journal* (Philadelphia), March 9, April 10, 1782.

61. Joseph Reed to Robert Morris, July 27, 1781, in Hazard *et al.* (eds.), *Pennsylvania Archives*, 1st Ser. Vol. IX, 311; Brunhouse, *Counterrevolution*, 75; John K. Alexander, "The Fort Wilson Incident of 1779: A Case Study of the Revolutionary Crowd," *William and Mary Quarterly*, XXXI (1974), 589–612.

62. Pennsylvania House Journal, November 25, 1775, February 23, April 1, 5, 11–15, 25, 1776; Mitchell and Flanders (eds.), *Statutes of Pennsylvania*, VIII, 538–44.

63. Pennsylvania House Journal, June 14, 1776; Mitchell and Flanders (eds.), *Statutes of Pennsylvania*, IX, 22–27, 167–69. The revolutionary government eventually repealed the double tax on nonservers, but the Constitutionalists continued to pass discriminatory taxes over Republican opposition throughout the war. *Ibid.*, X, 31–32; Brunhouse, *Counterrevolution*, 97–150.

64. Mitchell and Flanders (eds.), *Statutes of Pennsylvania*, IX, 29–33, 55–59, 312–14; "At a General Meeting of the Citizens of Philadelphia, and Parts Adjacent, at the State-House Yard in This City, on Tuesday the 25th of May 1779," in Shipton (ed.), *Early American Imprints*, No. 16463.

65. Mitchell and Flanders (eds.), *Statutes of Pennsylvania*, IX, 325–26, X, 114–15, 195–200; "State of Pennsylvania Paper," November 14, 1782, in Hazard *et al.* (eds.), *Pennsylvania Archives*, 1st Ser. Vol. IX, 665.

66. Mitchell and Flanders (eds.), *Statutes of Pennsylvania*, IX 230–35, 309–10, 360–72, 443–48, X, 238–43, XI, 81–89; summary of tax accounts to October, 1782, in Hazard *et al.* (eds.), *Pennsylvania Archives*, 3rd Ser. Vol. V, 206–32; state of excise collectors' accounts, *ibid.*, 233–37.

67. Pennsylvania House Journal, March 24, 1779, March 20, 1782; for continuing complaints, see "A Citizen," in *Pennsylvania Packet*, February 8, 1783; *Pennsylvania Journal*, November 28, 1783.

68. Mitchell and Flanders (eds.), *Statutes of Pennsylvania*, IX, 97–103, 152–56, 230–35, 326–36, 360–72, 443–48, X, 385–90.

69. *Pennsylvania Gazette*, February 5, 1777; Brunhouse, *Counterrevolution*, 109; Nevins, *American States*, 512.

70. Franklin to Robert Morris, December 25, 1783, in John Bigelow (ed.), *The Complete Works of Benjamin Franklin* (10 vols.; New York, 1887–88), IX, 138.

71. Philadelphia commissioners to President Reed, August 3, 1781, and to President William Moore, January 11, 1782, and David Rittenhouse to Reed, [May], 1781, all in Hazard *et al.* (eds.), *Pennsylvania Archives*, 1st Ser., Vol. IX, 119, 328–29, 478–79; Reed to Philadelphia commissioners, July 20, August 6, 1781, *ibid.*, 2nd Ser., Vol. III, 510–11.

72. Philadelphia commissioners to supreme executive council, [January], 1780, *ibid.*, 1st Ser., Vol. VIII, 80–81; Reed to tax commis-

sioners, March 9, 1780, and Berks County commissioners to Reed, March 8, 1780, *ibid.*, 124–25; supreme executive council minutes, *ibid.*, 1st Ser., Vol. XII, 244–45; opinions of Nicholas Waln and Jonathan Sergeant, *ibid.*, VIII, 49, 81–82; Edward Ford, *David Rittenhouse, Astronomer-Patriot, 1732–1796* (Philadelphia, 1946), 107–108.

73. William Henry to Reed, February 17, June 13, 1781, in Hazard *et al.* (eds.), *Pennsylvania Archives*, 1st Ser., Vol. VIII, 730, Vol. IX, 205; Timothy Matlack to tax commissioners, July 11, 1781, and Reed to tax commissioners, August 4, 1781, *ibid.*, 2nd Ser., Vol. III, 497–98, 512; Lancaster County commissioners to Dickinson August 16, 1783, *ibid.*, 1st Ser., Vol. X, 82.

74. Adam Whitman to Reed, March 10, 1780, *ibid.*, 1st Ser., Vol. VIII, 129–30; Bucks County commissioners to Reed, May 14, 1781, *ibid.*, 2nd Ser., Vol. III, 487; Joseph Hart to President Moore, March 3, 1782, *ibid.*, 1st Ser., Vol., IX, 507–508; Lancaster County commissioners to Dickinson, August 16, 1783, and Jacob Smyser to Dickinson, August 5, 1783, and Northampton County commissioners to Dickinson, August 25, 1783, all *ibid.*, 1st Ser., Vol. X, 77, 82, 92.

75. Reed to Chester County commissioners, April 22, 1780, and to Berks County commissioners, August 28, 1781, *ibid.*, 2nd Ser., Vol. III, 394, 526–27; Lieutenant William Henry to Reed, June 13, 1781, *ibid.*, 1st Ser., Vol. IX, 205; Pennsylvania House Journal, March 5, 1782; *Freeman's Journal*, May 7, 1783.

76. Reed to Charles Pettit and Clement Biddle, May 10, 1781, in Hazard *et al.* (eds.), *Pennsylvania Archives*, 1st Ser., Vol. IX, 129–30; Reed to Washington, undated, quoted in Albert S. Bolles, *Pennsylvania, Province and State: A History* (2 vols.; New York, 1899), II, 72; Reed to William Henry, July, 1780, in Hazard *et al.* (eds.), *Pennsylvania Archives*, 1st Ser., Vol. VIII, 423–24.

77. Mitchell and Flanders (eds.), *Statutes of Pennsylvania*, X, 448–57; *Pennsylvania Packet*, October 28, 1780.

78. Paine, "The Crisis Extraordinary," October 4, 1780, and "The American Crisis," No. 10, March 5, 1782, both in P. S. Foner (ed.), *Complete Writings of Paine*, I, 171–85, 196–207; Rittenhouse to Moore, and Philadelphia commissioners to Reed, May 2, 1781, in Hazard *et al.* (eds.), *Pennsylvania Archives*, 1st Ser., Vol. VIII, 662, Vol. IX, 116; Reed to A. McClean, April 8, 1781, *ibid.*, IX, 59.

79. James Finley to Dickinson, April 28, 1783, and Bucks County commissioners to Dickinson, August 5, 1783, and Cumberland County commissioners to Dickinson, August 14, 1783, and Northampton County commissioners to Dickinson, August 25, 1783, all in Hazard *et al.* (eds.), *Pennsylvania Archives*, 1st Ser., Vol. X, 40–41, 77, 79–80, 92; Northumberland County petition, November 25, 1778, *ibid.*, 2nd Ser., Vol. III, 250–52.

80. William Irvine to Moore, July 5, 1782, and Christopher Hayes to Moore, September 20, 1782, and depositions of John Robinson, June 20, and of Hugh Brackenridge, July 4, 1782, all *ibid.*, 1st Ser., Vol. IX, 572–76, 637–38.

81. Bucks County commissioners to Dickinson, July 31, 1783, *ibid.*, 75–76; Reed to Chester County commissioners, April 22, 1780, *ibid.*, 2nd Ser., Vol. III, 394.

82. Lancaster County commissioners to Dickinson, August 16, 1783, *ibid.*, 1st Ser., Vol. X, 82; Whitman to Reed, March 10, 1780, *ibid.*, 1st Ser., Vol. VIII, 129–30; Reed to William Henry, September 22, 1780, in "Letters to William Henry of Lancaster, Pennsylvania, 1777–1783," *Pennsylvania Magazine of History and Biography*, XXII (1898), 109–10; *Pennsylvania Gazette*, November 15, 1780; Pennsylvania House Journal, September 22, 1780; John F. Roche, *Joseph Reed: A Moderate in the American Revolution* (New York, 1957), 180–81.

83. "A Hint to the Whigs," *Pennsylvania Packet*, February 13, 1783.

84. Reed to William Henry, December 19, 1780, in Hazard *et al.* (eds.), *Pennsylvania Archives*, 1st Ser., Vol. VIII, 667–68; Dickinson to assembly, January 23, 1783, *ibid.*, 4th Ser., Vol. III, 894–904.

85. Reed to William Henry, July, 1780, *ibid.*, 1st Ser., Vol. VIII, 423–24, and to Washington, undated, quoted in Bolles, *Pennsylvania*, II, 72; *Freeman's Journal*, February 12, March 26, 1783.

CHAPTER SIX

1. Address of Sundry Inhabitants of the County of Guilford to Governor Martin [March, 1775], in Saunders (ed.), *Colonial Records of North Carolina*, IX, 1160–61; Martin to Dartmouth, March 10, April 20, October 16, 1775, and to General Thomas Gage, March 16, 1775, *ibid.*, IX, 1157, 1166–68, 1228, X, 265–66; William Hooper to Robert Morris, May 27, 1777, in "Letters to Robert Morris, 1775–1782," Collections of the New-York Historical Society, XI (New York, 1879), 427–30.

2. Joseph Hewes to Samuel Johnston, June 5, 1775, in Burnett (ed.), *Letters*, I, 112–13; Thomas Burke to the governor, September 2, 1777, *ibid.*, II, 472; Hooper to Johnston, May 23, 1775, in Saunders (ed.), *Colonial Records of North Carolina*, IX, 1280–81.

3. North Carolina Provincial Congress Journal, August 25, September 7, 1775, April 22, May 9, July 4, 1776.

4. Instructions to delegates, September, 1775, November, 1776, in Saunders (ed.), *Colonial Records of North Carolina*, X, 239–42, 870a–870f.

5. Douglass, *Rebels and Democrats*, 131–32. The constitution of 1776 granted every county two representatives, thus ending the preferential system that had allowed some low-country counties to have five.

6. Samuel Johnson to James Iredell, December 7, 9, 1776, in Griffith McRee (ed.), *Life and Correspondence of James Iredell* (2 vols.; New York, 1857–58), I, 337–38; James Iredell, "Creed of a Rioter," *ibid.*, 335–36.

7. Saunders *et al.* (eds.), *State Records of North Carolina*, XXIV, 6–9, 109–13, 134–35.

8. *Ibid.*, 200–204, 221–22, 317–18, 344–47, 390–94, 429–39.

9. Nevins, *American States*, 365–67, 468; R. D. W. Conner, *The History of*

North Carolina: The Colonial and Revolutionary Periods, 1684–1783 (Chicago, 1911), 433.

10. Saunders *et al.* (eds.), *State Records of North Carolina*, XXIV, 437–39; Nevins, *American States*, 356–57; William K. Boyd, "Currency and Banking in North Carolina, 1790–1836," *Trinity College Historical Society Papers*, X (1914), 55–58.

11. Saunders *et al.* (eds.), *State Records of North Carolina*, XXIV, 325–26; North Carolina Senate Journal, August 13, 19, 1778; Alexander Martin to Abner Nash, November 10, 1780, in Saunders *et al.* (eds.), *State Records of North Carolina*, XV, 151; Thomas Burke to the house, April 16, 1782, *ibid.*, XVI, 6; William Skinner to Governor Richard Caswell, March 5, 1778, *ibid.*, XIII, 63; Conner, *History of North Carolina*, 433–34.

12. James Iredell to his wife, May 18, 1780, May 23, 1783, in McRee (ed.), *Iredell Correspondence*, I, 446, II, 46–47; James Hogg to Iredell, May 17, 1783, and Iredell to Pierce Butler, March 14, 1784, *ibid.*, II, 45–46, 93–94.

13. Virginia Provincial Congress Journal, July 17, August 26, 1775, June 12, 1776; Hening (ed.), *Statutes of Virginia*, IX, 219–25, 286–89.

14. Landon Carter to Washington, May 9, 1776, in Force (ed.), *American Archives*, VI, 390; Richard Henry Lee to Patrick Henry, April 20, 1776, in James C. Ballagh (ed.), *The Letters of Richard Henry Lee* (2 vols.; New York, 1911–14), I, 176–79.

15. Roger Atkinson to Samuel Pleasants, November 23, 1776, in A. J. Morrison (ed.), "Letters of Roger Atkinson, 1769–1776," *Virginia Magazine of History and Biography*, XV (1907–1908), 357; George Mason to R. H. Lee, May 18, 1776, in Robert A. Rutland (ed.), *The Papers of George Mason, 1725–1792* (3 vols.; Chapel Hill, 1970), I, 271–72; Main, "Government by the People," 402–403.

16. Virginia House Journal, November 3–4, 1777; *Virginia Gazette* (Purdie), September 26, 1777.

17. Pendleton to William Woodford, January 16, 1778, in David J. Mays (ed.), *The Letters and Papers of Edmund Pendleton, 1734–1803* (2 vols.; Charlottesville, 1967), I, 246; Virginia House Journal, December 13, 1777, January 10, 19–23, 1778; Hening (ed.), *Statutes of Virginia*, IX, 349–68. Rutland (ed.), *Mason Papers*, I, 375n–77n, credits Mason with drafting the reformed tax bill.

18. Virginia House Journal, November 7, 1779; Hening (ed.), *Statutes of Virginia*, X, 199–201; Pendleton to Madison, December 3, 1781, in Mays (ed.), *Pendleton Papers*, II, 381–82; R. H. Lee to Hannah Corbin, March 17, 1778, in Ballagh (ed.), *Letters of R. H. Lee*, I, 392–94.

19. Pendleton to Woodford, May 24, 1779, in Mays (ed.), *Pendleton Papers*, I, 286; Hening (ed.), *Statutes of Virginia*, IX, 547–52, X, 9–10.

20. The various plans are described in Julian P. Boyd (ed.), *The Papers of Thomas Jefferson* (19 vols. to date; Princeton, N.J., 1950–), II, 221n–24n. The plan finally adopted merely admonished tax officials to find "some general mode" for making assessments within each county. Hening (ed.), *Statutes of Virginia*, IX, 547–52.

21. Pendleton to Woodford, January 31, 1778, May 24, 31, 1779, in Mays

(ed.), *Pendleton Papers*, I, 246, 286, 290; Hening (ed.), *Statutes of Virginia*, X, 9–14.

22. Hening (ed.), *Statutes of Virginia*, X, 9–14.

23. Joseph Jones to Madison, November 18, 1780, in Worthington C. Ford (ed.), *Letters of Joseph Jones of Virginia, 1777–1787* (Washington, D.C., 1889), 46–50.

24. Jones to Madison, December 2, 8, 1780, in W. C. Ford (ed.), *Letters of Joseph Jones*, 57–60, 62–63; Pendleton to Madison, December 4, 1780, in Mays (ed.), *Pendleton Papers*, I, 325.

25. Hening (ed.), *Statutes of Virginia*, IX, 349–68, 445–56; R. H. Lee to Mason, June 9, 1779, in Rutland (ed.), *Mason Papers*, II, 514.

26. Jefferson to Samuel Huntington, December 30, 1779, in J. P. Boyd (ed.), *Jefferson Papers*, III, 250; *Virginia Gazette* (Dixon and Hunter), April 6, 1776.

27. Hening (ed.), *Statutes of Virginia*, X, 79–81, 435; Virginia House Journal, October 15, November 9, 1779, May 18, June 21, 1780; Jefferson to Bernardo de Gálvez, November 8, 1779, and to Thomas Lee, January 30, 1780, in J. P. Boyd (ed.), *Jefferson Papers*, III, 168, 279–80.

28. Culpeper County collectors to the governor, March 29, 1781, in William P. Palmer (ed.), *Calendar of Virginia State Papers* (11 vols.; Richmond, 1885–93), I, 606; Pendleton to Madison, April 15, 1782, in Mays (ed.), *Pendleton Papers*, II, 389–91; Jaquelin Ambler's replies to questions by Madison, 1782, in Gaillard Hunt (ed.), *The Writings of James Madison* (9 vols.; New York, 1900–1910), I, 270–71.

29. Hening (ed.), *Statutes of Virginia*, X, 501–17, XI, 140–45.

30. *Ibid.*, X, 165–71, 182–83, 292–93, 357–58, 435; Albert O. Porter, *County Government in Virginia: A Legislative History, 1607–1904* (New York, 1947), 137; Hamilton J. Eckenrode, *The Revolution in Virginia* (Boston, 1916), 202–203.

31. Jones to Madison, May 25, 1783, in W. C. Ford (ed.), *Letters of Joseph Jones*, 105–106; L. G. Tyler, *Letters of Tylers*, I, 83–84, 136; Mary T. Armentrout, "A Political Study of Virginia Finance, 1781–1789" (Ph.D. dissertation, University of Virginia, 1934), 68.

32. Mason to Patrick Henry, May 6, 1783, in Rutland (ed.), *Mason Papers*, II, 769–73; Pendleton to Madison, May 26, 1783, in Mays (ed.), *Pendleton Papers*, II, 447–48; Jefferson to Madison, December 8, 1784, in J. P. Boyd (ed.), *Jefferson Papers*, VII, 557.

33. "The Farmer," in *Virginia Gazette*, May 18, 25, 1782; St. George Tucker to Theodorick Bland, May 2, 1782, in Charles Campbell (ed.), *The Bland Papers: Being a Selection from the Manuscripts of Colonel Theodorick Bland, Jr.* (2 vols.; Petersburg, 1840–43), II, 79.

34. Tucker to Bland, May 2, 1782, in Campbell (ed.), *Bland Papers*, II, 78–79; Pendleton to Madison, October 8, 1781, in Mays (ed.), *Pendleton Papers*, I, 372–74; Hening (ed.), *Statutes of Virginia*, X, 233–37, 347–50; Jones to Madison, November 5, 1780, in W. C. Ford (ed.), *Letters of Joseph Jones*, 40–42; Armentrout, "Virginia Finance," 62.

35. Robert Ewing to Jefferson, February 12, 1781, and Isaac Avery to

Jefferson, March 16, 1781, in J. P. Boyd (ed.), *Jefferson Papers*, IV, 587–88, V, 153–54; George Rice to the governor, February 14, 1781, and Colonel W. Curle to the governor, February 26, 1781, in Palmer (ed.), *Calendar*, I, 516, 542; Albemarle County petition, February 14, 1781, *ibid.*, 515.

36. Hening (ed.), *Statutes of Virginia*, X, 404–405, XI, 79–80, 105, 169–70, 194; Virginia Council Journal, April 1, 1783; Jones to Madison, May 31, 1783, in W. C. Ford (ed.), *Letters of Joseph Jones*, 109; Armentrout "Virginia Finance," 72.

37. *Virginia Gazette*, May 31, 1783.

38. Benjamin Harrison to Morris, November 7, 1777, in *Magazine of History*, XXIII (1916), 251–53.

39. Jefferson to Philip Mazzei, May 31, 1780, in J. P. Boyd (ed.), *Jefferson Papers*, III, 405; Virginia House Journal, June 6, 1780; Armentrout, "Virginia Finance," 31–33.

40. Virginia House Journal, June 22, 1780; Kate Mason Rowland, *The Life of George Mason, 1725–1792* (2 vols.; New York, 1892), I, 355; Armentrout, "Virginia Finance," Chap. 2.

41. Jones to Madison, November 10, 18, 25, 1780, in W. C. Ford (ed.), *Letters of Joseph Jones*, 43, 45–50, 53–57; R. H. Lee to Samuel Adams, November 10, 1780, in Ballagh (ed.), *Letters of R. H. Lee*, II, 210–12; L. G. Tyler, *Letters of Tylers*, I, 76.

42. Madison to Jefferson, April 16, 1781 (and enclosure), February 25, 1783, in Hunt (ed.), *Madison Writings*, I, 129–32, 384n–86n; Madison's notes on debates in Congress, January 28, 1783, I, 342.

43. Harrison to Congress, January 21, 1782, in H. R. McIlwaine (ed.), *Official Letters of the Governors of Virginia, 1776–1783* (3 vols.; Richmond, 1926–29), III, 131, and to Morris, March 28, 1782, in *Magazine of History*, XXIII (1916), 258–60; Morris to Jefferson, February 25, 1784, in J. P. Boyd (ed.), *Jefferson Papers*, VI, 563.

44. Hening (ed.), *Statutes of Virginia*, XI, 171.

45. South Carolina Provincial Congress Journal, June 14, 1775; Ramsay, *History of South Carolina*, I, 103.

46. South Carolina Provincial Congress Journal, November 15, 1775, March 6, 1776; Cooper and McCord (eds.), *Statutes of South Carolina*, IV, 361–63, 365–74.

47. Henry Laurens to John Laurens, January 22, 1775, quoted in William E. Hemphill and Wylma A. Wates (eds.), *Extracts from the Journals of the Provincial Congresses of South Carolina, 1775–1776* (Columbia, 1960), xxiii; Douglass, *Rebels and Democrats*, 43–44; Main, *Political Parties*, 268–69; Main, "Government by the People," 403–404; Schaper, "Sectionalism," 359–69. The best summary account of legislative politics in revolutionary South Carolina is Jerome J. Nadelhaft, "The Revolutionary Era in South Carolina, 1775–1788" (Ph.D. dissertation, University of Wisconsin, 1965). I have relied on it in this section.

48. Cooper and McCord (eds.), *Statutes of South Carolina*, IV, 635–74.

49. *Ibid.*, 413–22; South Carolina House Journal, September 6, 1779, February 8–9, 23, 1780; Nadelhaft, "Revolutionary Era," 117–19; Walsh,

"Christopher Gadsden," 201; Richard Walsh, *Charleston's Sons of Liberty: A Study of the Artisans, 1763–1789* (Columbia, S.C., 1959), III.

50. Henry Laurens to John Laurens, March 15, 1778, in "Correspondence Between Hon. Henry Laurens and His Son, John, 1777–1780," *South Carolina Historical and Genealogical Magazine*, VI (1905), 103–106; Rawlins Lowndes to Henry Laurens, March 30, 1778, in *South Carolina Historical and Genealogical Magazine*, X (1909), 172–73.

51. Henry Laurens' notes on debates at Congress, September 13, 1779, in Burnett (ed.), *Letters*, IV, 417; John Rutledge to delegates in Congress, December 8, 1780, in Joseph W. Barnwell (ed.), "Letters of John Rutledge," *South Carolina Historical and Genealogical Magazine*, XVIII (1917), 46; Charles G. Singer, *South Carolina in the Confederation* (Philadelphia, 1941), 47.

52. Cooper and McCord (eds.), *Statutes of South Carolina*, IV, 506–507, 576–82; Frank Zornow, "Tariff Policies in South Carolina, 1775–1789," *South Carolina Historical Magazine*, LVI, (1955), 31–44.

53. Edward Rutledge to Arthur Middleton, August, 1782, in Barnwell (ed.), "Correspondence of Arthur Middleton," 20–22.

54. Merrill Jensen, "The American People and the American Revolution," *Journal of American History*, LVII (1970), 14–15; Walsh, *Sons of Liberty*, 117–21; Walsh, "Christopher Gadsden," 201–203; David Ramsay to Benjamin Rush, July 11, 1783, in Robert L. Brunhouse (ed.), "David Ramsay, 1749–1815: Selections from His Writings," *Transactions of the American Philosophical Society*, n.s., Vol. LV, Pt. 4 (1965), 75.

55. "Democratic Gentle-Touch," in *Gazette of the State of South Carolina* (Charleston), July 29, 1784; Cooper and McCord (eds.), *Statutes of South Carolina*, IV, 627–37; Nadelhaft, "Revolutionary Era," 130–33; Ramsay, *History of South Carolina*, II, 107.

56. Governor Wright to Dartmouth, January 3, 1775, in "Letters from Sir James Wright [1773–1782]," Collections of the Georgia Historical Society, III (Savannah, 1873), 229–30; Georgia Provincial Congress Journal, July 8, 12, 1775.

57. Chandler (ed.), *Colonial Records of Georgia*, XIX, 87–99; Coleman, *Revolution in Georgia*, 155–65; Nevins, *American States*, 413; C. C. Jones, *History of Georgia*, II, 364–75.

58. Joseph Clay to Henry Laurens, October 21, 1777, in *Letters of Joseph Clay, Merchant of South Carolina*, Collections of the Georgia Historical Society, VIII (Savannah, 1913), 52–57; Coleman, *Revolution in Georgia*, 92–93, 163–67.

59. Chandler (ed.), *Colonial Records of Georgia*, XIX, 363–79; Coleman, *Revolution in Georgia*, 190–91; William B. Stevens, *A History of Georgia* (2 vols.; New York and Philadelphia, 1847–59), II, 344–45.

60. Maryland Provincial Congress Journal, December 8, 1775; William Eddis, *Letters from America*, ed. Aubrey C. Land (Cambridge, Mass., 1969), 101–104; John A. Archer, *The Provincial Government of Maryland (1774–1777)* (Baltimore, 1895), 23–24, 32.

61. "A Watchman," in *Maryland Gazette* (Annapolis), August 15, 1776;

Phillip A. Crowl, *Maryland During and After the Revolution: A Political and Economic Study* (Baltimore, 1943), 19–29. The best study of revolutionary politics in Maryland is Hoffman's *Dissension*.

62. *Maryland Gazette*, August 22, 1776; Charles Carroll to his father, August 20, October 4, 1776, in Charles Carroll Papers, Maryland Historical Society, Baltimore; Hoffman, *Dissension*, Chaps. 8, 9.

63. "A Declaration of Rights and the Constitution and Form of Government, Agreed to by the Delegates," Annapolis, 1776, in Shipton (ed.), *Early American Imprints*, No. 14836. Although Maryland's provincial poll taxes in the late colonial period were primarily religious taxes, they were bitterly resented and attacked. See Vivian, "Poll Tax Controversy in Maryland."

64. Maryland Session Laws, February, 1777, XXI, XXII, March, 1778, VII, October, 1778, VII, March, 1779 XI, July, 1779, V, October, 1779, XXV, November, 1782, VI, in Early State Records; Maryland House Journal, January 9, 1781; Charles Carroll to his father, April 4, 1777, in Carroll Papers; Hoffman, *Dissension*, 207–10.

65. Maryland Session Laws, February, 1777, XXI, XXII, March, 1778, VII, March, 1779, XI, July, 1779, V, October, 1780, XXV, November, 1782, VI, in Early State Records.

66. Maryland House Journal, January 9, 1781; Maryland Senate Journal, March 20, 1779, December 31, 1782, June 2, 1783; Main, "Government by the People," 401–402; Main, *Political Parties*, 212–13.

67. Maryland House Journal, December 15, 1779; Maryland Senate Journal, December 21, 23, 1779; "A Sentry," in *Maryland Gazette*, March 3, 1780; Maryland Session Laws, October, 1780, XLV, in Early State Records; Crowl, *Maryland*, 43–45; Kate Mason Rowland, *The Life of Charles Carroll of Carrollton, 1737–1782* (2 vols.; New York, 1898), II, 23–30.

68. William Eddis to Robert Eden, July 23, 1777, in *Maryland Historical Magazine*, II (1907), 107; John Chalmers to [?], August 20, 1780, in Collections of the Massachusetts Historical Society, 4th Ser., Vol. X (Boston, 1871), 797–801; Henry Dickinson to Thomas S. Lee, July 24, 1780, in Browne *et al.* (eds.), *Archives of Maryland*, XLV, 25–26; *Maryland Gazette*, August 9, 1781.

69. Browne *et al.* (eds.), *Archives of Maryland*, XLVII, 64–65.

70. Maryland Session Laws, October, 1780, XXI, November, 1782, VI, XXIV, in Early State Records.

71. *Ibid.*, October, 1780, XXV, May, 1781, III; council of state to William Merritt, February 23, 1780, and to Cecil County tax collector, March 31, 1780, in Browne *et al.* (eds.), *Archives of Maryland*, XLIII, 94, 125.

72. *Maryland Gazette*, March 3, 1780, July 26, August 9, 1781; Maryland Session Laws, February, 1777, XXI, XXII, October, 1780, XXV, May, 1781, III, November, 1782, VI, in Early State Records; Maryland Senate Journal, March 20, 1779.

73. *Maryland Gazette*, January 3, 1782; Maryland Session Laws, October, 1780, XXI, November, 1782, XXIX, in Early State Records.

74. Robert Morris to Benjamin Harwood, October 15, 1782, in Morris-Harwood Papers, Maryland Historical Society, Baltimore.

EPILOGUE

1. Merrill Jensen, *The New Nation: A History of the United States During the Confederation, 1781–1789* (New York, 1950), 85–90.

2. *Virginia Gazette*, May 10, 1783.

3. *Ibid.*, August 2, 1783; *Freeman's Journal*, March 14, 1787.

4. *Connecticut Courant*, January 6, 13, 20, 1784, February 5, 12, 19, 1787.

5. See, for example, Newport *Mercury*, February 6, 20, 1786; Jabez Bowen, "To the Freemen of the State of Rhode Island," Providence, 1786, in Shipton (ed.), *Early American Imprints*, No. 19521.

6. Poll taxes continued to yield one third of state revenues. R. J. Taylor, *Western Massachusetts*, 38.

7. "From a Boston Paper," *Freeman's Journal*, March 14, 1787; "Probus," in *Massachusetts Centinel* (Boston), May 5, 1787.

8. *State Gazette of South Carolina* (Charleston), December 8, 1788.

9. "Cassius" [James Sullivan], in *Massachusetts Gazette*, November 16, 1787.

10. Braintree town meeting, July 3, 15, September 25, 1786, in Samuel A. Bates (ed.), *Records of the Town of Braintree, 1640–1793* (Randolph, Mass., 1886), 555–68; Richard D. Hershcopf, "The New England Farmer and Politics, 1785–1787" (M.A. thesis, University of Wisconsin, 1947).

11. "Centinel," in *Pennsylvania Gazette*, February 2, 1785. Brunhouse, *Counterrevolution*, contains a summary account of the politics of postrevolutionary finance in Pennsylvania.

12. See, for example, Ephraim Douglas to Dickinson, July 11, 1784, in Hazard *et al.* (eds.), *Pennsylvania Archives*, 1st Ser., Vol. X, 588; Michael Hahn to John Nicholson, December 15, 1786, *ibid.*, XI, 97–98. Delaware faced similar problems. *Delaware Laws*, II, 904–905.

13. Deposition of Philip Jenkins, June 7, 1784, in Hazard *et al.* (eds.), *Pennsylvania Archives*, 1st Ser., Vol. X, 594–95; Douglas to Secretary Armstrong, May 29, 1784, *ibid.*, 581–83; Hayes to Dickinson, June 14, 1784, *ibid.*, 279; proclamation by Dickinson, June 28, 1784, *ibid.*, 4th Ser., Vol. III, 969; Washington County commissioners to Secretary Armstrong, July 9, 1784, *ibid.*, 1st Ser., Vol. X, 587; Dorsey Pentecost to Council of state, April 16, 1786, *ibid.*, 757–58.

14. Hahn to Nicholson, December 15, 1786, *ibid.*, 1st Ser., Vol. XI, 97–98; Thomas Hartley to William Bradford, Jr., January 5, 1787, and to Charles Biddle, June 4, 1787, *ibid.*, 114–15, 156–57.

15. Elizabeth Holt (ed.), *Laws of the State of New York, Passed at the First Meeting of the Seventh Session of the Legislature of Said State, Beginning the 12th Day of February, 1784, and Ending the 12th Day of May Following* (New York, 1784), 83–89.

16. Hamilton's speech to New York assembly, February 17, 1787, in Syrett (ed.), *Hamilton Papers*, IV, 94–95; Hamilton to Gouverneur Morris, April 7, 1784, *ibid.*, III, 529.

17. Jay to Francis Hopkinson, March 29, 1786, and to Jefferson, October 27, 1786, and to Washington, June 27, 1786, all in Johnston (ed.), *Papers of John Jay*, III, 187–88, 212, 204–205.

18. Madison to James Monroe, October 5, 1786, in Hunt (ed.), *Madison Writings*, I, 251–52.

19. Thomas Johnson, late sheriff of Louisa County, to Patrick Henry, January 19, 1785, in Palmer (ed.), *Calendar*, IV, 82; Virginia House Journal, December 10, 1784, November 12, 1784; L. Wood to Governor Edmund Randolph, April 17, 1787, in Palmer (ed.), *Calendar*, IV, 270; petition of Peyton Stern, July, 1785, in Mays (ed.), *Pendleton Papers*, II, 484–85.

20. Depositions of William Crabtree, March 10, 1786, of Thomas Berry, March 14, 1786, and of Arthur Bowen, May 4, 1786, in Palmer (ed.), *Calendar*, IV, 98, 102–103, 129.

21. James McClurg to Madison, August 22, September 10, 1787, in *Proceedings of the Massachusetts Historical Society*, 2nd Ser., Vol. XVII (1903), 472–73, 474.

22. Pendleton to Patrick Henry, July 31, 1786, in Mays (ed.), *Pendleton Papers*, II, 483–84.

23. Saunders *et al.* (eds.), *State Records of North Carolina*, XXIV, 543–46, 802–803; "Extract of a Letter from a Gentleman in the State of Franklin to a Gentleman in Augusta," *Georgia State Gazette* (Augusta), March 24, 1787.

24. Cooper and McCord (eds.), *Statutes of South Carolina*, IV, 528–29. Georgia followed with its first ad valorem tax the next year. Coleman, *Revolution in Georgia*, 204–205.

25. "Cato" [George Clinton], New York Journal, December 16, 1787, in Paul L. Ford (ed.), *Essays on the Constitution of the United States, 1787–1788* (Brooklyn, 1892), 271–73; see also [Melancthon Smith], "An Address to the People of the State of New York," 1788, in Paul L. Ford (ed.), *Pamphlets on the Constitution of the United States, 1787–1788* (Brooklyn, 1888), 102–108; "A Manifesto of a Number of Citizens from Albany County," New York *Journal*, April 26, 1788, in Cecelia Kenyon (ed.), *The Antifederalists* (New York, 1966), 361–65.

26. "The Address and Reasons of Dissent of the Minority of the Convention of the State of Pennsylvania to Their Constituents," *Pennsylvania Packet*, December 18, 1787; George Bryan, "Centinel No. 1," 1787, in Kenyon (ed.), *Antifederalists*, 8–9.

27. Jonathan Elliot (ed.), *The Debates in the Several State Conventions, on the Adoption of the Federal Constitution* (5 vols.; Philadelphia, 1941), III, 57, 285.

28. William Lancaster to the North Carolina ratifying convention, July 30, 1788, in Kenyon (ed.), *Antifederalists*, 415; William Davis to Iredell, January 22, 1788, in McRee (ed.), *Iredell Correspondence*, II,

217–18. Similar arguments could be cited at length. Federalists insisted that the national government would "doubtless accommodate the taxes to the customs and convenience of the several states" and denied that poll taxes or, indeed, any direct taxes would be levied by the national government after ratification. "A Citizen of New Haven" [Roger Sherman], New Haven *Gazette*, December 4, 1788, in P. L. Ford (ed.), *Essays*, 236; "Aristedes" [Alexander Hanson], "Remarks upon the Proposed Plan of a Federal Government, Addressed to the People of Maryland," 1788, in P. L. Ford (ed.), *Pamphlets*, 253. Again, similar arguments could be cited at length.

 29. See, for example, Rufus King to Theodore Sedgwick, June 10, 1787, quoted in J. R. Pole, "Shays's Rebellion: A Political Interpretation," in Jack P. Greene (ed.), *The Reinterpretation of the American Revolution* (New York, 1968), 431.

 30. Jameson, *American Revolution*, 9.

Bibliography

MANUSCRIPT COLLECTIONS

Franklin Delano Roosevelt Library, New Hyde Park, New York
    Livingston-Redmond. Papers.
Historical Society of Pennsylvania, Philadelphia
    Miscellaneous Broadsides.
    Penn, John. Manuscripts.
    Penn, Thomas. Letterbooks.
Maryland Historical Society, Baltimore
    Carroll, Charles. Papers.
    Morris-Harwood. Papers.
Massachusetts Historical Society, Boston
    Livingston, William. Papers.
    Paine, Thomas Treat. Papers.
New Jersey Historical Society, Newark
    Stevens, John. Papers.
New-York Historical Society, New York City
    Duane, James. Papers.
    Livingston, Robert R. Papers.
    Livingston, Walter. Letterbook.
Public Record Office, London
    Colonial Office. Papers.
    Admiralty Office. Papers.

NEWSPAPERS

Annapolis *Maryland Gazette*, 1763–84.
Augusta *Georgia State Gazette*, 1786–87.
Baltimore *Maryland Journal*, 1773–84.
Boston *Gazette*, 1763–84.
Boston *Massachusetts Centinel*, 1784–87.
Boston *Massachusetts Gazette*, 1763–87.
Burlington *New Jersey Gazette*, 1777–78.
Charleston *Gazette of the State of South Carolina*, 1777–84.
Charleston *South Carolina Gazette*, 1763–75.
Charleston *South Carolina Gazette and Country Journal*, 1765–75.
Charleston *State Gazette of South Carolina*, 1785–88.
Chatham *New Jersey Journal*, 1779–83.
Fishkill *New York Packet*, 1777–83.
Hartford *Connecticut Courant*, 1764–87.
New Haven *Connecticut Journal*, 1767–84.
New Haven *Gazette*, 1788.
New London *Connecticut Gazette*, 1763–84.

Newport *Mercury*, 1763–86.
New York *Gazette Revived in the Weekly Post-Boy*, 1763–73.
New York *Journal*, 1766–76, 1783–88.
New York *Packet*, 1783–86.
Philadelphia *Freeman's Journal*, 1781–87.
Philadelphia *Pennsylvania Gazette*, 1763–85.
Philadelphia *Pennsylvania Journal*, 1763–84.
Philadelphia *Pennsylvania Packet*, 1771–87.
Portsmouth *New Hampshire Gazette*, 1763–84.
Poughkeepsie *New York Journal*, 1778–82.
Providence *Gazette*, 1763–84.
Savannah *Georgia Gazette*, 1763–70.
Trenton *New Jersey Gazette*, 1778–84.
Williamsburg *Virginia Gazette*, 1763–80.
Worcester *Massachusetts Spy*, 1775–84.

PRINTED PRIMARY SOURCES

Adams, Charles Francis, ed. *The Works of John Adams*. 10 vols. Boston: Little, Brown, 1850–56.

Bacon, Edwin M., ed. *Supplement to the Acts and Resolves of Massachusetts*. Boston: G. H. Ellis, 1896.

Balch, Thomas, ed. *Letters and Papers Relating Chiefly to the Provincial History of Pennsylvania*. Philadelphia: Crissy and Markley, 1855.

Ballagh, James C., ed. *The Letters of Richard Henry Lee*. 2 vols. New York: Macmillan, 1911–14.

Barber, John, and Henry Howe, eds. *Historical Collections of the State of New Jersey*. New York: S. Tuttle, 1844.

Barnwell, Joseph W., ed. "Correspondence of Hon. Arthur Middleton, Signer of the Declaration of Independence." *South Carolina Historical and Genealogical Magazine*, XXVI (1925), 183–200, XXVII (1926), 1–29, 51–80, 107–55.

————, ed. "Letters of John Rutledge." *South Carolina Historical and Genealogical Magazine, XVIII* (1917), 42–49, 59–69, 131–42, 155–67.

Bartlett, John R., ed. *Records of the Colony of Rhode Island and Providence Plantations, in New England*. 10 vols. Providence: A. C. Greene, 1856–65.

Batchellor, Albert S., *et al.*, eds. *Provincial [and State] Papers of New Hampshire*. 40 vols. Concord: State of New Hampshire, 1867–1943.

Bates, Samuel A., ed. *Records of the Town of Braintree, 1640 to 1793*. Randolph, Mass.: D. H. Huxford, 1886.

Bigelow, John, ed. *The Complete Works of Benjamin Franklin*. 10 vols. New York: G. P. Putnam's Sons, 1887–88.

[Boston, Massachusetts]. *A Report of the Record Commissioners of the City of Boston, Containing the Boston Town Records, 1758–1769*. Boston: City of Boston, 1886.

[Boston, Massachusetts]. *A Report of the Record Commissioners of the City of Boston, Containing the Boston Towns Records, 1770–1777*. Boston: City of Boston, 1887.

[Boston, Massachusetts]. *A Report of the Record Commissioners of the City of Boston, Containing the Selectmen's Minutes From 1764 Through 1768*. Boston: City of Boston, 1889.

[Boston, Massachusetts]. *A Report of the Record Commissioners of the City of Boston, Containing the Selectmen's Minutes From 1769 Through 1775*. Boston: City of Boston, 1893.

Boyd, Julian P., ed. *The Papers of Thomas Jefferson*. 19 vols. to date. Princeton, N.J.: Princeton University Press, 1950–.

Boyd, Julian P., and Robert J. Taylor, eds. *The Susquehannah Company Papers*. 11 vols. Ithaca, N.Y.: Cornell University Press, 1962-71.

Boyd, William K., ed. *Some Eighteenth-Century Tracts Concerning North Carolina*. Raleigh, N.C.: Edwards and Broughton, 1927.

Browne, William H., *et al.*, eds. *Archives of Maryland*. 72 vols. Baltimore: Maryland Historical Society, 1883–1972.

Brunhouse, Robert L., ed. "David Ramsay, 1749–1815: Selections from His Writings." *Transactions of the American Philosophical Society*, New Series, Vol. LV, Pt. 4 (1965).

Burnett, Edmund C., ed. *Letters of Members of the Continental Congress*. 8 vols. Washington, D.C.: Carnegie Institution of Washington, 1921–36.

Butterfield, Lyman H., ed. *Adams Family Correspondence*. 2 vols. Cambridge, Mass.: Harvard University Press, 1963–65.

———, ed. *The Diary and Autobiography of John Adams*. 4 vols. Cambridge, Mass.: Harvard University Press, 1961.

Calvert Papers, The. Publications of the Maryland Historical Society, XXXIV. Baltimore: Maryland Historical Society, 1894.

Campbell, Charles, ed. *The Bland Papers: Being a Selection from the Manuscripts of Colonel Theodorick Bland, Jr.* 2 vols. Petersburg: E. and J. Ruffin, 1840–43.

Chandler, Allen D., ed. *The Colonial Records of the State of Georgia*. 26 vols. Atlanta: Franklin-Turner, 1904–16.

Channing, Edward, and A. C. Colledge, eds. *The Barrington-Bernard Correspondence.* Cambridge, Mass.: Harvard University Press, 1912.

Cohen, Hennig, ed. "Four Letters from Peter Timothy, 1755, 1768, 1771." *South Carolina Historical Magazine,* LV (1954), 160–65.

Colden Letterbooks, The. Collections of the New-York Historical Society, IX–X. New York: New-York Historical Society, 1877–78.

Colonial Records: Minutes of the Provincial Council of Pennsylvania from the Organization to the Termination of the Proprietary Government. 16 vols. Harrisburg: E. K. Meyers, 1852–53.

Concord [New Hampshire] Town Records, 1732–1820. Concord: Republican Press Association, 1894.

Cooper, Thomas, and D. J. McCord, eds. *The Statutes at Large of South Carolina.* 10 vols. Columbia, S.C.: A. S. Johnston, 1836–41.

"Correspondence Between Hon. Henry Laurens and His Son, John, 1777–1780." *South Carolina Historical and Genealogical Magazine,* VI (1905), 3–12, 47–52, 103–10, 137–43.

"Correspondence of Governor Eden." *Maryland Historical Magazine,* II (1907), 1–13, 97–110, 227–44, 293–309.

Crosby, J., ed. "Annals of Charlestown, in the County of Sullivan, New Hampshire." Collections of the New Hampshire Historical Society, IV, 101–38. Concord: New Hampshire Historical Society, 1834.

Deane Papers, The. Collections of the New-York Historical Society, XIX–XXIII. New York: New-York Historical Society, 1887–91.

[Delaware, State of]. *Laws of the State of Delaware [1770–1797].* 2 vols. Newcastle: Samuel and John Adams, 1797.

Duane, William, ed. *Extracts from the Diary of Christopher Marshall, Kept in Philadelphia and Lancaster, During the American Revolution, 1774–1781.* Albany: J. Munsell, 1877.

Eddis, William. *Letters from America.* Edited by Aubrey C. Land. Cambridge, Mass.: Harvard University Press, 1969.

Elliot, Jonathan, ed. *The Debates in the Several State Conventions, on the Adoption of the Federal Constitution.* 5 vols. Philadelphia: J. B. Lippincott, 1941.

Felt, Joseph B., ed. *Statistics of Taxation in Massachusetts.* Collections of the American Statistical Association, Vol. I, Pt. 3. Boston: Marvin, 1847.

Fitch Papers: Correspondence and Documents During Thomas Fitch's Governorship of the Colony of Connecticut, 1754–1766. Collections of the Connecticut Historical Society, XVII–XIX. Hartford: Connecticut Historical Society, 1918–21.

Foner, Philip S., ed. *The Complete Writings of Thomas Paine.* 2 vols. New York: Citadel Press, 1945.

Force, Peter, ed. *American Archives: A Documentary History of the Origin and Progress of the North American Colonies.* 9 vols. Washington, D.C.: Government Printing Office, 1837–53.

Ford, Paul L., ed. *Essays on the Constitution of the United States, 1787–1788.* Brooklyn: Historical Printing Club of Brooklyn, 1892.

———, ed. *Pamphlets on the Constitution of the United States, 1787–1788.* Brooklyn: privately published, 1888.

———, ed. *The Writings of Thomas Jefferson.* 10 vols. New York: G. P. Putnam's Sons, 1892–99.

Ford, Worthington C., ed. *Letters of Joseph Jones of Virginia, 1777–1787.* Washington, D.C.: Department of State, 1889.

———, ed. "Unpublished Letters of Edmund Pendleton." *Proceedings of the Massachusetts Historical Society,* 2nd Ser. Vol. XIX (1906), 107–67.

Foster, H. D., *et al.,* eds. *The Records of the Town of Hanover, New Hampshire, 1761–1818.* Hanover: Town of Hanover, 1905.

Handlin, Oscar, and Mary Handlin, eds. *The Popular Sources of Political Authority: Documents on the Massachusetts Constitution of 1780.* Cambridge, Mass.: Harvard University Press, 1966.

Hastings, Hugh, ed. *The Public Papers of George Clinton, First Governor of New York, 1777–1795, 1801–1804.* 10 vols. New York and Albany: State of New York, 1899–1914.

Hazard, Samuel, *et al.,* eds. *Pennsylvania Archives.* 138 vols. Harrisburg and Philadelphia: E. K. Meyers and others, 1852–1935.

Hemphill, William E., and Wylma A. Wates, eds. *Extracts from the Journals of the Provincial Congresses of South Carolina, 1775–1776.* Columbia: South Carolina Department of Archives, 1960.

Hening, William W., ed. *The Statutes at Large: Being a Collection of All the Laws of Virginia.* 13 vols. Richmond: Samuel Pleasants, 1809–23.

Higginbotham, Don, ed. *The Papers of James Iredell.* 2 vols. Raleigh: North Carolina Division of Archives and History, 1976.

Hoadly, Charles J., ed. *The Public Records of the Colony of Connecticut.* 15 vols. Hartford: Case, Lockwood and Brainard, 1850–90.

Hoadly, Charles J., and Leonard W. Labaree, eds. *The Public Records of the State of Connecticut.* 9 vols. Hartford: Case, Lockwood and Brainard, 1894–1953.

Holt, Elizabeth, ed. *Laws of the State of New York, Passed at the First Meeting of the Seventh Session of the Legislature of*

Said State, Beginning the 12th Day of February, 1784, and Ending the 12th Day of May Following. New York: Elizabeth Holt, 1784.

Holt, John, ed. *Laws of the State of New York, Commencing with the First Session of the Senate and Assembly, After the Declaration of Independence, and the Organization of the New Government of the State, Anno 1777.* Poughkeepsie: John Holt, 1782.

Hunt, Gaillard, ed. *The Writings of James Madison.* 9 vols. New York: G. P. Putnam's Sons, 1900–1910.

Jenkins, William S., ed. *Records of the States of the United States: A Microfilm Compilation Prepared by the Library of Congress in Association with the University of North Carolina.* Washington, D.C.: Library of Congress, 1949–.
Series A. Legislative Records.
Series B. Statutory Law.
Series D. Administrative Records.
Series E. Executive Records.

Johnson, Henry P., ed. *The Correspondence and Public Papers of John Jay.* 4 vols. New York: G. P. Putnam's Sons, 1890–93.

Journals of the Provincial Congress, Provincial Convention, Committee of Safety of the State of New York, 1775–1777. 2 vols. Albany: State of New York, 1842.

Keith, Alice B., ed. *The John Gray Blount Papers.* 2 vols. Raleigh: North Carolina Division of Archives and History, 1952–59.

Kennedy, John P., ed. *Journals of the House of Burgesses of Virginia, [1761–1776].* 4 vols. Richmond: E. Waddy, 1905–1907.

Kenyon, Cecelia, ed. *The Antifederalists.* New York: Bobbs-Merrill, 1966.

Kimball, Gertrude S., ed. *The Correspondence of the Colonial Governors of Rhode Island, 1723–1775.* Boston and New York: Houghton, Mifflin, 1902–1903.

Knollenberg, Bernard, ed. *Correspondence of Governor Samuel Ward, May 1775–March 1776.* Providence: Rhode Island Historical Society, 1952.

Labaree, Leonard W., and William B. Willcox, eds. *The Papers of Benjamin Franklin.* 20 vols. New Haven: Yale University Press, 1959–76.

Lee Papers, The. Collections of the New-York Historical Society, IV–VII. New York: New-York Historical Society, 1872–76.

Letterbook of John Watts, Merchant and Councillor of New York. Collections of the New-York Historical Society, LXI. New York: New-York Historical Society, 1928.

Letters and Papers of Cadwallader Colden. Collections of the New-

York Historical Society, L–LVI, LXVII–LXVIII. New York: New-York Historical Society, 1918–37.

"Letters from Henry Laurens to His Son John, 1777–1780." *South Carolina Historical and Genealogical Magazine*, III (1902), 86–96, 139–49, 207–15, IV (1903), 26–35, 99–107, 215–20, 238–77, V (1904), 3–14, 70–81, 125–42.

"Letters from Sir James Wright [1773–1782]." Collections of the Georgia Historical Society, III, 180–375. Savannah: Georgia Historical Society, 1873.

Letters of Joseph Clay, Merchant of South Carolina. Collections of the Georgia Historical Society, VIII. Savannah: Georgia Historical Society, 1913.

Letters of the Hon. James Habersham, 1756–1775, The. Collections of the Georgia Historical Society, VI. Savannah: Georgia Historical Society, 1904.

"Letters to Robert Morris, 1775–1782." Collections of the New-York Historical Society, XI. New York: New York Historical Society, 1879.

"Letters to William Henry of Lancaster, Pennsylvania, 1777–1783." *Pennsylvania Magazine of History and Biography*, XXII (1898), 106–13.

Lincoln, William, ed. *The Journals of Each Provincial Congress of Massachusetts in 1774 and 1775 and of the Committee of Safety.* Boston: Dutton and Wentworth, 1838.

McIlwaine, H. R., ed. *Official Letters of the Governors of Virginia, 1776–1783.* 3 vols. Richmond: State of Virginia, 1926–29.

McRee, Griffith, ed. *Life and Correspondence of James Iredell.* Appleton, 1857–58.

Maryland Hall of Records. *Calendar of Maryland State Papers.* 8 vols. Annapolis: Maryland Hall of Records, 1943–58.

[Massachusetts, State of]. *The Acts and Resolves, Public and Private, of the Province of Massachusetts Bay.* 21 vols. Boston: State of Massachusetts, 1869–1922.

Maury, Ann, ed. *Memoirs of a Huguenot Family.* New York: G. P. Putnam's Sons, 1853.

Mays, David J., ed. *The Letters and Papers of Edmund Pendleton, 1734–1803.* 2 vols. Charlottesville: University Press of Virginia, 1967.

Metcalf, Henry H., *et al.*, eds. *Laws of New Hampshire.* 10 vols. Manchester, N.H.: John B. Clarke, 1904–22.

Mitchell, James T., and Henry Flanders, eds. *The Statutes at Large of Pennsylvania from 1682 to 1801.* 17 vols. Harrisburg: State of Pennsylvania, 1896–1915.

Morris, Richard B., ed. *John Jay: The Making of a Revolutionary. Unpublished Papers, 1745–1780.* New York: Harper and Row, 1975.

Morrison, A. J., ed. "Letters of Roger Atkinson, 1769–1776." *Virginia Magazine of History and Biography,* XV (1907–1908), 345–59.

Muddy River and Brookline Town Records, 1634–1838. Boston:

New Haven Colony Historical Society Papers. 9 vols. New Haven: New Haven Colony Historical Society, 1865–1918.

[New Jersey, State of]. *Minutes of the Provincial Congress and Council of Safety of the State of New Jersey, 1775–1776.* Trenton: Naar, Day and Naar, 1879.

[New York, State of]. *The Colonial Laws of New York, from 1664 to the Revolution.* 5 vols. Albany: J. B. Lyon, 1894.

[New York City]. *Minutes of the Common Council of the City of New York, 1665–1766.* 8 vols. New York: Dodd, Mead, 1905.

[New York City, Chamber of Commerce]. *Colonial Records of the New York Chamber of Commerce, 1768–1784.* New York: J. F. Trow, 1867.

O'Callaghan, E. B., ed. *Documents Relative to the Colonial History of the State of New York.* 15 vols. Albany: Weed, Parsons, 1853–87.

———, ed. *The Documentary History of the State of New York.* 4 vols. Albany: Weed, Parsons, 1850–51.

Palmer, William P., ed. *Calendar of Virginia State Papers.* 11 vols. Richmond: State of Virginia, 1885–93.

Pitkin Papers: Correspondence and Documents During William Pitkin's Governorship of the Colony of Connecticut, 1766–1769. Collections of the Connecticut Historical Society, XIX. Hartford: Connecticut Historical Society, 1921.

Powell, William S., *et al.,* eds. *The Regulators in North Carolina: A Documentary History, 1759–1776.* Raleigh: North Carolina Division of Archives and History, 1971.

Revolutionary Correspondence from 1775 to 1782, comprising Letters Written by Governors Nicholas Cooke, William Greene, John Collins, Jonathan Trumbull . . . [and others]. Collections of the Rhode Island Historical Society, VI. Providence: Rhode Island Historical Society, 1867.

[Rhode Island, Colony of]. *[Acts and Resolves] at the General Assembly of the Governor and Company of the English Colony of Rhode Island and Providence Plantations, in New England, in America [1755–1783].* Newport: Colony of Rhode Island and State of Rhode Island, 1755–84.

Rutland, Robert A., ed. *The Papers of George Mason, 1725–1792.* 3 vols. Chapel Hill: University of North Carolina Press, 1970.

Ryden, G. H., ed. *Letters to and from Caesar Rodney, 1756–1784.* Philadelphia: University of Pennsylvania Press, 1933.

Saunders, William L., ed. *The Colonial Records of North Carolina.* 10 vols. Raleigh, N.C.: Nash Brothers, 1886–90.

Saunders, William L., et al., eds. *The State Records of North Carolina.* 26 vols. Goldsboro, N.C.: Nash Brothers, 1886–1907.

Schull, Gideon D., ed. *Journals of Captain John Montressor, 1757–1775.* Collections of the New-York Historical Society, XIV. New York: New-York Historical Society, 1882.

Selections from the Correspondence of the Executive of New Jersey, from 1776 to 1786. Newark: Newark Daily Advertiser, 1848.

Shipton, Clifford K., ed. *Early American Imprints, 1639–1800: A Microprint Compilation by the American Antiquarian Society.* Worcester, Mass.: American Antiquarian Society, 1955–.

Staples, William R., ed. *Annals of the Town of Providence, from Its First Settlement to the Organization of the City Government.* Providence: Knowles and Vose, 1843.

Street, Alfred B., ed. *The Council of Revision of the State of New York.* Albany: W. Gould, 1859.

Sullivan, James, ed. *Minutes of the Albany Committee of Correspondence, 1775–1778.* 2 vols. Albany: University of the State of New York, 1923–25.

Syrett, Harold C., ed. *The Papers of Alexander Hamilton.* 25 vols. New York: Columbia University Press, 1961–77.

Taylor, Robert J., ed. *Massachusetts, Colony to Commonwealth: Documents on the Formation of Its Constitution, 1775–1780.* Chapel Hill: University of North Carolina Press, 1961.

Thorpe, Francis N., ed. *The Federal and State Constitutions, Colonial Charters, and Other Organic Laws of the States, Territories and Colonies Now or Heretofore Forming the United States of America.* 7 vols. Washington, D. C.: Government Printing Office, 1909.

Trumbull Papers, The. Collections of the Massachusetts Historical Society, IX–X. Boston: Massachusetts Historical Society, 1885–88.

Walker, Lewis B., ed. *The Burd Papers: Selections from Letters Written by Edward Burd, 1763–1828.* Pottsville, Pa.: Standard Publishing, 1899.

Whitehead, William A., et al., eds. *The Archives of the State of New Jersey.* 36 vols. Newark: State of New Jersey, 1880–1941.

Willard, Margaret W., ed. *Letters on the American Revolution, 1774–1776.* Boston: Houghton, Mifflin, 1925.

Wilson, Rufus R., ed. *Burnaby's Travels Through North America.* New York: A. Wessels, 1904.

SECONDARY SOURCES

BOOKS

Adams, James T. *New England in the Republic, 1776–1850.* Boston: Little, Brown, 1926.

Akagi, Roy H. *The Town Proprietors of the New England Colonies.* Philadelphia: University of Pennsylvania Press, 1924.

Archer, John A. *The Provisional Government of Maryland (1774–1777).* Baltimore: Johns Hopkins University Press, 1895.

Bailyn, Bernard. *The Ideological Origins of the American Revolution.* Cambridge, Mass.: Harvard University Press, 1967.

Barker, Charles A. *The Background of the Revolution in Maryland.* New Haven: Yale University Press, 1940.

Becker, Carl. *The Eve of the Revolution.* New Haven: Yale University Press, 1920.

————. *The History of Political Parties in the Province of New York, 1760–1776.* Madison: University of Wisconsin Press, 1909.

Beer, George L. *British Colonial Policy, 1754–1765.* New York: P. Smith, 1933.

Belknap, Jeremy. *The History of New Hampshire.* 3 vols. Boston: published by the author, 1791–92.

Bolles, Albert S. *Pennsylvania, Province and State: A History.* 2 vols. New York: J. Wanamaker, 1899.

Bonomi, Patricia. *A Factious People: Politics and Society in Colonial New York.* New York: Columbia University Press, 1971.

Bridenbaugh, Carl. *Cities in Revolt: Urban Life in America, 1743–1776.* New York: Alfred A. Knopf, 1955.

Brown, Robert E. *Virginia, 1705–1783: Democracy or Aristocracy?* East Lansing: Michigan State University Press, 1964.

Brunhouse, Robert L. *The Counterrevolution in Pennsylvania.* Harrisburg: Pennsylvania Historical Commission, 1942.

Carroll, Charles. *Rhode Island: Three Centuries of Democracy.* 4 vols. New York: Lewis Publishing, 1932.

Caruso, John A. *The Appalachian Frontier.* Indianapolis: Bobbs-Merrill, 1959.

Caulkins, Francis M. *History of Norwich, Connecticut, from Its Possession by the Indians, to the Year 1866.* Hartford: n.p., 1866.

Channing, Edward. *A History of the United States.* 6 vols. New York: Macmillan, 1905–25.

Cochran, Thomas. *New York in the Confederation: An Economic Study.* Philadelphia: University of Pennsylvania Press, 1932.

Colbourn, H. Trevor. *The Lamp of Experience: Whig History and the*

Intellectual Origins of the American Revolution. Chapel Hill: University of North Carolina Press, 1965.

Coleman, Kenneth. *The American Revolution in Georgia, 1763–1789.* Athens: University of Georgia Press, 1958.

Conner, R. D. W. *The History of North Carolina: The Colonial and Revolutionary Periods, 1684–1783.* Chicago: Lewis Publishing, 1911.

Crowl, Phillip A. *Maryland During and After the Revolution: A Political and Economic Study.* Baltimore: Johns Hopkins University Press, 1943.

Cunningham, Charles E. *Timothy Dwight, 1752–1817.* New York: Macmillan, 1942.

Dangerfield, George. *Chancellor Robert R. Livingston of New York, 1746–1813.* New York: Harcourt, Brace, 1960.

Daniell, Jere R. *Experiment in Republicanism: New Hampshire Politics and the American Revolution, 1741–1794.* Cambridge, Mass.: Harvard University Press, 1970.

Dietz, Frederick C. *English Public Finance, 1485–1641.* 2 vols. New York: Barnes and Noble, 1964.

Dill, Amos A. *Governor Tryon and His Palace.* Chapel Hill: University of North Carolina Press, 1955.

Dorfman, Joseph. *The Economic Mind in American Civilization.* 5 vols. New York: Viking Press, 1946–59.

Douglas, C. H. J. *Financial History of Massachusetts.* New York: Columbia University Press, 1892.

Douglass, Elisha P. *Rebels and Democrats: The Struggle for Equal Political Rights and Majority Rule During the American Revolution.* Chapel Hill: University of North Carolina Press, 1955.

Dowell, Stephen. *A History of Taxation and Taxes in England, from the Earliest Times to the Present Day.* 4 vols. New York: A. M. Kelley, 1965.

Eckenrode, Hamilton J. *The Revolution in Virginia.* Boston: Houghton, Mifflin, 1916.

Ernst, Joseph A. *Money and Politics in America, 1755–1775: A Study in the Currency Act of 1764 and the Political Economy of Revolution.* Chapel Hill: University of North Carolina Press, 1973.

Ferguson, E. James. *The Power of the Purse: A History of American Public Finance, 1776–1790.* Chapel Hill: University of North Carolina Press, 1961.

Fisher, Edgar J. *New Jersey as a Royal Province, 1738 to 1776.* Columbia Universty Studies in History, Vol. XLI, No. 107. New York: Longmans, Greene, 1911.

Flick, A. C. *Loyalism in New York During the American Revolution.* New York: Columbia University Press, 1901.

Flippin, Percy S. *The Financial Administration of the Colony of Virginia.* Johns Hopkins University Studies in History and Political Science, Vol. XXXIII, No. 2. Baltimore: Johns Hopkins University Press, 1915.

Foner, Eric. *Tom Paine and Revolutionary America.* New York: Oxford University Press, 1977.

Ford, Edward. *David Rittenhouse, Astronomer-Patriot, 1732–1796.* Philadelphia: University of Pennsylvania Press, 1946.

Foster, William E. *Stephen Hopkins, a Rhode Island Statesman.* Rhode Island Historical Tracts, 1st Ser., No. 19. 2 vols. Providence: S. S. Rider, 1884.

Fry, William H. *New Hampshire as a Royal Province.* Columbia University Studies in History, Vol. XXIX, No. 2. New York: Longmans, Greene, 1908.

Gerlach, Larry. *Prologue to Independence: New Jersey in the Coming of the American Revolution.* New Brunswick, N.J.: Rutgers University Press, 1976.

Gipson, Lawrence H. *Connecticut Taxation, 1750–1775.* New Haven: Connecticut State Tercentenary Commission, 1933.

———. *Jared Ingersoll: A Study of American Loyalism in Relation to British Colonial Government.* New Haven: Yale University Press, 1920.

———. *The Coming of the Revolution, 1763–1775.* New York: Harper and Row, 1962.

Gordon, Thomas F. *The History of Pennsylvania from Its Discovery by Europeans to the Declaration of Independence in 1776.* Philadelphia: Carey, Lea and Carey, 1829.

Grant, Charles S. *Democracy in the Connecticut Frontier Town of Kent.* New York: Columbia University Press, 1961.

Gray, Lewis C. *History of Agriculture in the Southern United States to 1860.* 2 vols. Washington, D.C.: Carnegie Institution of Washington, 1933.

Greene, Evarts B. *The Provincial Governor in the English Colonies of North America.* New York: Longmans, Greene, 1898.

Greene, Evarts B., and Virginia D. Harrington. *American Population Before the Federal Census of 1790.* New York: Columbia University Press, 1932.

Greene, Jack P. *The Quest for Power: The Lower Houses of Assembly in the Southern Royal Colonies, 1689–1776.* Chapel Hill: University of North Carolina Press, 1963.

———, ed. *The Reinterpretation of the American Revolution.* New York: Harper and Row, 1968.

Gregg, Alexander. *History of Old Cheraws*. New York: Richardson, 1867.

Hall, Van Beck. *Politics Without Parties: Massachusetts, 1780–1791*. Pittsburgh: University of Pittsburgh Press, 1972.

Halsey, Edmund, *et al*. *History of Morris County, New Jersey*. New York: W. W. Munsell, 1882.

Hancock, Harold B. *The Loyalists of Revolutionary Delaware*. Newark: University of Delaware Press, 1977.

Harrington, Virginia D. *The New York Merchants on the Eve of the Revolution*. Columbia University Studies in History, No. 404. New York: Columbia University Press, 1935.

Hart, Albert B., ed. *The Commonwealth History of Massachusetts, Colony, Province and State*. 5 vols. New York: States History, 1927–30.

Hendrick, Burton J. *The Lees of Virginia*. Boston: Little, Brown, 1935.

Hoffman, Ronald. *A Spirit of Dissension: Economics, Politics and the Revolution in Maryland*. Baltimore: Johns Hopkins University Press, 1973.

Hutchinson, Thomas. *The History of the Colony and Province of Massachusetts Bay*. 3 vols. London: M. Richardson, 1760–1828.

Hutson, James H. *Pennsylvania Politics, 1746–1770: The Movement for Royal Government and Its Consequences*. Princeton, N.J.: Princeton University Press, 1972.

Jameson, J. Franklin. *The American Revolution Considered as a Social Movement*. Princeton, N.J.: Princeton University Press, 1926.

Jellison, Richard M., ed. *Society, Freedom and Conscience: The Coming of the Revolution in Virginia, Massachusetts and New York*. New York: W. W. Norton, 1976.

Jensen, Merrill. *The American Revolution Within America*. New York University Press, 1974.

———. *The Founding of a Nation*. New York: Oxford University Press, 1968.

———. *The New Nation: A History of the United States During the Confederation, 1781–1789*. New York: Alfred A. Knopf, 1950.

Jones, Charles C. *The History of Georgia*. 2 vols. Boston: Houghton, Mifflin, 1883.

Jones, Frederick R. *History of Taxation in Connecticut, 1639–1776*. Johns Hopkins University Studies in History and Political Science, Vol. XIV, No. 8. Baltimore: Johns Hopkins University Press, 1896.

Kemmerer, Edwin W. *Path to Freedom: The Struggle for Self-*

Government in Colonial New Jersey, 1703–1776. Princeton, N.J.: Princeton University Press, 1940.

Kennedy, William. *English Taxation, 1640–1799.* London: G. Bell and Sons, 1913.

Kim, Sung Bok. *Landlord and Tenant in Colonial New York: Manorial Society, 1664–1775.* Chapel Hill: University of North Carolina Press, 1978.

Kurtz, Stephen G., and James H. Hutson, eds. *Essays on the American Revolution.* Chapel Hill: University of North Carolina Press, 1973.

Lefler, Hugh T., and William S. Powell. *Colonial North Carolina.* New York: Scribners, 1973.

Lincoln, Charles H. *The Revolutionary Movement in Pennsylvania, 1760–1776.* Philadelphia: University of Pennsylvania Press, 1901.

Lincoln, William. *History of Worcester, Massachusetts, from Its Earliest Settlement to September, 1836.* Worcester: C. Hersey, 1862.

Livingston, Edwin B. *The Livingstons of Livingston Manor.* New York: Knickerbocker Press, 1910.

Lovejoy, David S. *Rhode Island Politics and the American Revolution, 1760–1776.* Providence: Brown University Press, 1958.

Lundin, Leonard. *The Cockpit of the Revolution: The War for Independence in New Jersey.* Princeton, N.J.: Princeton University Press, 1940.

Lynd, Staughton. *Antifederalism in Dutchess County, New York: A Study of Democracy and Class Conflict in the Revolutionary Era.* Chicago: Loyola University Press, 1962.

———. *Class Conflict, Slavery, and the United States Constitution.* Indianapolis: Bobbs-Merrill, 1968.

McCormick, Richard P. *Experiment in Independence: New Jersey in the Critical Period, 1781–89.* New Brunswick, N.J.: Rutgers University Press, 1950.

Main, Jackson T. *Political Parties Before the Constitution.* Chapel Hill: University of North Carolina Press, 1973.

———. *The Sovereign States.* New York: Watts, Franklin, 1973.

Mark, Irving. *Agrarian Conflicts in Colonial New York, 1711–1775.* Columbia University Studies in History, No. 469. New York: Columbia University Press, 1940.

Martin, James K. *Men in Rebellion: Higher Governmental Leaders and the Coming of the American Revolution.* New Brunswick, N.J.: Rutgers University Press, 1973.

———, ed. *The Human Dimensions of Nation Making: Essays on*

Colonial and Revolutionary America. Madison: State Historical Society of Wisconsin, 1976.

Martyn, Charles. *The Life of Artemas Ward.* New York: A. Ward, 1921.

Mason, Bernard. *The Road to Independence: The Revolutionary Movement in New York.* Lexington: University of Kentucky Press, 1966.

Mayer, Kurt B. *Economic Development and Population Growth in Rhode Island.* Providence: Brown University Press, 1953.

Mays, David J. *Edmund Pendleton, 1721–1803: A Biography.* 2 vols. Cambridge, Mass.: Harvard University Press, 1952.

Monaghan, Frank. *John Jay.* New York: Bobbs-Merrill, 1935.

Morgan, Edmund S., and Helen Morgan. *The Stamp Act Crisis: Prologue to Revolution.* New York: Collier Books, 1963.

Morris, Richard B., ed. *The Era of the American Revolution.* New York: Columbia University Press, 1939.

Morton, Richard L. *Colonial Virginia.* 2 vols. Chapel Hill: University of North Carolina Press, 1960.

Nevins, Allan. *The American States During and After the Revolution, 1775–1789.* New York: Macmillan, 1924.

New York State, Department of Archives. *The American Revolution in New York: Its Political, Social and Economic Significance.* Albany: University of the State of New York, 1926.

Paige, Lucius R. *History of Hardwick, Massachusetts.* Boston: Houghton, Mifflin, 1883.

Polishook, Irwin R. *Rhode Island and the Union, 1774–1795.* Evanston, Ill.: Northwestern University Press, 1969.

Porter, Albert O. *County Government in Virginia: A Legislative History, 1607–1904.* New York: Columbia University Press, 1947.

Purcell, Richard J. *Connecticut in Transition, 1775–1818.* Middletown, Conn.: Wesleyan University Press, 1963.

Ramsay, David. *The History of South Carolina from Its First Settlement in 1670 to the Year 1808.* 2 vols. Charleston: W. J. Duffie, 1858.

Read, William T. *Life and Correspondence of George Read.* Philadelphia: J. B. Lippincott, 1870.

Ripley, William Z. *The Financial History of Virginia, 1609–1776.* Columbia University Studies in History, Vol. IV, No. 1. New York: Columbia University, 1893.

Roche, John F. *Joseph Reed: A Moderate in the American Revolution.* New York: Columbia University Press, 1957.

Rodney, Richard S. *Colonial Finances in Delaware.* Wilmington, Del.: Wilmington Trust, 1928.

Rogers, George C. *Evolution of a Federalist: William Loughton Smith of Charleston, 1758–1812.* Columbia: University of South Carolina Press, 1962.

Rowland, Kate Mason. *The Life of Charles Carroll of Carrollton, 1737–1782.* 2 vols. New York: G. P. Putnam's Sons, 1898.

———. *The Life of Geogre Mason, 1725–1792.* 2 vols. New York: G. P. Putnam's Sons, 1892.

Scharf, John T. *History of Maryland from the Earliest Period to the Present Day.* 3 vols. Baltimore: J. B. Piet, 1879.

Schlesinger, Arthur M. *The Colonial Merchants and the American Revolution, 1763–1776.* Columbia University Studies in History, Economics, and Public Law, Vol. LXXVIII, No. 182. New York: Columbia University, 1918.

Selsam, J. Paul. *The Pennsylvania Constitution of 1776: A Study in Revolutionary Democracy.* Philadelphia: University of Pennsylvania Press, 1936.

Shepherd, William R. *History of Proprietary Government in Pennsylvania.* Columbia University Studies in History, Vol. VI. New York: Columbia University, 1896.

Singer, Charles G. *South Carolina in the Confederation.* Philadelphia: University of Pennsylvania Press, 1941.

Sirmans, M. E. *Colonial South Carolina: A Political History, 1663–1763.* Chapel Hill: University of North Carolina Press, 1966.

Smith, Jonathan. *Peterborough, New Hampshire, in the American Revolution.* Peterborough: Peterborough Historical Society, 1913.

Smith, Joseph E. A. *The History of Pittsfield Massachusetts from the Year 1734 to the Year 1800.* Boston: n.p., 1869.

Smith, William R. *South Carolina as a Royal Province, 1719–1776.* New York: Macmillan, 1903.

Snell, James P. *History of Sussex and Warren Counties, New Jersey.* Philadelphia: Everts and Peck, 1881.

Spaulding, E. Wilder. *His Excellency George Clinton, Critic of the Constitution.* New York: Macmillan, 1938.

Stevens, William B. *A History of Georgia.* 2 vols. New York and Philadelphia: D. Appleton and E. H. Butler, 1847–59.

Sydnor, Charles. *American Revolutionaries in the Making.* New York: Collier Books, 1962.

Taylor, Robert J. *Western Massachusetts in the Revolution.* Providence: Brown University Press, 1954.

Thayer, Theodore G. *Pennsylvania Politics and the Growth of*

Democracy. Harrisburg: Pennsylvania Historical and Museum Commission, 1953.

Trumbull, Jonathan. *Jonathan Trumbull: Governor of Connecticut, 1769–1784*. Boston: Little, Brown, 1919.

Tyler, Lyon G. *The Letters and Times of the Tylers*. 3 vols. Richmond and Williamsburg: Whittet and Shepperson, 1884–96.

Upton, Richard F. *Revolutionary New Hampshire: An Account of the Social and Political Forces Underlying the Transition from Royal Province to American Commonwealth*. Hanover, N.H.: Dartmouth College Publications, 1936.

Walsh, Richard. *Charleston's Sons of Liberty: A Study of the Artisans, 1763–1789*. Columbia: University of South Carolina Press, 1959.

Whitney, Edson L. *Government of the Colony of South Carolina*. Johns Hopkins University Studies in History and Political Science, Vol. XIII, No. 1–2. Baltimore: Johns Hopkins University Press, 1895.

Willison, George F. *Patrick Henry and His World*. Garden City, N.Y.: Doubleday, 1969.

Wood, Gordon S. *The Creation of the American Republic, 1776–1787*. Chapel Hill: University of North Carolina Press, 1969.

Young, Alfred F. *The Democratic Republicans of New York: The Origins, 1763–1797*. Chapel Hill: University of North Carolina Press, 1967.

————, ed. *The American Revolution: Explorations in the History of American Radicalism*. De Kalb: Northern Illinois University Press, 1976.

Zeichner, Oscar. *Connecticut's Years of Controversy, 1750–1776*. Chapel Hill: University of North Carolina Press, 1949.

ARTICLES

Alexander, John K. "The Fort Wilson Incident of 1779: A Case Study of the Revolutionary Crowd." *William and Mary Quarterly*, XXXI (1974), 589–612.

Bassett, John S. "The Regulators of North Carolina, 1765–1771." *Annual Report of the American Historical Association*, (1894), 141–212.

Boyd, Julian P. "The Sheriff in Colonial North Carolina." *North Carolina Historical Review*, V (1928), 151–80.

Boyd, William K. "Currency and Banking in North Carolina, 1790–1836." *Trinity College Historical Society Papers*, X (1914), 51–86.

Boyer, Paul S. "Borrowed Rhetoric: The Massachusetts Excise Controversy of 1754." *William and Mary Quarterly*, XXI (1964), 328–51.

Braley, Abner L. "Provisional Government of Massachusetts." In *The Commonwealth History of Massachusetts, Colony, Province and State*, edited by Albert B. Hart, III, 64–86. New York: States History, 1929.

Bushman, Richard L. "Massachusetts Farmers and the Revolution." In *Society, Freedom and Conscience: The Coming of the Revolution in Virginia, Massachusetts and New York*, edited by Richard M. Jellison, 77–124. New York: W. W. Norton, 1976.

Conley, Patrick T. "Revolution's Impact on Rhode Island." *Rhode Island History*, XXXIV (1975), 121–28.

Cowen, David L. "Revolutionary New Jersey, 1763–87." *Proceedings of the New Jersey Historical Society*, LXXI (1953), 1–23.

Dewey, Davis R. "Economic and Commercial Conditions." In *The Commonwealth History of Massachusetts, Colony, Province and State*, edited by Albert B. Hart, III, 341–45. New York: States History, 1929.

———. "Finance and Paper Money (1692–1775)." In *The Commonwealth History of Massachusetts, Colony, Province and State*, edited by Albert B. Hart, II, 192–221. New York: States History, 1928.

East, Robert A. "The Massachusetts Conservatives in the Critical Period." In *The Era of the American Revolution*, edited by Richard B. Morris, 349–91. New York: Columbia University Press, 1939.

Ernst, Joseph A. "The Robinson Scandal Redivivus: Money, Debts and Politics in Revolutionary Virginia." *Virginia Magazine of History and Biography*, LXXVII (1969), 146–73.

Ferguson, E. James. "Currency Finance: An Interpretation of Colonial Monetary Practice." *William and Mary Quarterly*, X (1953), 153–80.

Fuhlebruegge, E. A. "New Jersey Finances During the American Revolution." *Proceedings of the New Jersey Historical Society*, LV (1937), 167–90.

Gould, E. R. "Local Self-Government in Pennsylvania." *Pennsylvania Magazine of History and Biography*, VI (1882), 156–73.

Gray, Lewis C. "The Market Surplus Problems of Colonial Tobacco." *Agricultural History*, II (1928), 1–34.

Greene, Jack P. "Foundations of Political Power in the Virginia House of Burgesses, 1720–1776." *William and Mary Quarterly*, XVI (1959), 485–506.

———. "The North Carolina Lower House and the Power to Appoint Public Treasurers, 1711–1775." *North Carolina Historical Review,* XL (1963), 37–53.

Handlin, Oscar, and Mary Handlin. "Revolutionary Economic Policy in Massachusetts." *William and Mary Quarterly,* IV (1947), 3–26.

Harlow, Ralph V. "Economic Conditions in Massachusetts During the American Revolution." *Publications of the Colonial Society of Massachusetts* XX (1920), 163–91.

Hoober, Richard T. "Finances of Colonial New Jersey." *Numismatist,* XIII (1950), 72–86, 152–58, 206–16, 336–47.

Jensen, Merrill. "The American People and the American Revolution." *Journal of American History,* LVII (1970), 5–35.

Kaminski, John P. "Democracy Run Rampant: Rhode Island in the Confederation." In *The Human Dimensions of Nation Making: Essays on Colonial and Revolutionary America,* edited by James K. Martin, 243–69. Madison: State Historical Society of Wisconsin, 1976.

Kay, Marvin L. "Provincial Taxes in North Carolina During the Administrations of Dobbs and Tryon." *North Carolina Historical Review,* XLII (1965), 440–53.

———. "The Payment of Provincial and Local Taxes in North Carolina, 1748–1771." *William and Mary Quarterly,* XXVI (1969), 218–40.

Kemmerer, Donald L. "A History of Paper Money in Colonial New Jersey, 1668–1775." *Proceedings of the New Jersey Historical Society,* LXXIV (1956), 107–44.

Klein, Milton M. "Democracy and Politics in Colonial New York." *New York History,* XL (1959), 221–46.

Kulikoff, Allan. "The Progress of Inequality in Revolutionary Boston." *William and Mary Quarterly,* XXVIII (1971), 375–412.

Lockridge, Kenneth A. "Social Change and the Meaning of the American Revolution." *Journal of Social History,* VI (1973), 403–39.

McAnear, Beverly. "Mr. Robert R. Livingston's Reasons Against a Land Tax." *Journal of Political Economy,* XLVIII (1940), 63–90.

Main, Jackson T. "Government by the People: The American Revolution and the Democratization of the Legislatures." *William and Mary Quarterly,* XXIII (1966), 391–407.

———. "Social Origins of a Political Elite: The Upper House in the Revolutionary Era." *Huntington Library Quarterly,* XXVII (1964), 147–58.

———. "The Distribution of Property in Colonial Connecticut." In *The Human Dimensions of Nation Making: Essays on Colonial and Revolutionary America,* edited by James K. Martin, 54–104. Madison: State Historical Society of Wisconsin, 1976.

Mohl, Raymond A. "Poverty in Early America, a Reappraisal: The Case of Eighteenth-Century New York City." *New York History,* L (1969), 5–27.

Moody, Robert E. "Samuel Ely: Forerunner to Shays," *New England Quarterly,* V (1932), 105–34.

Morison, Samuel E. "Remarks on Economic Conditions in Massachusetts, 1775–1783." *Publications of the Colonial Society of Massachusetts,* XX (1920), 191–92.

————. "The Struggle over the Adoption of the Constitution of Massachusetts, 1780." *Proceedings of the Massachusetts Historical Society,* 3rd Ser., Vol. L (1917), 353–410.

Nash, Gary B. "Poverty and Poor Relief in Pre-Revolutionary Philadelphia." *William and Mary Quarterly,* XXXIII (1976), 5–30.

Pole, J. R. "Shays's Rebellion: A Political Interpretation." In *The Reinterpretation of the American Revolution,* edited by Jack P. Greene, 416–34. New York: Harper and Row, 1968.

Robinson, Maurice H. "A History of Taxation in New Hampshire." *Publications of the American Economic Association,* 3rd Ser., Vol. III (1902), 639–872.

Schaper, William A. "Sectionalism and Representation in South Carolina." *Annual Report of the American Historical Association,* I (1900), 242–463.

Shipton, Clifford K. "The New England Frontier." *New England Quarterly,* X (1937), 25–36.

Spencer, Charles W. "Sectional Aspects of New York Provincial Politics." *Political Science Quarterly,* XXX (1915), 396–424.

Vivian, Jean H. "The Poll Tax Controversy in Maryland, 1700–1776: A Case of Taxation *with* Representation." *Maryland Historical Magazine,* LXXI (1976), 151–76.

Walsh, Richard. "Christopher Gadsden: Radical or Conservative Revolutionary?" *South Carolina Historical Magazine,* LXIII (1962), 195–210.

Weir, Robert M. "North Carolina's Reaction to the Currency Act of 1764." *North Carolina Historical Review,* XL (1963), 183–99.

Whittenburg, James P. "Planters, Merchants and Lawyers: Social Change and the Origins of the North Carolina Regulation." *William and Mary Quarterly XXXIV* (1977), 215–38.

Wiener, F. B. "Rhode Island Merchants and the Sugar Act." *New England Quarterly,* III (1930), 464–500.

Zornow, Frank. "Tariff Policies in South Carolina, 1775–1789." *South Carolina Historical Magazine,* LVI (1955), 31–44.

DISSERTATIONS AND THESES

Armentrout, Mary T. "A Political Study of Virginia Finance, 1781–1789." Ph.D. dissertation, University of Virginia, 1934.

Bates, Whitney K. "The State Finances of Massachusetts, 1780–1789." M.A. thesis, University of Wisconsin, 1948.

Burbank, H. H. "The General Property Tax in Massachusetts, 1775–1792." Ph.D. dissertation, Harvard University, 1915.

Cohen, Joel A. "Rhode Island and the American Revolution: A Selected Socio-Political Analysis." Ph.D. dissertation, University of Connecticut, 1967.

Hershcopf, Richard D. "The New England Farmer and Politics, 1785–1787." M.A. thesis, University of Wisconsin, 1947.

Kinnaman, John A. "The Internal Revenues of Colonial Maryland." Ph.D. dissertation, Indiana University, 1955.

Loucks, Rupert C. "Connecticut in the American Revolution." M.A. thesis, University of Wisconsin, 1959.

Nadelhaft, Jerome J. "The Revolutionary Era in South Carolina, 1775–1788." Ph.D. dissertation, University of Wisconsin, 1965.

Saladino, Gaspare J. "The Economic Revolution in Late Eighteenth-Century Connecticut." Ph.D. dissertation, University of Wisconsin, 1964.

Index